DISMANTLING THE
PYRAMID

GOVERNMENT...BY THE PEOPLE...

PAUL VON WARD *1939-*

**DELPHI
PRESS**

UK
421
V65

Published by Delphi Press, a division of Delphi Research Associates, a non-profit, tax exempt organization incorporated in the District of Columbia. For information, address Delphi Press, Suite 2970, 475 L'Enfant Plaza, Washington, D.C. 20024.

First Edition

Library of Congress Cataloging in Publication Data

Von Ward, Paul, 1939-
    Dismantling the pyramid.

    Bibliography: p. 229-231,

    1. Bureaucracy—United States. 2. United States—Politics and government. I. See also Ward, Paul Von   II. Title.

JK421.V65   353'.01   80-85441
                                   AACR2

ISBN 0-939202-13-1
ISBN 0-939202-14-X (pbk.)

Table of Contents

Preface

With each new Administration there is a resurgence of hope that the bureaucratic problem will be effectively tackled. However, before long the enthusiasm is inevitably dampened by the intractability of the system and the frailty of current management theories. Each generation has confronted the reality that bureaucratic reform is something more than choosing the right technique or getting the right team together.

History has shown that over time traditional social organisms become incapable of preventing their own internal fragmentation and hardening of the arteries. Their hierarchical structures become so complex that separatist forces are inevitable. Resource demands become excessive. The *raison d'etre* shifts inward and a changing external environment leaves them in its backwash. Internal dynamics build in dysfunctionalisms, even during a successful period, which eventually render them out of phase with a new era.

This is the state in which Americans now find their institutions of national government, and particularly the permanent bureaucracy of the Executive Branch. We are now at a crossroads. We must find a way to revitalize the federal service or suffer the consequences of its entropy. But we confront the existence of an organic being, the self perpetuating bureaucracy, that is governed by laws of social dynamics that are impregnable to superficial reorganizations and structural tinkering.

The social contract philosophy espoused by 17th and 18th Century thinkers formed the base for an institutional innovation that gave society a chance to break the seemingly inexorable rule of growth and decay. With implementation of the concept of government by the governed, they believed a society should be able to assess its course and adjust its institutions in a process of continuing self-renewal. Some of the more prescient founders conceived the American institutional revolution as a permeable system of government that would benefit from a continual flow of new blood and ideas, susceptible to peaceful internal reform.

During the last two hundred years decisions have been taken, consciously or by default, that moved the operation of the American national government away from these novel principles and in the direction of more traditional social institutions that lack the built-in renewal mechanism. That form of bureaucracy, nurtured by a symbiotic relationship with Congress, partisan politics, and a large range of special interests and supported by myths apparently immune from serious intellectual challenge, has now fallen into the same rut that spelled decline for all its predecessors.

Bureaucracy as we now know and experience it in our national government is at odds with democracy. To turn back the tide and return greater control of the machinery of government to the people, giving our society another chance at self-renewal, will take a rethinking of our current institutional assumptions, roles, and relationships. We must move beyond bureaucracy to a new form of government organization.

The last thirty years have seen many different attempts at reform, from the Hoover Report of the 40's to President Carter's Reorganization Project. But when one takes part in and/or closely observes such efforts he or she quickly realizes that we have not learned from our past mistakes. That has been my experience in government, as both a public official and management consultant.

Reform is not achievable through our partisan political process. Participation in politics is today most often based on the desire of individuals to get something out of government for themselves. We cannot expect the special interest-based nature of our system of governance to nurture an initiative for change. The lack of any substantial reform in government as a result of so traumatic an experience as Watergate clearly indicates how little can be expected from the current system.

Effective reform of the Washington system of governance hinges on a dramatic change in the internal culture of the administrative public service, with an opening up of the bureaucracy to public scrutiny and involvement. To demonstrate, despite 30 years of experience to the contrary, that it is conceivable, and therefore within the realm of possibility, to have a peaceful internal institutional revolution is the purpose of this book.

I trust that it offers useful insights into the bureaucratic process and the complexity of social entities charged with the responsibility of governance. It contains both words of caution and words of optimism; the caution is required by the existence of large amounts of chaos and conflict and the seemingly insurmountable obstacles to rational progress, yet it is tinged with hope based on the belief that the first step toward improvement is an elementary understanding of the current realities.

For the leader who wishes to lead there is a warning of limits that can only be overcome by new institutional approaches that avoid the traditional superficial management strategies.

For my reform-minded colleagues in the public service, I trust they will read the material as I intend it, as a stimulant to internal reflection and self-renewal. I know of no finer group of individuals, filled with the highest order of dedication and potential—needing only to release themselves from the tangled gauze of their outmoded myths. And many of them are trying in various ways to overcome our self-made stumbling blocks. A fond hope would be that this book serve as a catalyst to greater commitment and concerted effort on their part.

Regardless of the good intentions of many insiders, it is ultimately upon the tax-paying, aware and concerned citizenry that the success of bureaucratic reform rests. A closed, ossifying organism such as our federal bureaucracy cannot salvage itself. The spark from a few must be followed up with sustained public involvement in the process of institutional revolution. For those of you who empathize with the views set forth here, *Dismantling the Pyramid* is intended to give you another tool with which to start something happening.

Paul Von Ward
Washington, D.C.
December, 1980

Introduction

1
Organizations and Societal Decline

> ... all experience hath shown, that mankind are more disposed
> to suffer, while evils are sufferable, than to right themselves by
> abolishing the forms to which they are accustomed.

> The U.S. Declaration of Independence

The United States of America has entered its 3rd Century of political independence. Most people agree the society is involved in a significant period of transition. Many wonder whether in the coming decades America will continue to be a creative, humanly fulfilling, and leading force on the planet, a model for "life, liberty, and the pursuit of happiness." Some draw threat and strength balance sheets that fill many intelligent and thoughtful observers of the American scene with pessimism. Even among the less gloomy there are nevertheless serious reservations about our ability to take effective action quickly enough to avoid serious social and economic perturbations during the next decade or so. There is widespread concern whether we can continue for long to beat back crisis after crisis.

Some observers would argue that it is simply the end of the United States flowering phase, like that of British, Holy Roman and Spanish Empires in different centuries over the past 500 years. Several intellectuals, like Henry Kissinger in one of his highly publicized nonattributable airborne discussions with reporters, have expressed the view that perhaps the United States has reached its creative peak and will now inexorably follow the way of all previous "empires," unable to escape the apparently immutable social law of periodic growth and decline.

In contrast, some believe it is possible to break free from the vicious cycle that has always haunted societies of the past. Jean-Francois Revel in his book *Without Marx or Jesus*[1] argued that if any society on earth has the potential to give birth to the next generation of social progress it is the United States of America.

Revel's view is by no means generally accepted. At an international symposium on the future of democracy sponsored by the French government in Athens in October of 1977 many intellectuals from both industrialized and Third World countries argued that Western-style democracy was bankrupt, that it did not have the moral fiber and institutional resilience to overcome long-term economic and social problems. Arthur Schlesinger, at that meeting, defended the concept of democracy which provides the people of nations with democratic institutions the means to get rid of stagnating leaderships. If the concept is valid, the question still remains whether people will exercise their freedom to use those principles to keep their self-governing institutions in working order.

C. Wright Mills, in *The Causes of World War Three*,[2] wrote his contention that "men are free to make history" and that some people are freer than others, depending on the specific kinds of social structure they have inherited or created. He argued that fate, in either its philosophical or sociological conception, only works its way when certain events are beyond the influence of an identifiable group of people who are powerful enough to make decisions with consequences, being able to predict them, and who can be held accountable for their acts. Those conditions are basically inherent in modern consciously designed societies such as the United States. Therefore, we cannot absolve ourselves of the responsibility for the consequences of our leaving future events to fate. We have created huge organizations to help shape our destiny and their products are our responsibility.

C. Northcote Parkinson,[3] in his reviews of the alternating rise and fall of civilizations in the East and West, postulates that most major societies at the time of going into an eclipse during the last four or five millenia have manifested overblown bureaucracies. But he sees them as manifestations of an already weakened people, not the cause of the decline. What role does American bureaucracy play in the growth and demise of our society?

Do such interpretations of human development on the planet Earth apply to the United States? What are the forces acting on it and how well is it responding? Is concern for the nation's long-term vitality well founded? Are we entering a creative middle age or a passive senescence?

Despite quantum leaps in the scope of human knowledge and technological skills during the past few decades the rages of violent international conflict, internal societal schisms, man-made threats to our environment, and unfilled human needs pose greater dangers for the society's long-term survival and cultural progress than ever before. As problems become more complex and monumental and the world more interdependent this society's ability to mobilize itself and adapt to cope with them seems to diminish. The phenomenal technological advances of the twentieth century have not been matched by our social and psychological pace of maturation; man's social inventions do not work as well as his machines. The latter are more susceptible to direct control, but they too have many unintended by-products. Much of our technology has created more difficulties than it solved. Americans only need to consider the imminent energy crises, survey their decaying cities and countryside, check the deteriorating infrastructure, and observe the declining rate of innovation in an increasingly competitive world to realize that many threats are being inadequately responded to by their society's institutions. The more knowledgeable realize that the U.S. does not have to neglect social problems in order to maintain adequate security; there is enough waste to pay for more than twice what citizens now receive for their tax dollars. We have reached a point where our major cultural systems are actually depleting irreplaceable resources, human and material, instead of operating in a self-sustaining mode. Our overall muscle tone is poor; we have become a flabby society, unable to pull ourselves together quickly and effectively enough.

As inflation and unemployment persist at levels Americans consider debilitating, as the overall quality of life is seen as continuing to deteriorate, and as complex international problems such as rational use of energy resources are ineffectively tackled, more and more people are concerned about the inability of the society's institutions to cope with them. Why is it that the rational systems we have created to deal with those problems are incapable of doing so? What are the connections between the larger problems of a society's life cycle and its consciously created institutions?

Jimmy Carter and many who voted for his Presidency apparently believed that serious reorganization within government would turn things around. Warren Burger, speaking from his perspective as Chief Justice, has called for an overall review of the evolution of our national institutions of government to assess how we have gotten off track. The 1980 campaign revealed an even greater sense among citizens that the country needed a dramatic shift.

Some would blame the mass media for a weakened, consumption-oriented society. Others would blame coddling approaches to education. The historical richness of an untapped continent is seen by some as having developed excessive hedonism. The demise of religious influence has been described as both cause and effect.

The issues alluded to by these various explanations are interrelated. The future of a society and the futures of its specific institutions are largely interdependent. The warp and woof of that pattern must be understood if we are to get better control of our destiny.

What are the characteristics of this state of entropy? How does one get a handle on the ills of a society? That challenge is very complex in our large, and more consciously created than most, society. Even to intellectually grasp it boggles the imagination. It is difficult to calculate the right size bite for analysis. What are the definable components? How can we both conceptually and in practical action terms select the most effective starting point?

What is the role of the central government in the malaise? With its power the federal bureaucracy ought to be an effective force contributing to a process of societal self-renewal. If it is not, is that failure a cause or a symptom? The case seems clear that a key, if not *the* element in America's troubles as it opens its 3rd Century, is the federal bureaucracy. It is the single most important institution, in terms of sheer size and the many facets of its influence, in our society. That is why we must start with the bureaucracy if we want to do something about the lethargy of our society.

This introduction deals in a general way with the above issues and the following chapters focus specifically on the federal bureaucracy and its relationship to them. They address the puzzle of crucial importance to us if we refuse to resign ourselves to fate: whether societal self-renewal is possible, and if so, under what circumstances.

The Global Maelstrom

The relative position of the United States in the world has changed dramatically; we are no longer the comparative economic, technological and morally overwhelming giant we were at the end of World War II. We share nuclear military power with almost a dozen other nations. We feel the economic competition of Western Europe and Japan. We are dependent on the continued good will of Middle Eastern and other oil-exporting countries for almost one-half of our fossil fuel energy requirements. The Vietnam debacle and policies of intervention in the affairs of other nations tarnished our world image. And a world in which we helped create a new level of concern for economic equity, social justice, and quality of life now challenges our own performance in these very spheres.

The 35-year post-war restructuring of military, economic, political, resource, environmental, social, and ideological relationships has so changed the environment in which our national government must operate that its eyes, when they are focused outward, hardly recognize the landscape. Other nations have moved ahead of us in material standards of living and in the more important general quality of life. Around the world forces of political fragmentation, social unrest, burgeoning populations and dislocations, competition for control of resources, and armed aggressions and potential for them move more and more beyond our control, even as their impact on our society increases. The future health of our country is inextricably linked to the success of others in coping with this array of issues. The globe has become a highly interdependent place where our ability to successfully function within it depends on a whole new range of knowledge, skills, and institutional resources.

What are the questions of global interdependence which loom so large for our 3rd Century institutions? Will sufficient energy be available for our basic requirements, for those of other industrial nations and for the developing countries at an economically viable price until alternative energy sources are operational? Will primary resources, such as minerals and basic manufacturing materials, be available in adequate quantities and at feasible prices to user nations? Will the international trade and finance system be able to resolve the conflicting needs of the developing and industrial nations? Can it even handle large balance of payments deficits by industrialized countries much longer? In the U.S. we seem unable to aggressively redress our standing through free market competition. What will be the outcome of so many nations literally becoming armed camps, with weapons that can destroy the globe many times over? World military expenditures are approaching $500 billion, with the U.S. the leading exporter. Can irreparable damage to the world environment be avoided? Will we drastically change our climate or make parts of the planet uninhabitable from toxic chemicals or radioactive wastes? There is now only 1.8 U.S. meals per capita available each day.* The U.N. conservatively projects a 49 percent increase in population in two decades. Will a revolution of frustrated "have-nots" sweep northward? Will a new rash of regional or global epidemics be avoided? As all these items are added to the public policy agenda it becomes clear that questions of political and social interpenetration cannot be ignored by governments. The future viability of our own nation and others is undermined by our failure to take strategic preventive measures and to make internal adjustments.

Domestic Changes

In the same period things have changed dramatically at home too. The national top priorities of post-war defense, economic recovery and expansion, and the fulfillment of the technological age have been joined by concerns for maintenance of jobs, social justice, and quality of life. There is greater concern about the future of our global biosphere, the maintenance of human rights, and coping with the economics of living in a post-industrial era—all of which bring us closer to the problems faced by developing nations and their order of priorities. But as these new values have emerged the national capacity for realizing many of them seems to have been weakened.

The relative rates of technical and social innovation have slowed down. Technological breakthroughs are coming more and more frequently from outside the U.S. New concepts of work and social organization are being imported more often than they blossom here.

We do not seem capable of providing new opportunities for gainful and meaningful employment for all able citizens. Conversely we do not have the capacity in our national institutions to cope with the wrenching about of sectors of our workforce as other nations outstrip us in productivity or enjoy more favorable labor costs. (In recent years the increase in U.S. productivity has been below 3 percent, and continues to decrease, while labor costs have been rising at a rate of well over 8 percent.) Rather than becoming a service society, one might just as well say we have become a self-service society. The current acquisitive mentality of asking for more and giving less pervades most sectors of society. At the same time the hardcore percentages of disadvantaged citizens seem largely unimproved.

*And much of that is wasted by self-indulgent people around the globe.

The combined challenge of maintaining a high and equitably distributed standard of living, continuing to increase productivity, and making the necessary adjustments in our economic structure to cope with changing markets and international competition is one of the top threats to our 3rd Century public institutions. Our record to date in achieving solutions to growing inflation, runaway energy demands, unemployment, and skyrocketing taxes does not inspire confidence; the result is considerable malaise among consumers, investors, and businessmen. All these factors are inter-related and derive from our government regulated and frequently tax supported, obese and wasteful institutions. Yet some citizens still wonder why charts show the U.S. average well below several other countries on quality of life standards.

Enhancement of the quality of life in the face of growing energy constraints, the aging of our capital intensive infrastructure, and a still increasing population with expanding aspirations, is currently impossible without a heretofore nonexistent mobilization of public and private human and other resources. Our systems of criminal and civil justice, health care, and the provision of welfare support for the needy are all factors related to the general quality of life that require fundamental overhauling. Included in this latter problem is the increasing needs of an older age citizenry.

Even such a superficial summary of urgent issues raises the question of whether mankind, and our society in particular, has mature enough institutions to cope satisfactorily with the global problems of an interdependent, nuclear, post-industrial age. It seems ironical that whereas the human race, in the form of many individuals and their collective understanding, has the knowledge to solve these problems, the behavior of the primary actors, our national institutions, makes it appear that we are only capable of muddling along. But the problem is even greater than gearing public organizations up to cope better with today's crises; they must address our sins of omission. Currently the society's leadership groups are doing little work on long-term issues, and that is done in a piecemeal fashion.

Public Organization: The Problem and the Answer

Problems of this order of magnitude cannot be resolved by individuals acting alone, nor even by small groups acting in concert. A mechanism for large-scale, planned cooperation is required, and that means formal, public arrangements. In many cases an organization appears to be the bane of one's existence, yet it is the only hope for salvation. Non-organization or a return to a globe of scattered little villages is not a feasible alternative; there are too many of us and the problems of living together are too complex. Formally established organizations are here to stay and our only viable recourse is to learn how to use them to better serve us.

Societies over the globe are faced with a dilemma regarding these public entities. While the need becomes more urgent for such mechanisms to cope with complex problems, many that transcend political and natural boundaries, people in increasing numbers are realizing that most formal organizations as conceived and structured today are not capable of meeting the demands placed upon them. Yet the nation is after all only an aggregate of various institutions (organic sectors of people) and their activities. So we must concern ourselves with the day-to-day renewal of selected pivotal institutions of our society: the family, education, industry, neighborhoods, and governments. All are interrelated and need attention.

No one collection of people in society bears all the responsibility for either the present flabby nation nor for leading the campaign to shape it up. Educational facilities, the isolated family, religious bodies, political and other public groups, and large businesses all contribute to the problem and are potential sources of constructive action. In traditional societies religion may be the most potent force (*a la* recent events in Iran); in small nations a single industry or group of families may be all powerful; in underdeveloped countries social trends may result from free-for-all tactics of exploitation by outsiders, but for a fairly large number of modern industrialized countries institutions have been consciously established to take responsibility for treating many societal issues. Most of these nations are now undergoing citizen questioning of their institutional effectiveness. The specific variations are rooted in cultural concepts and to analyze one requires that we look at the whole society; this book focuses on the American experience.

Businesses that are too large, families that are too small, religions that are too otherworldly, and agriculture that is managed like a production line detract from the development of self-sustaining and self-renewing social units whose integration would result in a strong resilient society. Turning that around requires the thinking of new thoughts by questioning minds; a re-education of large sectors of society is called for.

Obviously the Washington bureaucracy is to a large extent reflective of the values, attitudes, and priorities of the society at large. The government cannot be held responsible for America's wasteful materialism, our misguided vision of ourselves as a "Chosen Nation," our underdeveloped sense of community, our gullibility to mass fads and our self-imposed intellectual and emotional isolation from the rest of the world. Neither can it claim credit for our willingness to try new things. The workers in government are unlikely to eradicate the negatives, but they could do a better job of consciously and systematically emphasizing the positive.

Clearly Congress also contributes to the floundering, but that story would require an entire additional book. In many ways Congress is very similar to the Executive bureaucracy: closed, largely self-perpetuating, inwardly focused, with the arrogance of elitism, and planning for the last war. The mutually-benefiting relationships of many of its members with parts of the bureaucracy and with special, primarily economic, interests help to reinforce many of the bureaucratic faults. Whether this triangular relationship produces padded defense contracts, special tax loopholes, exceptions to wage and price constraints, subsidies for a particular industry, grants and contracts for pet institutions or projects, or simply restraint from interference in one's bureaucratic or private enterprise, the effect is the same: Certain special interests are benefited to the detriment of the general public and the priorities of the society at large.

Part of our difficulty lies in the institutions of education. In fact, the situation is analogous to government. Early, our citizens saw a need for public mechanisms to educate better more children, so public funding was provided and institutions established. Now the goals of those institutions have become their own survival and the imposition of their "wisdom" on others. An integral component of a strategy for attacking the problem of outmoded educational institutions will be a change from an approach of "teaching the kids what they ought to know" to helping them "learn how to learn." Unfortunately recent disillusionment with several new approaches (such as the voucher system for encouraging competition among schools and the learning contract between student and teacher) has caused retrogression to the already discredited traditional mode. People become disappointed with the experiments because we are still using as indicators of success uniform tests of limited areas of conceptual knowledge and are incapable of assessing such things as motivation, creativity, attitudes toward life and work, and survival skills for the new age.

I do not imply that a few teachers are not already doing some things in those areas, but as the concepts of bureaucracy are reshaped the pressures for such simplistic standards, as the basis for tenure, promotions, and federal grants, will be reduced and teachers can stop "operating"[4] a curriculum and start working and playing with their students in an adventure of self-directed growth. But that brings us back again to the question of institutional resilience.

Institutional Lethargy

As the operations of institutions become more abstruse, large quantities of human and material resources are siphoned off by activities that neither produce nor provide services which contribute to the intellectual and material development of the larger community. In the business sector this leads to excessive costs which are only sustained by similarly uncritical "customers" and a monopolistic web of laws and institutional arrangements. In this respect the legal and medical professions are probably the two largest groups, but educators and public administrators fall close behind.

In other words, we have reached a point where far too many creative energies and resources which should be available for new departures are soaked up by the wasteful mammoth organizations that are the homes of most employed individuals in our society. The organizations may be monolithic as government, highly integrated as a chemical manufacturing firm, or looseknit as the medical profession in a large city, but the end result is the same: people on the outside pay for the inefficiency and self-coddling of those on the inside. In most instances the hidden purpose of these institutions appears to be their own aggrandizement. The legal profession is able to do it through the guise of helping government, i.e., making it more complicated. Ours is no longer a competitive, entrepreneurial society that rewards innovations and risk-taking and encourages thoughtful economies. It has developed an interlocking set of bureaucratic social organisms that, in their own self-interest, detract from society's ability to continually adapt; the behaviors they should have outgrown cannot be discarded.

Individually, a majority of citizens are aware of the loose motion and waste in their workplaces and the society in general is fed-up with the stifling burdens of overly inflexible institutions. But they have no vision of how to effectively attack them and the result is only spasmodic flailing about by small groups, sometimes supported by voters in the rush to cut taxes, and a general mood of despair about coping. The only recourse perceived by most is to turn inward and try to take care of self. Some would say we have fulfilled Alexis de Tocqueville's[5] prediction that Americans might "finally become so engrossed in a cowardly love of immediate pleasure that their interest in their own future and that of their descendants may vanish and that they will prefer tamely to follow the course of their destiny rather than make a sudden energetic effort necessary to set things right." We are in a state of internal conflict, dissatisfied with the course of events and yet apparently resigned to the passive and often cushy role of victim. Without the ability to overcome this languor, the ultimate outcome in our society will be even more atrophied institutions and some collapses, with the price ultimately being a global setback to man's hopes for a new world order. Political, social and economic ideals which motivate humans all over the planet will lose much of their force, along with centuries of skills honed to help bring them into reality. Whether the collapse is just around the corner or decades away, it is inevitable unless we find some way to bring about effective congruence between our espoused principles of a consciously self-managing society and our current institutional practices.

Lethargy in Government

In the face of daily challenges, both global and from within, America's institutions of government continue more often than not to be lethargic. The federal institution of government, charged with the pivotal role of public leadership, becomes more and more cumbersome and unresponsive, unable to keep up with current problems and totally incapable of seeing things whole and planning and carrying out a coherent course of action oriented toward the future. The partisan political process does not seem capable of producing an elected and appointed leadership with the ability to manage the government bureaucracy in a way that elicits effective performance. Neither is the bureaucracy itself producing such leadership talent. Without effective leadership, and left to its own devices, the machinery of government is largely incapacitated in the face of the nation's more serious external and self-inflicted threats to its well being.

While new government programs spend billions, the problems they were designed to attack persist or become more virulent. Note the records of the Department of Energy and the Law Enforcement Assistance Agency as examples. Institutions whose mandates include anticipating likely international problems seem to be caught ill-prepared when the crisis comes. Note the U.S. behavior around the Iranian crisis.

A recent study in the Netherlands found certain public service organizations so complex that 50 to 60 percent of staff time is devoted to internal communication efforts. The Dutch found this environment conducive to "planned opportunism," bargaining for public resources among "merchantmen," and "gamesmen" mapping personal strategies through the tangled mesh. The size and degree of complexity and fragmentation in the U.S. makes such a description even more relevant here.

We have a situation where some of the country's best and most motivated people have been brought together to work on the public's business, given plenty of resources to do so, and yet they find themselves unable to deliver what one could reasonably expect given their qualifications and aspirations.

The overall result is a lethargic organism; the bureaucracy is unable to deliver timely, concerted efforts that directly relate to the priority issue at hand. Its structures and mentality render it involuted: an octopus tangled in its own tentacles.

Bureaucratic Millstone

Apart from the fact that it is an obvious mess, there are two basic reasons for the choice of bureaucracy as the best place to start conscious societal renewal: our publicly financed institutions were created with at least the implicit, if not always the express provision that they would assume the responsibility for leadership in general social dilemmas. Citizens believe that is what they are paying for and they have, for the most part, divested themselves of a sense of responsibility for and the maintenance of capabilities to resolve them. Secondly, and perhaps more importantly, government bureaucracies now sit astride practically every path to solutions for national and global problems, through their power of regulation, taxation, certification and allocation. As a function of its size, the number of people and resources, and constraining power the

Washington bureaucracy is perhaps the most pervasive influence in every sector of American society. Bureaucracy is both the medium and the obstacle to needed social change, if not the cause of the problem in the first place.

On to the question of size, in 1975 the U.S. economy totaled $1 and 1/2 trillion, with the federal government share of that at $500 billion. The federal sector was 32 percent of the Gross National Product and 40 percent of national income. It directly employed over 2.9 million civilians in 1977. Its paperwork alone costs $100 billion per year. Perhaps more than one-half of the overall resources consumed by the federal government are non-productive transfers of funds; payments to people who produce little or nothing is simply another form of welfare. And here I am not talking about welfare recipients but employees.

During the first half of the century, national government expenditures multiplied nearly three times faster than the nation's economy.[6] Since the end of World War II the internal profile of the federal budget and its uses have changed dramatically, adding another reason why bureaucracy is the logical starting place for institutional reform; state and local governments are supported by and follow the lead from Washington. These domestic programs of the federal budget have seen a sevenfold growth in the last 20 years, with an accompanying decisive change in the nature of the impact of Washington bureaucracy on the society at large. The federal payroll is only the tip of the iceberg; much of the federal budget finances services at the state and local levels. The divided federal system has been *de facto* nullified; the national government is now asked to finance any type of local government activity without anyone defending the principles of federalism. A recent calculation showed $80 billion a year flowing from Washington to state and local treasuries. Three-fourths of that went through 492 separate categorical grant programs, each with its own bureaucracy and constituents.

Government outlays at all levels equal one-third of the country's total output. A large percentage of that is now diverted from direct investment in more socially useful endeavors by virtue of the waste endemic in bureaucracy. Employment in government increased 139 percent between 1952 and 1972, 3 and 1/2 times faster than the civilian labor force and four times faster than the population. Now one out of between four and five American workers is on some government payroll. And that does not include the millions whose whole or partial salary derives from government contracts and grants.

The tentacles of federal bureaucracy now penetrate just about every part of the fabric of our society, through rules, procedures, and reporting requirements for obtaining federal largesse. We now spend more than a third of our time working for the government, paying taxes and filling out forms. Many business decisions are made on the basis of possible tax deductions and write-offs, not on the basis of good business sense. Fear that the government might intervene, or withdraw support, inhibits many from trying new ventures. Even for a group to be a religion, the IRS has to approve it.

Within the last ten years, on top of long standing regulatory agencies such as the Interstate Commerce Commission and the Federal Communications Commission, we have created additional regulatory units employing more than 80,000 people. Their purposes are to protect the environment (EPA), consumers (CPSC), highway travelers (NHTSA), and workers (OSHA) and others. While the need is recognized, many now wonder if the bureaucratic method is the best way to ensure health and safety and minimize expense and confusion. It is simply impossible to measure the magnitude of the sway about two million federal bureaucrats have on the lives of over 220 million Americans and of billions around the world.

When it does not have direct influence, government sets the standards to emulate for those who want to be on its good side. Higher education, as an example, is a case where both principles come into play. In 1978 the federal government provided 30 percent of all support, all conditional on institutional compliance with specific standards. The grants were accompanied by watchdogs-in-residence, review committees and tons of long forms to be filled out.

Also of critical importance is the example set by bureaucracy for students, and their professors, as they try to learn how the world works. As students are developing skills for coping with the world's problems, they look at the existing machinery and accept it as "the natural way" to function. They have few alternative conceptual patterns and none that get reinforced as does the Washington model. The academic way of life entails playing the bureaucrat's game in order to get the goodies, whether it be a Fulbright grant, a large research contract, special program support, or an eventual job. The element of society that has the time and resources to detect the faults and the potential for constructive change, those who inhabit academia, are coopted into colluding with the bureaucracy by the support the feds provide. The most likely independent force for institutional renewal in our society has thus been neutralized.

Public Dissatisfaction

Only infrequently has America had such periods of dissatisfaction with the performance of its national institutions as it has today, and they have usually been associated with periods of war or severe economic depression. Never has there been such all-encompassing lack of faith that some organization, if given enough resources, could pull the rabbit out of the hat. The last two decades have also convinced most Americans that a simple change of personalities in leadership roles is not the answer. They have come to understand that national institutions are beyond the influence of a few individuals and that larger programs are not necessarily better. The drive for a constitutional amendment to balance the budget reflects this judgment.

With this increased awareness of the complexity of social, technical, and economic forces has come frustration; disillusionment with the traditional indirect representation processes of government had led more and more people to try to take the matter into their own hands. For the average citizen, a Proposition 13-type reaction seems to be the most potent course of action. Others have resorted to passive, covert taxpayer resistance or other forms of self-protection. In some countries the violent protest route is taken more often than in the U.S., but this nation also has its share—frequently cloaked in the crime statistics. Those with enough money simply work around the system to their own ends.

Yet despite the shock of political violence, the Vietnam war, the scandals of Watergate, high inflation and chronic poverty, and the failures of leadership, there remains a belief that the basics of our system are valid. People know there are serious problems, but the realities of payoffs and corruption, self-serving government by special interests, and lackluster day-to-day behavior by public officials and employees do not erase the view that the fundamental principles of the American democratic constitution are sound. Many sense and some few articulate well the understanding that the ideals of the Declaration of Independence are a viable foundation for a healthy and continually renewing society, if it can continue to move toward their full actualization. Unfortunately, there is no consensus on what actions should be taken to bring the actual practices of government into accord with these espoused ideals.

The flailing about is due to a lack of understanding of the dynamics of directed institutional change; the intellectual leadership of society has not articulated an effective theory of organizational reform that the public can support and take part in. For the first time in the country's history, however, there exists the communication and public interest group infrastructure that is a prerequisite to effective, widespread public participation in a remaking of national institutions. Nevertheless, until there is a widely-accepted vision of a new approach, there will only be ineffective public protests and beleaguered institutions will continue to defend the *status quo*.

Newspaper polls and everyday conversation make it clear that criticism of the quality of services funded from tax revenues is rising. Although there are complaints about the overall cost, the loudest criticism is that the service is lousy. Public opinion should motivate politicians and public employees to take action; its expressions of frustration are enough reason to do something dramatic. However, such displeasure is only a symptom. The underlying cause, the stultification of governmental organisms, should give rise to even more concern. The manifestation of government's endemic faults should cause those who are interested in long-term human prospects to become involved in current political institutional questions. This lack of vision should be foremost among intellectual and political concerns.

Why is it that in spite of all the dissatisfaction only 36% of the voters went to the polls in the 1978 general election? The fact that people are so dissatisfied and at the same time feel themselves so impotent means the society has reached a phase where the health of the nation as a social body is endangered; it is perceived by the body politic as too weak to throw off the malady. Simultaneously, the internal condition of central institutions is such that they are incapable of self-regeneration. Certain of their deeply engrained characteristics hamper the innovation that is necessary for self-correction and increased responsiveness to societal needs. When institutions not only become debilitated, but have built up a protective skin that successfully wards off external pressures for change, even though nourished with a continued diet of people and funds, they are well down the road to extinction. When institutional needs take precedence over human needs the larger society has reached a crisis point. And in the case of the U.S. national institutions of government, where their impact on the larger society is so pervasive, such hardening of the organizational arteries should galvanize aspiring leaders and responsible citizens into action.

3rd Century Challenge

If the greatest threat posed to the American society is the combination of the changed nature of the agenda of global problems and the lack of appropriate institutional capabilities to deal with them, then the challenge is to create a renaissance in outmoded organizations.

How can we impact on our current closed and atrophying structures to bring about reform, a revolution toward self-correcting social systems? What is an appropriate intervention strategy? I have tried to build the case for starting with the Washington-centered career government service. Some say we should let it slide into oblivion and private volunteer efforts will pull us into the New Age, but after several years of considering alternatives I remain convinced that reform of the bureaucracy is the key to the rebirth of a self-sustaining democratic society.

The focus of most of the material in this book then is the national government bureaucracy, primarily that operating in Washington. It is not an issue of bad people, lack of resources, or too complicated problems; it is a matter of ill-conceived organizations getting in the way. We need new concepts for structures and new assumptions about people and their governance. Perhaps the strategy set forth in this book sounds too simple, too elegant and uncluttered to engage effectively our complicated machinery that is government and its links with society. Yet we have built new institutions from plain concepts before. Why can't we do it again, from the debris of the current bureaucracy scattered around us?

Recognized Need for Reform

The institutional deficiencies of the federal bureaucracy and their relationship to ineffective societal action have been recognized for many years. The last thirty years have given rise to almost countless commissions, studies, and publications on the subject of reform in the federal bureaucracy. These have pointed out the need for change and in some instances offered legislative remedies. Some have dealt with the human factor and recommended changes in personnel practices. Others have focused only on shuffling around the current organization boxes. But none has helped us get our bureaucratic employees to become different kinds of workers, producing a better quality product. Most give a prescription for pushing on one part of the organization or another, but the result is like squeezing quicksilver; one gets control of a little piece with some pressure, but the rest slips away in different directions all across the board. None offered a way to get the whole thing into another form without shattering it any more than it already is.

For example, for the last 30 years the Department of State has been the direct object of an almost annual assault on the weaknesses of the foreign affairs apparatus. The long list of shattered hopes for reform lies like a row of skeletons beside the 19th Century trace to Pike's Peak. New ideas are introduced into the system, but before they take root another tack is taken. When semi-permanent changes are grafted on, they cause problems to surface elsewhere. A specific symptom gets treated and the reaction is a new, generally debilitating rash. And after so much effort the nation's central foreign policy institution is weaker than ever.

Observing much of the pulling and pushing that politicians and managers go through to improve bureaucratic performance reminds me of my boyhood experiences getting ready to go fishing and finding that my line was tangled into such a ball of knots that efforts to get it straightened out only seemed to make matters worse. Getting one knot loosened would increase the pressure in another or cause an entirely new one to be formed. My feelings are similar today, as I survey the federal bureaucracy and futile attempts to straighten it out.

Faced with such a mess and with such lack of success in our efforts to cope with it, we have no choice but to conduct a profound reassessment of our situation. Periodically individuals and groups must stop and take stock of where they are, where they have been and where they are going. Gail Sheehy with her popular book *Passages*[7] made the case that there is a need for such assessments on an individual and family scale, and it is equally clear that similar examinations must be made of larger institutions, and even societies, if they are not to become stuck in a non-growth or even degenerating rut. This law of nature, if you please, is required because of its corollary which ordains that success carries the seeds of its own destruction. Both personal and organizational strategies and structures require several profound reevaluations over the span of a full life-time.

Continual fiddling with the edges goes on all the time, but certain phases in a life cycle call for fundamental introspection and a reordering of perspectives and priorities; as Thomas Jefferson said, the coat made for a boy can no longer be expected to serve him as a man. The conflux of domestic and international events has brought our national institutions to just such a point, and perhaps not just coincidentally, at the beginning of our 3rd Century.

We have reached a wavering phase in our historical development when our progress and failures to date need to be evaluated for a new institutional departure. The shift from nomadic to agricultural society and the advent of nation states are perhaps comparable in magnitude to the incipient promise of this era: the creation of consciously self-correcting social institutions.

History and its varying explanatory theories are useful stimuli for our current analysis and development of social strategies, but we would be unwise not to consider the intellectual and communication advances that separate us from our predecessor societies. We have in fact made some progress in developing answers to the following questions:

- Are there inherent and immutable stages from conception to senility or is continual societal and institutional renewal possible?

- Can we design and operate different social arrangements that do not simply perpetuate, but actually improve themselves?

- Is there hope for changes in particular institutions that would stimulate change in the larger society?

I would reply that man is much more in charge of his own fate than most of us realize. In the constant struggle for power and control over a people's own destiny, democratic ideals provide a powerful tool for enlightened progress.

The institutions of our government have become too far removed from the people they were created to serve, too insensitive to changing circumstance, and actually constitute a hindrance to the continued well being and progress of our society. Yet knowledge about organization building and alternative approaches to management of them are available to correct existing faults and maintain the principles that are the foundation of our American democratic society.

We have the capacity to solve the problems of our wasteful and smothering institutions; we only need the will. We cannot escape by asking the government to do it, because the government ought to be us.

Whether you believe in social evolution that is determined in some way (destiny) or serendipitous (chance) and whether you are a nationalist or globalist, it is clear that the current era is unparalleled in history for the potential planet-wide impact of any group's behavior; and it is equally clear that the United States still exercises greater global influence than any other single social entity. The economic and communication influences of our country have been and remain for the time being almost overwhelming in their cultural impacts on the rest of the world. Whether one wishes it or not, what we do as a society in the next few decades will profoundly shape the course of events on this earth for all time. The realities of time and place make it not chauvinistic to perceive of ourselves in such a manner. Consequently, it is irresponsible to be passive beings, resigned to the toss of the dice or the inexorable impulses of unattended social forces. Just to attempt to tackle intellectually the rethinking of an institution is a horrendous task, the massing of action is almost unthinkable, but it is conceivable and therefore can be done.

If we are willing to reaffirm the objective, intrinsic in the founding of our nation, of assuming as much control as possible over our own destiny, our challenge becomes how to do it in a complex society with its future development primarily limited to renewing that which already exists. Constrained from going out and creating new institutions on a new frontier; starting a new cycle elsewhere, how can we build on what we already have? How can we take advantage of the present plateau of social and technical development to renew ourselves for a New Age?

A Launch Pad

Each person who takes it on himself to proclaim sweeping generalizations about the historical context of a particular period and throw out such challenges makes it easy for others to decry his lack of sufficient knowledge of the past or to protest his presumptuousness about trends yet to unfold. After all, there are no generally accepted constants to which one can safely tie such conclusions and predictions. Nevertheless, every person acts according to either explicit or implicit conclusions about the future course of human events, and the individual who is motivated to attempt in a public way to reshape those trends must be willing to claim some vision. It is a recognition of the inadequacy of human pre-vision combined with a sense of urgency about acting that shapes the propositions set forth here. They are offered not as infallible truths, but as one person's visions of a possible turning point in American, and perhaps global, evolution. Your reaction to them, whether agreeing or disputing, will in itself impact on the very process discussed here; none of us can avoid the role we play in the future that is inherent in our acts of today.

In order to comprehend better the weaknesses of our current organizations and to discern ways to make them work for us, we must, before plunging into the actual maelstrom, stand back and become aware of the perceptual patterns through which we interpret reality. Such an approach is required if we are to improve on the random, headline news story-type discussion that characterizes most American thinking on the problems of bureaucracy.

Most of us are aware that the reality of the external world is not simply and wholly implanted on our brains. We do not directly experience social reality. Stimuli from the external environment are translated into our consciousness by and through a set of learned constructs or patterns which order our perceptions into some sort of logical and coherent whole that appears to make sense for the individual.[8] The way we react to much of reality is determined then not so much by the externalities as by the way we have categorized and interpreted them. In other words, we "see" what we are ready to see, creating our "personal worlds" with these internal pre-existing constructs. These *a priori* perceptual patterns are generally more real to the individual than reality. Consider a small girl traveling in Africa for the first time: upon seeing lions and elephants in the savannah she exclaimed, "This is almost like a real safari" (comparing the trip to her TV images). Another: "It's almost like a true romance" (*a la* a storybook tale). Similar preconceptions influence the way we look at organizational life.

The validity of these perspectives or personal constructs is a function of how reliable they are over time in allowing us to interact with the outside world and obtain consistent results from our initiatives. Do they make sense after some experience with external circumstances and the reactions of others? If we perceive that a specific person has certain needs and proceed to relate to him or her in a consistent manner and consistently observe the reactions we expected, we can assume that our perceptions were fairly accurate. In other words, we have generated a hypothesis about the nature of our friend and our experience has confirmed it. Such testing is the only way to confirm our internal guidance system.

We desperately need to test out our underlying assumptions about modern bureaucracy. The chapters that follow are designed to help accomplish that objective. They also offer some new concepts to move organizations beyond bureaucracy and a strategy to reassert democratic principles in government.

Part I
Problematic
Bureaucracy

2
Costly, Poor
Quality Chaos

> It is easier to discover another such new world as Columbus
> did, than to go within one fold of this which we appear to know
> so well.
>
> Henry Thoreau

Many are critical of big, bureaucratic government but it is difficult to really define the problem unless there is a clear picture of what ought to be. What are the purposes of government organizations in the first place? The answer to this question varies from one type of society to another. In a traditional monarchy the aim is to carry out the king or queen's command, in a dictatorship it is to control the people, but in a democracy the objective is to secure for all citizens their rights and to carry out commonly agreed upon operations for their benefit. None of these models are pure in the belief system of any country today, but they do represent relative emphases. All, however, presuppose a societal leadership role that anticipates the impacts of today's acts and pursues optimal courses of action for the future. Included is the implicit responsibility for assuring the survival of the society.

It is only after some clarification about the purpose of a governmental entity that one can really address the question of effectiveness; it must be measured vis-a-vis some standard or expectation. The United States Government was established as a function of our Constitution, "to form a more perfect union, establish justice, insure domestic tranquility, provide for the common defense, promote the general welfare, and secure the blessings of liberty to ourselves and our posterity."

To accomplish these ends the constitutional conventions of the original thirteen states gave power to the Congress to establish public offices to collect taxes, borrow, coin and manage federal monies; to regulate commerce with other nations and among the states; to handle naturalization; to provide postal service and roads; to protect copyrights and patents; to run a system of justice; and to maintain military forces. · Over the past 190 years we have, through Amendments to the Constitution, legislation, and executive fiat, added other functions: protection of the environment, support for education, health care assistance, individual and community assistance, aid to agriculture, support of the arts and humanities, provision of public transportation, management of public resources, and others.

These additions moved in the direction of giving government the means to create programs, to be responsible for the development of certain sectors in society, and to provide services traditionally left to other institutions. As our society evolved we asked the government to take over from church and local groups various welfare functions. As concepts of equity emerged, we asked the central government to become the honest broker in collecting and distributing the dole. As government got bigger we assigned it even greater responsibility for research and development. From the roles of protector and facilitator, we broadened its mandate to become our shaper and leader.

Implicit in our enhancing the role of the national government was the expectation that it could do the tasks well and efficiently; we assumed it would be under our control and would essentially do our bidding. Now a majority of us wonder at both the cost and the way the job is handled.

When tax-paying citizens assess the products of these public entities they not only find their costs out of proportion, but go away from contact with the bureaucracy feeling that the transaction has been a demeaning experience. Columnist William Raspberry writes of a general desire to "grade" the service given by public employees. The voter response to denunciation of the federal bureaucracy by both major 1976 Presidential candidates came as no surprise; the 1980 voter disillusionment with it was even greater. The general view in America today is that the organizations we created to serve us now seem more often to serve themselves or special interest groups. The 20th Century pressures of many different interest groups for extraordinary government support or largesse have backfired and most people have ended up paying for more than they get in return. It has become clear that the competitiveness of special interest group government does not result in the greatest good for the overall society.

Rather than debating whether we erred in assigning government too many functions, let us assume for now that we want our public institutions to carry out the mandates established by existing statutes. Starting from there, what is the problem? The way we define the issues shapes the design of a public response. Therefore it is very important that we carefully craft that analysis. As will be seen in Chapter 5, misleading definitions of the problem have thwarted past reformers.

In the Club of Rome report on resource limits to growth, the term "world problematique" was used to convey a sense of the multifaceted nature of the predicament facing mankind. The use of the second word as English in that manner is a distortion of the French, but sometimes when it is necessary to coin a new phrase such hybridization is justified. Therefore, I will use, for the discussion in this book, the term "bureaucratic problematique" to label the overall malaise that afflicts the many elements that make up the social organism of our national bureaucracy. The portrait drawn of that malaise must lead to new insights if individuals and groups are to find the analysis conducive to effective personal action.

The "bureaucratic problematique" appears to me to be comprised of three levels: the symptoms, the apparent sources or media, and the causes. The levels are interdependent and interactive, but it is necessary to separate out the components to enable people to shape alternative concepts and courses of action for themselves. As we will see, past reform strategies have not directly dealt with the causes.

Following this three level schema I focus in Chapter 2 on the symptoms (the products and public behavior of the bureaucracy) and some of the dysfunctional or counterproductive media from which the symptoms directly flow. Among these media are ill-conceived structures and procedures and misused personnel resources. In Chapters 3 and 4 I try to go below the surface to describe an unhealthy psychological set and debilitating interpersonal norms. Invalid assumptions about human beings and their diminutive self-images, the basic causes of the problem, are examined.

One may characterize the overall "problematique" as essentially a failure of the career government service to carry out effectively and efficiently the functions ascribed to it. Part of the blame can also be laid at the feet of the transient political level officials who have been unable to define a leading role and have consequently maladroitly intruded in the organizational processes. But the latter does not mitigate the bankruptcy of the permanent career-service concept as now implemented by the bureaucracy and accepted by the public. In the current standoff nobody wins, and certainly not the average citizen. We have neither a political (representative) government nor a meritocratic one. The latter concept has not worked becaues of its internal dynamics and the situation has been aggravated by manipulations of politicians. As a result we have learned that something other than the spoils system or a sanitized meritocracy is required; new concepts are needed for America's 3rd Century. We need to develop a better approach to interactions among the elected public employees, their career colleagues and the general public. We need new approaches to internal organization.

In the last 30 plus years, governmental leaders have come and gone, striving for policy and performance improvements, but public organizations remain ineffective and continue to be bedeviled by their incompetence in self-management. People in government fail to understand and effectively cope with the outside world because they understand neither the internal influence of their own behavior nor their impact on the organization's collective public performance. Most people have thought of "the problem" as synonymous with the symptoms, and thereby failed to understand its most important part—the underlying human precepts.

Because of the confusion about problem definitions we fumble in contradictory directions at the same time. For example, the 1978 Civil Service Reform Act tends to politicize the bureaucracy at the same time it reinforces its insular tendencies. The Carter Administration, with only a partial definition of the problem aggravated the symptoms (through superficial reorganizations) and missed the mark with changes to the media (personnel control systems).

The Public Performance

What does the public in general think of the services its government provides? Each reader will have his or her own view, but there are some general opinions that merit review. The following excludes tales of kickbacks, Watergate, CIA misbehaviors, etc. It is an attempt to focus on the everyday routine, the iceberg below the surface, that accounts for our institutional problem of the century.

In the spring of 1977 the Carter Reorganization Project undertook a survey to determine which programs and agencies possessed the greatest public disrepute. It found dissatisfaction in all three categories that make up the product of the bureaucracy: *goods,* produced directly or through contract, *services* for the public and for other parts of government, and *policies* that regulate or otherwise impinge on the behavior of the private sector. Among the worst were: law enforcement, local and community economic development, human services, and administrative services.[1] The problems (actually only symptoms) were identified as duplication, overlap, fragmentation, lack of coordination, confusing rules, inefficiency, outmoded practices, and general lack of responsiveness to the public.

Congressional opinion was solicited as part of the survey. Receiving the dubious distinction of having the most complaints was the Labor Department's Office of Workmen's Compensation Program. It was characterized as extremely slow in processing claims, rude in treatment of claimants, and filled with incompetent employees. The Immigration and Naturalization Service was reported in mid-1977 to have a backlog of 146,000 immigration applications (a backlog of four years); applicants for naturalization had to wait six months, and even getting answers to simple questions took days. Other units that caught strong criticism were the Social Security Administration's disability insurance program, the Department of Housing and Urban Development, the Postal Service, and the Environmental Protection Agency. (Some units were complimented, notably the Veteran's Administration, the Passport Office of the Department of State and the Department of Agriculture's Forest Service.)

Most of the complaints related to services to groups with special problems or needs. Citizens who find themselves in those categories are treated as if the services were available only thanks to the sufferance of the bureaucrat. They are placed in the role of petitioner instead of that of claimant of a service provided for by law and paid for by taxes. News stories and any street corner conversation can validate the Administration's survey by revealing a widespread perception that something is dramatically wrong with both the quality of government services and the attitudes with which they are provided to the citizen.

Not only are the directly administered services wanting, but the indirect involvement of bureaucracy in daily living adds additional burdens. Everyone has his or her own horror story of excessive costs, time and psychological harassment by the bureaucracy which is ostensibly there to help us, but here is a typical example of the kind of help we could do without: a study by the Rutgers University Center for Urban Policy Research revealed that "excess" government regulations may boost the price of a new home by as much as 20 percent. Over a 30 year period for an average house in today's market that would mean almost $100 extra in the monthly cost of buying a home. It has been estimated that excessive product regulation may cost the consumer at least $500 per year. Citizens pay for both the higher costs and the excess expenses of the regulators; the latter is true even when the social ends of regulation are laudable. It is ironic that we continue to increase our taxes to enlarge the bureaucracy's role in order that it can find new ways to raise our cost of living.

Government itself falls victim to the inefficient services of the bureaucracy. Most of the internal customers of government service have reason to complain as much as non-government citizens. The General Services Administration, which provides logistical support for other units of government, came in for heavy criticism in the Administration survey. The GSA's Public Building Service spends almost $2 billion a year and has 20,000 employees; yet other agencies complain of the inadequacy of the space, cleaning, maintenance and security services which that budget is intended to provide. Early in this writing newspaper stories began to reveal the GSA scandal of kickbacks and non-competitive contracting practices pervasive in GSA.

Another example of double jeopardy for the taxpayer is the cases, discovered across many states, of government employees (federal, state, and local) who were also receiving welfare payments. While the practice is dishonest and shocking, the individuals involved may have felt themselves justified by the examples of retired military officers drawing both retirement checks and full-time government pay, Congressmen receiving their salaries and legal retainer fees from law firms or businesses their legislation nutures, government executives who use public resources to further their own business activities, etc. The principle is the same; only the mechanism varies.

While no justification for the bureaucrat on the take, it is true that for many groups our government has become solely a dispenser of largesse—a Santa Claus with a bag of gifts. Included are tax loopholes, like the $1.2 billion tax credit for oil companies who pay taxes abroad, welfare payments, non-product related grants and contracts, pork-barrel construction projects, industry subsidies (including the dairy industry), etc. Although authorized by legislation, it is for the most part a covert process, resulting from non-competitive practices and the sleight of hand that accompanies the passage of legislation with goodies tucked away in it for special groups. No public declaration of these impacts is required. Although this government property (basically money) which is given out as largesse comes from all taxpayers, there is no way for them to know how it is awarded and where it goes. In addition, the overhead involved in this transfer of wealth, generally to other wealthy,* is excessive; it is known as bureaucratic waste whether by the bureaucrats themselves or by wasteful government contractors.

A late 70s Congressional study revealed that a Defense Department contract administration service with a large staff and budget had failed to provide effective controls to eliminate duplication and costly overlap in defense contracts. Although the ratio of costs to dollars in excess profits extracted from defense contractors was not very profitable for the taxpayer, it was resented and military and industrial figures persisted in trying to get it abolished.

Obvious Symptoms

As bad as these complaints may appear, they are only the views of individual citizens as customers of government or relate to a specific product or particular behavior. An even worse picture materializes when one surveys the scene from the inside and sees how the pieces of the puzzle fail to fit together or when one compares large economic or social issues with what is actually being done about them. When all these specifics are laid out together, patterns of symptoms begin to emerge.

They generally fall into five categories, and the following descriptive phrases seem to capture their essence:
- nobody in charge
- too many actors
- take the easy way
- too expensive
- too self-centered

For every government job I had, but one, in almost 17 years of government service, these conditions existed. It was not clear who was ultimately responsible for the end product, even when there was a well-defined one; and that was not very often. We either got in each other's way or divided the task up into such little bits that they were meaningless. No one wanted to tackle the hard questions. When faced with any difficulty we most often decided a large, expensive new effort—in terms of people and money—was necessary. Individual decisions to accept responsibility or commit resources for a project were almost always a function of the perceived benefit to the future career of the individual employee. But let's go beyond my personal experience.

For each of these "generic symptoms" it should be useful for us to describe

---

*Interestingly enough, government gives most of its research money to big corporations despite the fact that an OMB study revealed that smaller firms produce many more innovations for the dollar spent.

them in behavioral or product terms, using specific examples for illustration, and to look at their immediate underpinnings or the media which nurture them. By the end of this analysis I hope we can begin to see their interrelationships and begin to have an understanding of the organic nature of the overall problem.

Nobody in Charge

During the weeks following the Three Mile Island nuclear plant accident in March, 1979 no one was sure what the local radiation dangers were, although eight federal government agencies were monitoring and collecting data in the area. They apparently were all looking at different things and no one seemed capable of putting it all in perspective. After the fact the White House's reaction was to name one of the eight (EPA) the lead agency.

There is no disputing that analyses are needed of such data for a variety of purposes, but there is no logical justification for the eight-fold duplication of personnel and equipment in the field. This example illustrates one-half of the problem with the current structuring of our bureaucracy; each entity believes that it must be an integral unit in itself. That means regardless of policy or service role each unit staffs itself as if no other agency of government can be depended upon. Even the security clearances given by some agencies are not acceptable to others. Consequently each must be self-contained with field personnel, data collectors and processors, analysts, professionals, administrators, managers, etc.—from top to bottom.

The other half of the structuring problem is that we have no overriding principle for assignment of roles. It is impossible to discover logic in agency tasks, to find a rational answer to the question who is where for what purpose? No consistent pattern has been followed in the assignment of responsibilities. The consequence of this disjointed and confusing landscape is that *no individual or collective coordination and focusing of priorities and strategies is possible in any single functional area of importance to the nation today.*

The government topography has conglomerate, sectoral departments such as Health and Human Services (formerly HEW), Housing and Urban Development (HUD), Transportation, and Energy. It includes constituency based departments such as Commerce, Labor, and Agriculture; issue-oriented units like the Environmental Protection Agency and the Arms Control and Disarmament Agency; and traditional area-focused ones like the Department of State (foreign relations) and the Department of the Interior. In addition, there is a myriad of non-departmental, but relatively independent units. They deal with such things as regulating the sale of securities, guaranteeing U.S. exports, providing farm credit, encouraging the arts and humanities, exploring space, assisting underdeveloped countries, producing and selling electric power, and taking care of veterans, etc.

If the superficial labeling is confusing, the delineation of specific responsibilities is downright incomprehensible. Activities relating to public utilities are scattered among or fall between the cracks of two departments and seven independent agencies. Welfare falls into three departments. Trade matters are divided among seven departments and ten independent or quasi-independent agencies. Agriculture has a bigger rural transportation office than the Department of Transportation. Pollution is supposed to be attacked by five departments and five agencies. Housing programs and policies fall under the purview of three departments and four agencies . . . and on and on. These examples do not include all the little commissions, bureaus, and offices hidden away in all kinds of places relating to these same issues. Even the weather is handled by at least two federal departments and two other organizations.

The result is inordinate fragmentation of responsibility and overlap of effort. And the converse is equally true; significant problem areas are left unattended. In this maze of conflicting roles central coordination from any single perspective, regardless of whether it is the White House or some other focus, is impossible. For example, while other units are charged to be concerned about the health of the American people, the volume of foreign trade, the food requirements of foreign nations, and the development of a self-adjusting domestic economy, the Agriculture Department establishes policies which cut wheat production, pay for storage of temporary surpluses, and militate against other productive uses of the land. Through the use of loans and supplementary payments, Agriculture's policies are disincentives to constructive changes in agricultural practices and contradictory to the aims of other agencies.

Given the lack of other overreaching principles of agency role allocation, the most consistently used one seems to be bureaucratic divisions that correlate with definable groups in society. Consequently each industry, each profession, each special interest group, and many self-defined sectors of society have their respective homes in the bureaucracy. This principle of organization facilitates the development of "iron triangles"[2]—the symbiotic relationships that bind private sector groups, units of the bureaucracy, and congressional subcommittees into self-protective associations. In these circumstances attempts at reorganization provoke turf battles that line everyone up against the President.*

Nowhere in government is there the institutional capacity to address and sort out such competing priorities in a manner that permits public understanding and confirmation. Congress itself created an Office of Technology Assessment that duplicates DOE, EPA, and CEQ studies.

One of the examples of unintended implications of this chaos and its susceptibility to special interest aggrandizement is the fact that almost 10

---

*Congressional rejection of President Carter's concept of a Department of Natural Resources is an example.

percent of the federal budget (Medicare and Medicaid) is a transfer of funds from those earning $10-15,000 (average taxpayer) to those earning above $75,000 (medical doctors) with questionable service being rendered. The same principle applies to the government-wide research grant program. These and other examples like them support Eugene McCarthy's observation that democracy in America has become socialism for the rich. Or for the politically powerful, as when a Senator's favorite organization gets a program development grant without competition.

Efforts to cut across these narrow perspectives by creating new bureaucratic units to serve a broader good, such as the concept of a Consumer Protection Agency, are doomed to failure.* What is needed is a rethinking of the concepts that render the bureaucracy into insulated, self-serving fragments in the first place. The current self-contained pyramid view of government units makes the reallocation of the government resource pie a competitive zero-sum game; public employees never cease their attempts to increase the size of the slices given to their respective offices, for their own use and for their clients. The result is that it is practically impossible to disband a unit. When President Carter announced the decontrol of fuel prices, bureaucrats in the Department of Energy had a ready-made answer for why overall personnel cuts would not be made.

Such continual gerrymandering of the bureaucratic turf brings public policies and programs that aim in unrelated directions. Many continue to serve out-moded ends, and only fortuitously complement new activities and national or global objectives.** Unfortunately, the practice of adding more people and money, i.e., more finite units, each time a new problem surfaces is supported by our cultural perspective that says more is better. Even within agencies powerful fiefdoms emerge with no effective cabinet level control. Consider the position of the Secretary who has an Assistant with the power that accrues to the mistress of a powerful White House aide or the backing of an industrial sector.

Managing within the organization seems to be no more successful than attempts to affect the outside world. The elected or appointed manager wonders what is wrong. He or she arrives on the job with a public mandate or at least a private sense of where the organization should be going. Problems are analyzed, plans are made, and goals are set, but what happens?

- The President orders relocation of tactical military installations. Twelve months later he learns they are still in place.
- A cabinet officer directs a revision in his department's hiring procedures. Six months later he discovers a change has been made, but not in the direction he wanted.

*I have participated in the meeting of representatives of several "iron triangle" partners in strategy sessions with the aim of insuring the sanctity of their resource allocations in the Congressional budget review of shifting public priorities.

**Foreign officials often express shock at our inability to sort out the confusion and internal competition. Most learn to take advantage of it in bi-lateral, agency based programs.

After a few months even the frustrated manager begins to ask "Who is in charge?" When Max Weber studied public institutions and postulated, "The question is always who controls the existing bureaucracy machinery,"[3] he was unable to foresee today's circumstances when the answer often is, "Nobody is!" And furthermore, it often appears that nobody can be! In public bureaucracies no single person or group can exercise significant control. It is no wonder that many see them as Frankensteinian creatures, raging out of control.

In our current system bureaucrats assume the unit of which they are a part is indispensable and that its continued existence is unquestionably in the public interest. Each agency and office within it has a tightly woven set of interpretations of public need to justify its own program. The rationale may be to help a needy group, control a greedy group, protect a national asset, defend our national interest, protect one group of citizens from another, punish evil doers, develop our resources, increase our national pride, or enhance the welfare of our people. Whatever it is, the explanation covers every activity the unit is engaged in, from policy-making to taking care of the buildings and physical needs of employees.

Interestingly enough, this fierce sense of responsibility to the "public interest" does not usually extend to the point where one's responsibility brings him into conflict with other units. In fact, when the bureaucrats are asked to take a role in bringing about change beyond their formal area of influence, very intelligent and well qualified people appear to lack competence, are passive, and capitulate easily to the countervailing forces from another bureaucratic unit. There is almost a mutual non-aggression pact—"You do not try to get into my domain, and I will not get into yours." This makes it almost impossible to debate publicly and at a high level issues where there are inter-unit differences of opinion. For example, the predicted great debate between State, led by Henry Kissinger, and the Department of Defense on national security policy that was to have occurred when James Schlesinger assumed charge of Defense never took place. The two bureaucracies appear to have decided to stay out of each other's sphere of influence. Admirable efforts (like the 1977-78 interagency committee to develop a new national urban policy that ended in a laundry list of all members' existing activities) to reshape the interagency profile of programs fail because nobody can be in charge.

An exchange from one agency's Congressional testimony illustrates the phenomenon:

Congressman: Many other agencies have programs very similar to yours. Shouldn't we put them all in one place to be more efficient and effective in achieving this national objective?
Deputy Secretary (well briefed by his bureaucratic staff): No, I would not want to do that. The bureaucratic problems might be too great. But, we should know what the others are doing so we can plan our activities

accordingly. After all, the different approaches are not really completely duplicative.

Congress, composed of those allegedly direct representatives of the people, has not been immune either. The geometrical increase in Congressional staff over the last decade to the current level of more than 20,000 (including 7,000 substantive aides) has resulted in considerable encroachment on the functions of the Executive and a burrowing into extraordinary detail and day-to-day questions by a Congress that has fragmented itself to relate to the fragmented bureaucracy. The end result is a weakened capacity to see things whole and to take the broad view in what should be the public process of debate and setting of national priorities. Spreading themselves so thinly frequently results in congressional requests of the bureaucracy to prepare both the questions and answers for hearings. Attempting to get so deeply involved with their specialized areas leaves Members of Congress in a position where they can not easily avoid deferring to spheres of influence and trading-off respective decisions with each other. Each member is also seduced into playing tit for tat because of desires to obtain deference when his or her area of the bureaucracy has legislation on the calendar. Without the capacity to take a broader critical perspective, and perhaps also from time to time for more venal reasons, Members are unable to challenge the legislative proposals that have grown out of the "iron triangles."

The lack of a self-adjusting principle for assigning roles, the pervasiveness of the self-contained (and self-perpetuating) concept of unit organization, the assumption of essentiality, and the existence of the mutual non-aggression principle all contribute to the symptom or condition where "nobody is in charge at any significant level." Although these factors contribute to our difficulties, they are not *per se* the fundamental problem. We will have to peel back another layer or two of our bureaucratic onion before a cause susceptible to constructive direct action is identified.

Too Many Actors

Not only are there too many units with fragmented and duplicative mandates, or lack thereof, but there are also too many people in each unit. There are too many chiefs, too many support staff, too many underworked people, and too few professionals actually getting something accomplished.

The symptom description should read, *more people than necessary are available for most routine tasks yet most government talent is untapped while many crucial activities are understaffed.*

How much of the human resource of government is wasted by its bureaucratic character? If we accept the idea that it does not matter how many people are on the government payroll because it is simply a way to redistribute income through a means more indirect than a simple welfare check, as one U.S. President reportedly did, the preceding question might not bother us. But even if the overall magnitude of the public payroll does not bother some people almost everyone would agree that the payrollees ought to be accomplishing something worthwhile. If you concur with that, then waste can be defined as people, money, time, and other resources that are non-essential to the production of agreed-on public ends.

In a bureaucratic setting there are several factors that result in people in irrelevant assignments. Their combined effect is a demand for far more people and other resources than would be required if the sole dynamic operating was a desire to get the job done in the most effective manner.

Let us take a typical federal entity of 300 people and see how it is staffed. What are the ramifications of these dynamics? At the top we have the "chief" with a special assistant or two and secretaries. Next come three deputy "chiefs,"* with secretaries, a staff assistant and special messenger (such senior personnel for some reason cannot be served by the same support staff as the rest of the organization). At the next level come fifteen office heads. And they all have deputies and staff aides (you are not considered to be really important unless you have deputies and staff aides, so that accounts for another 30 employees. Each office of any significance must have a research assistance or "go-fer"; another 15 people. Each office head must have a "span of control" so the result is at least thirty division chiefs. Some of these too must have subordinate units, so branch chief positions are created: perhaps forty-five more people. And of course all of these "officials" must have secretaries and typists. The titles may vary from agency to agency, but the pattern is the same. The distinguishing feature of these levels is that they do not do the actual work. They supervise and coordinate their subordinates and communicate and "liaise" with each other, and act as go-betweens linking the workers with people who need or can use the work produced.

The layers of overseers take up almost one-half of the resources of a bureaucratic organization and it is the judgment of many on the inside that up to two-thirds of them or almost 100 people in our hypothetical unit of 300 are usually inconsequential to the essential tasks of the unit. In most instances their presence only makes more difficult the accomplishment of the necessary tasks.** Because of the activities spawned by these layers, people in this group

---

*Everybody has to have a deputy, even though they (as one Deputy Secretary of a major Department said in a not totally facetious manner) often are there only to close a door after the principal. Other deputies only serve as foils for their would-be prima donnas.

**This excessive layering of non-functional supervisors demands more and more from the working level. In one agency I found a staff that estimated 60 to 70 percent of its time is spent cleaning up the mistakes of second echelon agency personnel who are not aware of real work issues and the activities

become attenders of meetings and meeting explainers, passers-on and interpreters of instructions, supervisors and supervisees, clearers-of-action-with-others, rumor merchants, liaisoners, and rewrite editors. To support them they have to have assistants-to, typers of internal papers, messengers for internal documents, and transmitters of internal telephone calls. This means millions of work hours devoted to activity that would be unneeded if we did not have such an artificially complicated system.

Our 300 person unit has at least 25 workyears (equivalent to that many full-time positions) devoted to writing instructions, filling out administrative and personnel forms, maintaining work records, auditing taxi and travel accounts, processing evaluation reports, etc. The whole unit spends another 5 person years just writing and reviewing the performance evaluation reports. And that does not count the hours lost by all employees discussing and worrying about their contents and the impact they will have on careers. The result of this is unmitigated waste of a minimum of 10 percent of the human potential in our sample unit.*

Outside the 300-person line unit, in the larger support bureaucracy, there is a corresponding excess in administrative staff to support the surplus people in the line operating unit. They show up in swollen numbers in the central personnel staff, in communication facilities, in payroll offices, in security operations, and in the general housekeeping functions.

The inappropriately utilized portion of the workforce related to built-in organic expansion and to excessive control and regulations may range from an optimistic 30 percent of the total workforce to a more likely 50 percent.

The topography of any bureaucracy that has been in existence for several years is splotched with pockets of people who are left out of the current action. Managers do not know what to do with them; they just leave them there carrying out routine and irrelevant functions year after year. At some point priorities or needs changed and these people did not adapt or, more likely, were by-passed as new managers put their own people in charge of the "important" new tasks. The by-passed ones may have been the favorites of preceding generations of managers. These are the people in some of what Rosabeth Kanter calls "stuck jobs";[4] they are at a dead end and know it, but keep plodding away for the financial security involved. The longer they stay in place the more unlikely it is that they or anyone else will attempt reinvigoration. Reorganizations and reassignments whirl about them, but never touch their quiet little domains which collect cobwebs and dust. Executives mistakenly believe they are being humane when they fail to disturb these little nests. More units are created as

of subordinate office and private groups. These senior officials serve as the model for Garry Trudeau's "Department of Symbolism," in the Doonesbury comic strip.

*To the extent that the bureaucratic model is applied in private sector organizations one will find comparable levels of superfluous activities.

managers feel frustrated at the lack of responsiveness to their initiatives. Unfortunately, society as a whole pays for it; the individuals themselves die a slow death, demoralized with a "what's the use" malaise, and with their talents lost to us all. The waste of human life in this manner by the bureaucracy cannot be overstated. The portion of the workforce that falls into this under-utilized, by-passed category depends on the size and age of the unit, but for traditional government bureaucracies as many as one-fourth of their complements may qualify.

The by-pass process used by managers may take the form of adding personal staff, so-called policy and planning units, and/or new layers and formal procedures. In the Department of State the Executive Secretariat,* the Policy and Planning Staff, the Office of the Counselor, and the Office of Management Operations are relatively recent examples of this phenomenon. The National Security Council at the White House level is a symbol of the presidentially perceived need to by-pass the Department of State in the field of foreign policy. Any number of other White House staffs have been created in response to perceived ineffectiveness among the more traditional bureaucracies. Although these creations are supposed to help the senior manager or the President cope with the inadequacies of the bureaucratic structure, they in fact exacerbate the problem by moving the head farther away from the hands and feet.

In addition to the systemically caused excesses of personnel there is blatant manipulation of the personnel system. Family members of Congressmen may be given make-do jobs, as well as the former secretaries of Senators. Former lovers of White House politicians may be sent to U.S. activities overseas. Alcoholic friends may be allowed to hang on to their jobs until retirement. All of these abuses of the merit system only add to the surplus.

What I have described here is the real "fat" in government bureaucracy. It is that huge part of the total workforce that is unnecessary for the currently assigned tasks and that by being rooted in place blocks the allocation of resources to pressing but under-attended priorities. Given this easily observable evidence the typical federal Department or agency wastes between one-half and two-thirds of its available resources, and the amount of waste increases with the age of the unit. Even in more operational oriented organizations which are lesser offenders the waste is probably as high as one-third to one-half. This is not to say that the individuals involved do not have anything to offer society for their salaries. They do, but it is largely untapped or misused. Neither is it necessarily to say that our society does not need a government workforce of about the existing size. It might, but it is certain that its actual accomplishments would be quite different. The majority of the public workforce would not be squandered on internal maintenance of the bureaucracy itself, as is now the case.

*Many other Departments have now emulated State and have such Secretariats and Management Information System offices for high officials.

The United States Government has the largest single collection of human talent on earth. That talent has the capacity to move us lightyears ahead in the struggle to create a safe, just and humane planet for all people. The government has social scientists, engineers, physical scientists, teachers, philosophers, poets, artists, managers, skilled technicians, planners, thinkers, and doers in sufficient quantity to engage the society at large in dramatic change for its own progress. But it is shackled by a bureaucratic tangle of our own creation. Today employees have to spend most of their time learning skills to cope with the bureaucracy. We need to devise a way to unleash their energy in constructive work.

Take the Easy Way

In this bird's eye overview of the performance of the problematic bureaucracy the third clearly visible trait is its tendency to focus on the little problems and to take the path of least resistance.

When viewing the end-products, it appears as if all the elements conspire to make the bureaucracy deal with the most minor issues, accept the easy way out, and produce the minimally acceptable level of performance. The FBI infiltrates student conferences and reports on marijuana smoking by Americans overseas, while the sectors of the economy dominated by syndicated criminals increase. HUD writes regulations on the locations of bathrooms in houses while thousands of people have no place to live at all. The Department of Agriculture teaches graduate courses in personal budgeting while non-competitive farming practices by huge corporations increase the price of food and simultaneously drive the family farm from the American scene. The IRS audits middle-income taxpayers to collect $200 more from each while businesses easily cover up millions in unpaid taxes. Thousands of government auditors check all official travel vouchers to catch penny errors while useless contracts are let for millions each year.

This marginal approach is also applied to serious problems such as the energy crisis of parallel, continuing escalations in prices and demand. Easy ways to shave here and there are proposed, such as Sunday closings of gas stations and raising the price of downtown parking. The result is that nothing is really saved and the real issues of social values and priorities are not addressed.

Naive politically appointed managers reinforce the focus on the periphery by inept attempts to gain control over the bureaucracy; they ask for easily quantifiable handles. As an example, one newly appointed deputy of a large agency began to look at analyses of trips and long distance telephone calls in an attempt to shape the substance of programs under his control. This deflected time and attention away from the questions of purpose and program effectiveness. Given the attention devoted to protecting one's turf and the procedural and interpersonal hassle required to accomplish even the most minute innovative effort, there is little time and energy available to tackle some of the bigger issues.

Bureaucrats, while not engaged in lower priority routine activities or producing tons of basically irrelevant paperwork, spend a considerable amount of time pushing their own pet projects or personal futures. After the initial flurry of public concern that results in the establishment of a new agency or program, the subsequent unit initiatives are generated internally or by outside individuals on the make and not by public needs. When these pet project grants are awarded to favored outsiders, nothing useful happens very often. And when it does not the recipient gets another contract to follow up and determine why.

The poor quality of this non-public performance is encouraged by other aspects of the bureaucracy which break down responsibilities into narrow tasks and reward short-term and easily quantifiable results. The tendency is to shirk responsibility for the big issues, avoid assuming new tasks because there is no easy way to get rid of outdated ones, and resist demands from society for courses of action that would force changes in the internal, safe and stable, bureaucratic order. This order protects itself from basic questions by a compartmentalization that ensures that cause and effect never meet.

Examples abound to indicate that even when there is a high degree of consensus on what should be done, it is still practically impossible for the members in the organization to take control over the course of internal events. Attempts to improve the nature of the federal product are easily repulsed by the mutually reinforcing bureaucratic elements that form an almost impregnable monolith.

> A senior management official of the State Department convened 13 task forces consisting of 250 carefully chosen employees. They made 500 specific recommendations to modernize the Department and got the Secretary's approval for them. Six years later not one of the significant changes had been effectively implemented.

What are the organizational factors that reinforce the tendency to take the easy way? They are structures, operating procedures, and managerial philosophy. Some illustrations of the way they influence employee behavior are discussed below.

Obviously many people who take jobs in the bureaucracy are motivated at the start to be creative, influential problem-solvers, or builders, but for most of them early disillusionment is inevitable. Only a few seem to be able to rise above the weight and distrust of the system and remain in control of themselves. New program starts fill the archives of government like half-finished monuments and stadia in under-developed countries, abandoned because the commitment and resources do not last long enough to finish them.

People quickly begin to view work in bureaucracies as a burden, not just because of the task to be done but also due to the conditions under which it must be accomplished—the non-essential attributes of bureaucracy imposed by our ineffective organizational structures and practices: the excessive layers of supervision, artificial channels of communications, paperwork and petty regulations that justify non-essential jobs. Even when the primary tasks of an organization are inherently meaningful and interesting, they degenerate under circumstances that neither demand creative performance nor are rewarding to creative people. Some estimate that as high as 50 percent of labor costs result from the distrust and lack of motivation engendered by "the system."

As a result of this antagonistic perception of the relationship between employer and employee we have come to assume that the nature of work is contrary to the nature of man and have concluded that even more controls must be installed. This is the underlying assumption of most modern management techniques and the 1978 Civil Service "reform legislation." When individuals come to the office, we ask them to forget their important interests and aspirations, their global perspectives, and their desires to create complete entities. Instead we demand they deal with fragments, never finish anything, and refrain from trying to find out how the whole thing turns out. Consequently they begin to restrict themselves and come to believe they are not capable of assuming responsibility.

We would have very different results if we recognized the personally rewarding nature of real work; we would find people refusing to do make-work that serves neither societal nor personal needs. The current system produces quite different kinds of people. Prevailing expectations, reward systems, and operating procedures have become powerful forces for a protect-yourself approach to work. The principle holds true regardless of what one is expected to produce; most federal employees now produce or process papers—an easy way to avoid real issues.

Useless paperwork is the primary product of the Washington bureaucracy. It, like so many other aspecs of bureaucracy, is both a cause and effect. It looms so large that Congress established one of the biggest study commissions ever, the Commission on Federal Paperwork with a staff of more than 200 and a budget of $10.5 million, to review the morass and make proposals for simplification and reduction. Such an objective is only a pipedream in the bureaucracy where to produce paper is to justify one's job. The culture instills the conviction that if what you are doing or thinking is not committed to memoranda, letters, or at least just on notes to the files, it must not be very valuable. The usefulness of a document for one's career depends on whether the individual's name is on it. Many a game is played to be listed as a principal contributor, or as administratively responsible. The broader the circulation a paper gets and the higher the recipients are in the hierarchy, the more status one has—and visibility and status are the name of the game. Self-confirmation and the ability to get ahead often depend on accumulation of such visible paper symbols.

Some strong beliefs promote the volume of paper: a lot of people cannot be trusted, the government must be run by the book and consistency is necessary. Paper is required because we have created such large structures with formidable layers and fragments that people need road maps to get anything done. The more people we put together the more guidelines we need, and vice versa. The cycle goes on. Reports and other papers prepared by the bureaucracy may too often be characterized by a quote from one of the draft reports of the aforementioned Commission: "fashioned to reflect a variety of personal interests such as ambitions or opportunities for career advancement." Others are prepared to "cover one's ass," as the saying goes in bureaucratic circles, when events threaten to expose fallacious judgments, omissions, or even reasonable mistakes. There are other lamentable reasons for producing paperwork: the overly cautious need to leave a "paper trail"; to communicate with people whom bureaucratic norms, interpersonal pique, or distance makes it difficult to meet face-to-face; and oftentimes to meet the capricious demands of the Congress and the public.

A large portion of the makework in public organizations comes from an illfounded assumption of need to monitor all that public workers do and how they do it. The attribution to all workers of the slothfulness or dishonesty of a few results in actually impeding more performance than it prevents waste or theft. The prevailing attitude of low trust described earlier has contributed to excessive layers of "supervisor/monitors" and strings of administrative roadblocks.

Generally, "monitors" do not know how to evaluate real performance, so in order to insure public accountability they use the time-clock approach. Instead of examining the quality of policy or product, the "monitors," or administrators, use things such as time sheets, meeting reports, and detailed travel vouchers. We spend thousands of dollars to try to save tens. We make all the workers come and leave together, thereby assuming the public is getting its money's worth, yet are unable to obtain coordinated effort between 8:00 a.m. and 5:00 p.m.

The lure of uniformity results in administrative pressures on employees to do the same thing the same way—"get the format right," "don't exceed the space limits," "fill in all the categories," "line the desks up this way," etc. For some inexplicable reason we believe uniformity of routine assures comparable levels of quality. The reality is quite opposite. Unique individuals blunt their creativity trying to force thoughts and actions into a common mold.

We also pay a very high price for the worker-watcher dichotomy in terms of mistrust and conflict. Those who really know how to do the job resent the amateur monitor's intrusions and these interpersonal conflicts have their own significant impact on the size and performance of the unit. In the continuing shuffle of officials in management positions, it is easy to slough off organizational commitments to individuals; jobs or tenure are promised by one team and denied by the next. While observing this pattern, it is no wonder employees spend so much time looking out for self.*

The growth of so-called administration and personnel professions has generated a great phalanx of controllers whose sole purpose is to administer the 30 volumes of internal accounting requirements and prohibitions and make sure there is no deviation; whether deviation be for personal or public gain is irrelevant. The rules have to be followed just because they exist; they exist because we have unnecessarily complicated our organizational structure and because we have only trained people how to devise new rules, to cover the loopholes of the previous set, not how to reduce our need for them. When the public abrogated its control over the public service, it welcomed the concept of bureaucratic rules to "keep them honest," but it failed to foresee the result: excessive rules do not keep dishonest people from cheating, but they do impede everyone from working effectively on new and difficult challenges.

How many fertile minds in bureaucracies are capable of bringing new strategies to play on the age old problems of war, disease, ignorance, and poverty? How many effective new approaches to resource use have been initiated by these in-house technocrats? In sum, how many innovative creations (technical and social) never see the light of bureaucratic day? Even the spasmodic efforts to reform the bureaucracy take the easy way out. Managers are unwilling to do the hard thinking, and acting, required to deal with real behavioral and performance problems. While recognizing the need for action, managers cannot seem to get past the mechanics of the formal system—but more on that later in the case of civil service reform.

Some question whether it is possible for bureaucratic organisms to produce important innovations with direct application to individual human needs. Most recent technological advances (computers, nuclear power, space capsules) seem to serve best the large type organizations which developed them. This rule seems to be even more valid when it comes to social innovations. Look at the complexity of most tax, welfare, and government regulation programs; they are generally misdirected overkills.**

Many experienced observers tell us that innovation usually can only come from outside the organization or from members who are marginal in the formal structural and career hierarchy. If these concepts are correct, then resources are wasted when the bureaucracy recruits creative applicants for service; they are only doomed to disappointment.

The career bureaucracy as a whole, because of the conditions that determine

---

*I recently observed one typical case of a woman who was forced to retire because it would have been difficult, although honorable, for the new personnel manager to follow through on previous commitments to place her after a reorganization.

**One recent Congressional survey of 20 government economic initiatives found they had generally had an impact different from their objectives. Nineteen years and $85.8 billion on training programs for the unemployed is generally seen as "a bust."

the behavior of individuals within it, takes the easy way out. Two of the big structural reasons for it, discussed earlier, are the fragmentation of roles, which is even worse within agencies than among them, and the fact that there are so many people without substantive jobs that too many try to keep a small piece of the action for themselves. Even when a bit of responsibility is given to an individual, the support system, over which he has no control, is so complicated and cumbersome that little can be accomplished in a timely fashion. It is not assumed that individuals can take on a whole task; the guiding precept appears to be to divide and control. People are often punished for advancing new ideas, and the converse, reward for innovation, occurs far too infrequently. There are also many psychological and interpersonal pressures that result in cautious behavior; they are discussed more fully in the next chapter.

Too Expensive

Two factors already discussed, unnecessary duplication of units and too many people within them, make the cost of goods and services provided to the public very expensive.

With the excess of personnel there is unnecessary communication, all of it superfluous to the actual need for internal communication, collaboration, and coordination. As an illustration, there are 4,000 laws that deal with federal contracting and 80,000 sets of specifications for purchases, yet no one believes the U.S. Government gets the best product at the best price. There are untold correspondence, meetings, briefings, getting clearances—all of it unnecessary were responsibility and full authority placed in those most directly involved with the work in question.

The operation of these bureaucratic factors results in the creation of what is commonly known as makework; something is done because people are available and operating procedures exist, not because it has to be done to accomplish a task for the public. Bureaucracy creates an internal cycle that generates work to react to the first effort, and then work to straighten out the differences between the two, and then more work to put it all together for someone higher up to review, and then a rework after the review, and then work for clearance with another part of the organization, and then a re-do for formal submission up the pyramid, and on and on. Frequently, when it is finally put together and massaged through dozens of people it is found that the effort has been overtaken by events or a senior official states it should have been done some other way in the first place.

If two assumptions go unquestioned, the belief in the efficacy of the unit's espoused *raison d'etre* and the self-contained bureaucratic pyramid, then serious doubts about numbers of people, amounts of funds expended, and the variety of his unit's activities never arise in the bureaucrat's mind. Consequently, one finds in government all kinds of offices, involved in make-work or tangential activities, whose existence is papered over (literally) by the lofty-sounding statements of organizational mission. There are examples of whole agencies whose original purposes for being have been by-passed by time (such as the Selective Service System). The more creative of them invent new rationales which permit expansions of budgets and personnel (such as DOE's Economic Regulatory Administration). Parkinson's Law is a reality. The U.S. Department of Agriculture, with its Graduate School and other non-farm related functions, is analogous to Parkinson's example of the British Admiralty that continued to grow as the size of the British Royal Navy decreased.

A corollary of the belief in unquestioned unit purpose is the blind faith in the agency's current technique of carrying out its work, the acceptance of the existing methodology as the best and most appropriate. The perpetuation of outmoded practices is supported by this assumption. Agencies continue to collect data and issue reports long after the need has passed, they maintain costly information distribution and accounting procedures long after practical experience has shown they are not worthwhile, and they reject without trial new analytic and validating principles.

There are at least two additional generic aspects of bureaucracy that raise the overhead costs: the overly complicated management systems and the pressures to be a full-budget spender. But beyond the management system engendered waste, we also have considerable squandering by individuals (encouraged by some of the self-images and elitist attitudes examined in the next chapter). These are not the big swindles uncovered by investigators from time to time; they are the day-to-day examples of disregard for the fact that the resources being used are public.

Examples ranging from the use of government telephone lines for personal long distance calls to the purchase of expensive new cars for new appointees abound throughout the bureaucracy. No one thinks twice about reproducing personal papers on government copy machines or spending thousands of dollars to redecorate perfectly good offices, or Ambassadorial residences, to personal tastes. When employees see their agency chiefs, office directors and Ambassadors satisfying whims there is little inclination to conserve office supplies and equipment. Senior officials who keep staff members on overtime outside normal working hours to aggrandize their sense of unique importance not only waste time and resources but detract from the day-to-day effectiveness of workers. This practice is widespread from the White House on down despite years of psychiatric evaluations that demonstrate its counterproductive impact on the quality of performance; in the culture of many units you are considered not to be important unless you "must" work late and on weekends. In contrast, many others "call in sick" from the farm just to avoid the tedium of the office.

The arrogance of power leads to even more blatant personalized excesses. As a junior officer at an overseas post about to receive a visit from the U.S. President, I was shocked to attend a planning meeting where an advance White House aide opened a briefcase full of money to "take care of local expenses." No receipts were required for the many unnecessary goods and services and all of us were given cash to up our economy class return air fares to first class status. By taking it we all colluded in the extravaganza. On the same trip one of the senior White House aides brought along his secretary as a part-time roommate. Considerable travel with sexual motivations is in evidence. While not being a moralist about the personal relations involved, it is disconcerting to see the diversion of travel funds needed for program purposes. Frequently priorities are set for such personal purposes, without regard to public needs.

Enough of the foibles of a largely amoral institutional culture. What are the more important systemic predispositions to waste? What is the superfluous that is considered normal as long as one accepts the bureaucratic perspective?

There are three big personnel groups; the civil service, the postal service and the military service. Then there are 45 excepted services scattered throughout the government such as the Foreign Service, the CIA, the Tennessee Valley Authority, the Public Health Service, etc. All of these categories have their special internal structures. It would not be stretching the truth too much to say that we have invented the most complicated and fragmented personnel structure that modern man with the help of his machines can devise.

The current patchwork system is so filled with holes and bursting seams that one must devote all available time keeping the thing from completely breaking down. Adding a new and stronger patch on one bare area only results in something weakening and giving way elsewhere. You find one hole in the regulations, maybe even an inadvertent one, and you change it. That sets something else aflutter and you go to remedy that miscarriage. Then you find that makes something else stop working and you have to rush to that breach.

We have created an incredibly costly internal system and refined it to the point where people can no longer understand it, much less control it. *Overwhelmed by expensive complicated procedures our institutions are too sapped of their energy and resources to deal successfully with the needs of the external world.*

The process of hiring new people is a nightmare; 4 to 11 months of red-tape and interoffice haggling is the norm. The merit promotion process is equally time consuming (three-fourths take more than 6 months) and a charade (only a few people really know of new jobs and are truly considered). There never seem to be the right people available to fill new priority tasks. Little is known about what talent is available in underworked offices. In other words, the personnel management function of the bureaucracy would be better labeled as regimented chaos. Its product is not efficiency, but demoralization. People anticipate the difficulty of getting anything done and consequently do not set very high expectations for their work, yet the spinning wheels cost millions.

The same characterization can be made of the procurement of goods and services. An employee who actually wants to get a job done finds himself unable to quickly obtain administrative support; materials take weeks to arrive, contracts and purchase orders require months to process, and assistance from other people is unavailable. One has to be a very senior official to cut through the red tape; lower level program officials are actually hampered by the administrative officials ostensibly hired to support them. The process is so complicated that outsiders in effect set the prices for government contracts; the bureaucrat has to spend so much time on process that he cannot deal with the substance of performance and costs.

Task forces, management analysts, system experts and organizational specialists galore spend years and millions of dollars devising ways to set up new bureaucratic systems and others must spend just as much time and money figuring out how to get around them.

Despite daily examples that there are too many procedural obstacles, or perhaps because of them, senior bureaucrats still respond to the lure of so-called modern management; they keep opting for mechanistic gimmicks and control techniques, all of which only add to the confusion and cost. Expensive technological and process developments, such as computer information processing, electronic communications, statistical analyses, and budgeting concepts, are grasped to the bosom to assuage the senior manager's fear of unresponsive bureaucrats. Often that lack of response is due to the fact that their hands and feet are tied. It takes on the average six months for a program manager to enter into a contract with an outside firm. It is no surprise that managers turn to non-competitive contracts or big friendly existing contractors through which work can be more quickly channeled.

When voters or legislatures reduce the funds for a bureaucracy the first things its leaders cut are the "end-of-the-line" people (such as teachers and firemen) and organizational units (such as field offices and small special purpose military units). Some of these decisions are motivated by a desire to pressure people to reverse the decisions adverse to the bureaucracy, but from the managing bureaucrat's position it is easier to cut those on the periphery; they are not so well entrenched nor able to play bureaucratic games as those nearer the headquarters (which is where most of the waste usually is). Secretaries' jobs are always cut before professionals, although the latter cannot function without clerical support. Externally developed cost-cutting efforts therefore affect little of the waste.

Another paradoxical phenomenon that leads to excessive demands on the taxpayer is the penalty that goes with saving money. If a unit finds it can get by for less than it budgeted for the year it is apt to find its requests for the next year reduced accordingly. More value is placed on plans that "come out right" than creative efficiencies. Consequently, every effort is made to spend all the money that is available, and to even ask for more to prove how crucial your program is. Entrepreneurs circle around the bureaucracy like vultures the last month of the fiscal year because they know all funds must be obligated to protect the administrator's reputation. These last few weeks produce more creativity than the rest of the year as officials come up with ingenious ways to spend the last cent.

Given these prevailing structural, managerial, and attitudinal conditions the excessive costs we pay for the governing bureaucracy should not be surprising to us.

Too Self-Centered

Perhaps it would be more palatable to citizens to pay too many people too much money to do small tasks in a disorganized system if what was accomplished could most often be perceived as an attempt to serve the general welfare. But the opposite is the impression given.

One of the most striking aspects of the performance of public bureaucracy is the arrogant and capricious way in which its members treat their fellow citizens: a modern example of the traditional "dog biting the hand that feeds it." Behind that behavior lie several elements of a rationale that determines how bureaucrats perceive their responsibilities to the public. Few consciously set out to behave that way, but the inherent assumptions and norms of the bureaucratic culture induce it. Even the populist politician when elected or appointed to the bureaucracy leaves behind the public's perspective as he or she is quickly melded into the select "power elite."[5] Such a transformation is illustrated by a comparison of a Jimmy Carter campaign speech with one of his mid-1977 ones. In 1975 he said the American people were concerned that government had lost its integrity and that no one represented the American people's perspectives and aspirations. In 1977 he said, "We are trying as best we can to make progress. It takes time to change the trends of history and reverse the bureaucratic mechanism." His 1980 behavior clearly indicated he had completed the transformation from champion of the public to spokesman of the bureaucracy. It appears that very few are immune from the insider-versus-the-outsider syndrome. If it affects so dramatically the attitude of the elected who come and go, as best epitomized in the Watergate mentality, it is no surprise that those who commit their entire lives, especially in units that consider themselves to be meritocratic elites, become staunch defenders of their bureaucratic fiefdoms. This belief of infallibility causes leaders to leave crazy people as Ambassadors, defend cohorts involved in illegal activities, and angrily denounce questions about the bureaucracy's integrity.

Bureaucrats generally see their fellow citizens as falling in one of three categories, all of which permit rationalization of the bureaucratic-outsider dichotomy. The most widespread attribution is "clod." I do not mean the term itself is often used—it is actually a rural colloquialism meaning a dull, stupid person—but the attitude clearly exists that the general public is too naive to really understand the nuances of complex issues which are best left to the ministrations of experts, i.e., the bureaucrats in question.

One sees this in the issuance of regulations. Requirements for public hearings and Congressional involvement notwithstanding, federal regulators preempt for themselves the making of law. A classic example was the 1970s large-scale expansion by bureaucratic fiat of the Food and Drug Administration's regulations, from a 1938 Act, without the benefit of a Congressional action. In effect, law was made by the bureaucracy. Some of it was needed, but the issue of concern here is the process. A similar example is the administration of the Health Services Finance Administration where bureaucrats quite openly take actions that impact on the practice of medicine, although such behavior is expressly forbidden by statute. Since the early days of the Interstate Commerce Commission the bureaucracy has increasingly arrogated the power to legislate.

The national security area of the bureaucracy is perhaps the most prone to take the secrecy stance. The weighing of strategic pros and cons, the assessment of foreign attitudes, the complicated building of decision models and scenario options are believed to be way above the comprehension of anyone but the insiders. The bureaucrat claims that John Q. Citizen cannot understand the factors entering into decision-making and therefore keeps the process and pertinent facts secret; the very secrecy ensures that public understanding will not increase. A General Accounting Office report estimated that more than 70 million documents are classified (restricted) each year. The bureaucrat, by his secrecy, guarantees that he is correct in belittling the level of knowledge of the public. Another such paradox is that much of the complicated analysis and modeling is required as a result of the secrecy about what we are doing. By collaborating in the international games of bureaucratic secrecy we reinforce the tendencies of other nations to play hide and seek games with us, which then requires that we devote tremendous resources to attempts at deciphering them. Few people in the bureaucracy understand that greater openness about capabilities and intentions would lead to greater predictability and enhanced stability and security in international relations as well as generate domestic confidence. Most are unable to escape their own self-imposed blinders, attributing to and thereby reinforcing in others the same attitudes they hold themselves.

Such an attitude was manifested in the Pentagon's handling of the proposed production of a neutron bomb. The Pentagon decided, with the then Energy Research and Development Administration (ERDA), to produce and deploy neutron enhanced radiation warheads and artillery projectiles in U.S. forces in Europe. Funds were requested in the ERDA fiscal year 1978 budget, yet the public and most of the Administration, including perhaps the outgoing and incoming Presidents, were not aware of the full import of this dramatic new generation of weapons. It only became public knowledge through an inadvertent reference to the new warhead in declassified transcripts of ERDA hearings before a Congressional appropriations committee. The Pentagon justified its secrecy on the basis of keeping the development from the Soviets, a probably futile aspiration, and the complexity of a tactical cost-benefit analysis of such a "clean" weapon, which requires a "sophisticated" understanding of the relative advantages of killing people without destroying their buildings or military shelters versus total leveling of an area.

The belief that the public cannot comprehend the implications of technical violations in the handling of uranium and place such infractions in a proper perspective may have motivated the staff of the Nuclear Regulatory Commission to keep secret an inspection report on uranium missing from a nuclear submarine fuel factory in Pennsylvania. When it was leaked to the press on Capitol Hill in 1977, two years after the report's preparation, the NRC staff quickly and fairly satisfactorily gave reassuring explanations of the incident. Early sharing of the report by the NRC with the public it is constituted to serve would have been much more credible and constructive, but perceiving of the public as a "bunch of clods" makes it easier to justify keeping things from them. The NRC's handling of Three Mile Island nuclear plant accident in 1979 showed that not much progress had been made in the interim.

This example also illustrates the "constituency" problem, where the members of bureaucratic units see themselves as relating solely to a particular sector of the public, e.g., teachers, airline companies, farmers, etc. This often turns into a sweetheart relationship, with exchanges of personnel, mutual political support, and even financial transactions to the benefit of both parties. The bureaucracy is loath to criticize the constituency which is its *raison d'etre* and does not wish to portray itself as having been ineffective in dealing with it. So a natural collusion evolves to keep the general public unaware of the real impact of the government's relations with each group.

This symbiotic relationship between a bureaucracy and its constituency was well illustrated in the Pentagon's withholding of B-1 bomber cost estimates in the last days of the Ford administration. An updated internal government estimate put the production cost as $112 million each, above the publicly stated figure of $93 million. Independent estimates placed the cost at $117 million, but no public discussion of the higher estimates took place for fear of jeopardizing Congressional and public support for construction of the bomber. Here again the bureaucracy arrogated for itself the right to deceive the public at large to its and its special constituency's benefit.

The idea that there exists a legitimate "right" to deceive one's "clients" in their own interest enjoys broad support among patronizing groups of physicians, ministers, and teachers in our society. As self-defined professionals they consider themselves able to know better what is best for the client. This attitude permits otherwise intelligent and humane people to decide not to inform people of health problems and interpersonal difficulties, to unilaterally take actions that affect patients, and to trade-off individual interests against some nebulous "larger good." They escape with their consciences intact by acceptance of the principle that it is all right to lie to a person if one believes that not to do so would cause the recipient distress. It is not surprising then to find public administrators, and bureaucrats in general, striving to be labeled professionals, arrogating the same so-called right for themselves. They also use the same rationale to cover up weaknesses in the procedures of government itself, such as the lack of a fail safe command system on the nuclear launch buttons.

A part of the NRC nuclear loss report mentioned above stated that both the firm and the NRC failed to inform individuals who had been exposed to excessive radiation, through faulty plant equipment, of that fact and its potential danger to them. Recent CIA admissions that it used hallucinogenic drugs on unaware employees, proposed 1975 Environmental Protection Agency experiments on unsuspecting subjects with carcinogenic fungicides, and the military's cavalier treatment of soldiers exposed to atomic-test radiation in the '50's, are examples of how the patron-client mentality influences bureaucratic behavior vis-a-vis the public.

These interlocking "client, constituent, and clod" stereotypes help shape how bureaucrats perceive of their responsibilities to the public and their corresponding behavioral patterns give us the kind of treatment that is labeled as "arrogant," "calloused," and "self-serving." The inherent assumptions, behavioral norms, and internal mechanics of the bureaucratic culture reinforce such behavior. *The problem is that the bureaucratic climate instills and perpetuates an arrogance that removes the government from the people it should serve.*

Although I have used rather negative terms to describe the attitudes of bureaucratic employees, and those labels may appear reasonable to the outside observer, those on the inside have a different perception of themselves. In their view they are trying to do the "right" thing.

In the final analysis, organizations succeed or fail depending on the integrity of individual employees. But the huge superstructure and control apparatus which has been built up takes away from the individual actor his autonomy and responsibility. In the end the basic function of government can thrive only to the degree that each actor reasserts his or her independence and acts in accordance with a sound understanding of the real world and the requirements of the public at large. Since the ultimate fate of organizational performance depends on the individual taking the appropriate action, it stands to reason that organizations would attempt to prepare their employees for such an august role by providing scope in terms of knowledge and experience. The opposite is what actually occurs in a bureaucracy. We have created a system so complex and so filled with inequities that there are few benefits, psychological or otherwise, to be derived from exercising a self-discipline that prohibits taking advantage of each event for oneself and one's personal office. What influence does that have on the public employee's outlook?

Ethical Perspective

Much that government does is unique and lacks well-defined traditional guidelines or cultural norms internalized by most members of society. With such a large degree of ambiguity, it is then necessary for bureaucrats to develop an institutional ethical framework within which "do's" and "don'ts" can be labeled. It is possible to distinguish a set of ethical constructs that have evolved in our federal career service regarding the relationship of government to the larger society.

In order to place these bureaucratic ethics within a larger context, one which affords comparison, I would like to refer to the scale of moral maturity developed by Lawrence Kohlberg of Harvard University.[6] Kohlberg has defined moral judgments as "judgments about the good and right of action ... (that) tend to be universal, inclusive, consistent, and to be grounded on objective, impersonal, or ideal grounds." From the individual's perspective they are seen as essentially expressions of the concept of justice.

For the most part bureaucratic ethics fall in Level IV, the "law and order" category, of his 6 category scale. During recent years considerable discussion has taken place within the bureaucracy about the ethics that should govern bureaucratic behavior. The primary debate seems to revolve around whether bureaucrats should owe their allegiance to the bureaucracy or to the public at large. The view that has prevailed is that the bureaucracy comes first. Note is taken of the public servant's oath of office, of the allegiance pledged to the Constitution and to the laws of the land, and of the idea that ours is a government of, by and for the people, but the debate generally concludes that the best way to meet those obligations is to do the best one can *within* the bureaucracy.

During the height of the struggle between Kissinger and the Congress over access to foreign policy information, Nathaniel Davis, a respected professional diplomat, wrote[7] to the Department of State and Foreign Service the following pertinent comments:

> Honorable public servants do not undermine their constituted superiors or colleagues ... In a policy disagreement, no (bureaucrat) has a right to prevail; nor to campaign against an adverse decision. What he should have is the opportunity to be heard as the decision is being made.

Although the article and a subsequent Davis speech to employees recognized real dilemmas and stipulated certain nuances or caveats, the point of view presented, which is an articulate expression of Level IV ethics, ignores the fact that the only time bureaucracy fears openness is when it is unwilling to be judged by the public. And that is exactly the time when dedication to the public interest should motivate bureaucrats to speak out. The view of the traditional bureaucrat would require an employee who disagrees with the hierarchy and cannot submit to the official line to get out of government service. If this concept were universally applied—and it is already applied too widely—the result would be a bureaucracy with no dissent to warn those on the outside of violations of the public trust. Revelations of just such infringements by intelligence and law enforcement agencies, exposed over the past few years, indicate the results of unconstrained application of bureaucratic ethics.

A paraphrase of Kohlberg's Level IV definition makes it specifically applicable to bureaucracy:

> There is orientation toward the organizational hierarchy, fixed rules and the maintenance of the bureaucracy. Right behavior consists of doing what one is told, showing respect for the chain of command, and maintaining the bureaucracy for its own sake.

This ethical context is a logical and organic extension of the other components of the bureaucratic mental set and other elements of bureaucracy: a self-arrogated elitism, a mistrust of outsiders (the public), self-serving reward systems, authoritarian structures, and defensive interpersonal games. All of the various parts of the bureaucratic organism discussed in the next two chapters complement and reinforce each other to give us the remote and self-protecting ethics of our public service.

A Performance Overview

This chapter has not been a definition of the problem; the factors described here are only symptoms and some of the second order contributing media in the overall "bureaucratic problematique." They indicate, however, that our central institution for social guidance and development cannot provide leadership, is overgrown, cannot tackle the big issues, and saps the society's resources, largely for its own self-preservation.

Notwithstanding the array of talent involved and instances of exceptional workmanship, *the overall performance of the federal bureaucracy is of very poor quality and unreasonably expensive.* Not only are the products slow in the making and poor in quality, but the manner in which they are delivered to the public is sorely lacking in the characteristics one has a right ot expect in a democratic society.

An independent, full-scale audit of the efficacy of a public bureaucracy undoubtedly would reveal that among all man's inventions it is unequaled in terms of inefficiency—never have there been such numbers who perform so many acts and consume so much time to accomplish so little. A cost-product analysis of even the simplest kind indicates that the input of human and financial resources is far beyond what one would expect from viewing the output. The contrast is even more striking when one includes only the "useful output" in the comparison. The quality of the product is usually in inverse relationship to the number of people and the amount of time spent on it; the more time and people involved the weaker the product. Generally, the farther the review of papers goes in the hierarchy from the involved workers who originate them, the poorer the quality, both in terms of the validity of the analysis and the quality of the recommendations. The actual product of the bureaucracy demeans the number of creative people who are attracted to it and then rendered incapable of actualizing themselves as they had expected. The difference between what they are capable of and what they actually produce is staggering.

If the output of public organizations fails the public's minimum expectations and if senior managers seem no longer to be in control, is it the fault of public employees? Are they only spending their time making life easy for themselves? Any study of individual employees would discover a resounding, "No!"

Perhaps even more than the assembly line workers described in HEW's study, *Work in America*,[8] public employees can hardly wait for the end of the day or the beginning of vacation. They resent being under-utilized and manipulated; they feel a lack of control over their own behavior and destinies. It is often only the economic security that such organizations provide that keeps them at their jobs.

> A professional employee believing he is responsible for informing Congress of illegal agency payments to contractors acts accordingly. He is fired. After months of publicity and appeals, he is rehired—only to be given a routine job.

> An employee loyally serves 35 years and one day quietly dissents on a policy issue. Her job is reorganized to force her into retirement.

The government's human organizations are inhuman zoos of steel and concrete and inhumane in their members' treatment of each other. In moments of reflection and with feedback from others, sensitive employers are shocked to recognize that they daily relate to subordinates and colleagues with exactly the same demeanor under which they chafe at the hands of others.

Although no exciting new words have been used to define the symptoms that afflict our government establishment, the five phrases on page 28 do capture their essence and also provide us a taxonomy that permits the ordered, deeper burrowing into their media and causes that is required before actions leading to real reform can be designed.

Is it really that bad? In this chapter we have reviewed the "bureaucratic problematique" as it can be easily perceived by any observer who wishes to devote some time to it. If you have no direct experience, you may ask government employees to whom you can talk in confidence whether it is really that bad. Ask your citizen friends what they think. The consensus of those many descriptions will beyond doubt confirm the picture drawn here.

But to describe a performance problem does not automatically provide an insight into what to do about it. For that we need some guide to the inner dynamics of things social, some understanding of why things work the way they do. For centuries maybe this understanding was inbred among members of simpler social organisms, but with the complexity of modernity our instincts seem now to have failed us. We seem to be lost, standing around wondering how we got into such a mess and unable to do anything about it.

Without a sound knowledge of their own institutions people cannot look outward and comprehend the forces that move their fellow citizens and other nations. To assume one can be an aware leader in the world-at-large without first being aware and in charge of one's own behavior is a grave error in judgment. The people who create cumbersome structures, overcompartmentalize ideas and people, and play bureaucratic games on the inside take the same approach in the larger world. If public officials cannot elicit the best from their own fellow workers, then they should not be too surprised when they fail in their public efforts.

As a nation we grew out of the forests and the fields, the villages and the small towns, and arrived in the city to build a new kind of world, a modern age, but we got so caught up in the new theories that we forgot the lessons of back home— that a person needs room, identity, space (linear and psychic) to breathe and think, and that one needs to be a part and at the same time architect and builder. Getting caught up in enjoying the goodies of the technological age we dissociated our past, cut the roots and left the knowledge behind, disdaining it for the new. Having burned the bridges to our sources we no longer have confidence that we possess other potential thought patterns to bring to bear on the problems of our organizational life.

What is needed is neither flailing attacks on bureaucrats, nor emotional defenses of organizational traditions. We simply need a critical look at the internal dynamics and underlying assumptions that appear to have trapped all of us, but upon which we are so ill-prepared to perceive and act.

3
Diverting and
Demotivating Complexity

> They are playing a game. They are playing at not playing a
> game. If I show them I see they are, I shall break the rules and
> they will punish me. I must play their game, of not seeing I see
> the game.
>
> R.D. Laing, *Knots*[1]

Chapter 2 described many of the obvious symptoms of the bureaucracy; now it
is time to go below the surface and dissect the innards that help shape them. We
have looked at the more visible performance issues: the fragmented and
duplicative formal structures, inappropriate behavior vis-a-vis the public,
employees stumbling over each other, and the overly complicated management
systems. What kind of people are inside? How do they work? And why?

We must peel back even more layers of our scarred onion if we are to address
the question of whether the waste, the cost and the chaotic, self-centered nature
of bureaucracy is inevitable. We must cut very deeply if we are to understand why
more than 30 years of attempted remedies for symptoms have not enhanced the
effectiveness of our public bureaucracy. We must go to the core of basic
assumptions about people and how their related systems are used to elicit desired
behaviors.

The hidden sources for the more easily visible problematic manifestations of
the bureaucracy are the answers to questions such as: What do the organism's
members think—about themselves, their roles, other people, and the outside
world? What are their emotional states? How do they relate to each other on a
day-to-day basis? How do the internal administrative processes actually affect
employees?

We now enter the domain that eludes most observers, unless they also live in
and directly experience the culture of bureaucracy; it includes the dynamics of
group psychology, unwritten and infrequently articulated assumptions and
attitudes, interpersonal norms, and the pervasive influence of an inappropriate
personnel system. These internal factors directly shape the disappointing public
performance of the organism described earlier. They are themselves influenced
over time in a reciprocal relationship with the poor quality products. It is almost
a vicious cycle: we have done so poorly that we cannot expect to do better. It
would be inaccurate to say I am about to expose cause and effect relationships;
reality is much more complicated than that. But there are direct linkages
between the less concrete media now to be described and the actual symptoms

that occupied our attention in the first chapter.

Before going any further it might be useful to try to label in a general way the onion-like layers of reality that comprise any social organism, including a cultural entity like the Washington bureaucracy. One reasonable set of categories is shown below. (The first level and part of the second were covered by the previous chapter.)

- Overt Behavior
- Formal Organizing Systems
- Available Human Talents
- Interpersonal Behavioral Style
- Individuals' Psychological Set
- Basic Assumptions
- Members' Self-Images

I use the onion metaphor due to the lack of a better commonly known physical analogue. It is too simplistic and does not reflect the reality of reciprocal relationships among the categories, nor the variegated patterns of influence flows among the many elements. Social and psychological reality is much more complicated, but more on that later. But such a hierarchy does let us analyze the data from within the bureaucracy in a manageable way.

What is the employees' vision of life within the bureaucracy and their perception of the symptoms? The following bit of imagery grew out of a few minutes of free time some employees had while waiting for what they all knew was going to be a boring bureaucratic staff meeting. Someone suggested it would be great to plan an animated cartoon to express the nature of life in a bureaucracy and the following images were described:

Man As Machine/Organization as Factory

Down stark corridors fragments of personalities flit past each other. Sometimes the geometrical shapes pause to move with stylized steps around the space between them. In those instances they make contact with opaque eyes and jerking hands in a way that keeps them apart, at the proper distance. At other times they line up and parade into rooms where internal computer-like programs point out the appropriate places to sit. There each being glances down his/her private agenda and proceeds to talk her/his way through it, pausing to give others the alloted air time and to organize what he/she will say next. Thoughts pass each other in the air like darkened ships in the night, or parry and thrust like drugged boxers to defend their own integrity. In both cases they make no progress toward synthesis.

In thousands of rooms individuals silently prepare to participate in hundreds of those meetings. The act of preparation is to quiet the fear bubbling inside that one will be found out. A ritual process is used. Its exercises are to psych out in advance what the other person is going to do while avoiding being found out oneself.

This beehive of unrelated machinations resembles nothing else so much as a huge factory with unconnected groups of machinery in a din of grinding and whirring that spits out bits and pieces of a puzzle for which the overlay has long been lost.

That description was sort of a composite, free-association exercise, but it conveys very strongly a sense of superficiality, stylized relations, alienation, unconnectedness, defensiveness or even fear, and the absence of a sense of purpose. It implies the individual wisdom to conceive of the design and work with others to reshape it was lost in a prior age. The vision of a whole has dissolved and only parts of its blueprint remain intact in the minds of a few, scattered helter skelterly in the warrens. The possessors of the clues do not generally recognize the value of what they have and the few who do are afraid to hold them up to the light for others with possibly matching pieces to see. The fear of standing out, calling and receiving no response, is so great that one stays quiet in an alienation that at least is familiar.

The reaction to this sense of anomie is very often that described below, regardless of the individual's personal competence or position in the hierarchy.

If I am seven layers down the chain of command, do not understand exactly what is requested of me, cannot really ask the big boss because of jealousy over prerogatives, have little clerical or administrative support, distrust my counterpart in another unit with whom I should work, am concerned about my next evaluation report and its impact on my salary for Junior's first year of college, feel that I cannot really design a course of action that allows me to do my best, believe that whatever I do will be taken by someone else for his or her own ends, know that I'll get rewarded for meeting the Chief's values, and have too little energy left to fight for a democratic vote on my work, what can I do? Or,

If I am heading a unit, but don't know what all my employees can do, have only the means to give orders and dispense positions, cannot know if I should trust the people who work for me, want to look good myself, fear other units encroaching on me, am not sure if the President likes my performance, do not have time to re-do everything, am not sure exactly what my mandate is and cannot seem to get my management systems to produce what I want, what can I do?

This vision more typically characterizes the career employee than the transitory political leadership, but it is surprising how many in the latter group quickly fall into the same mood. It is therefore, possible to make some generalizations about the bulk of government employees. Most see themselves passing time in an unreal world.

Human Talents Dulled

The human result is dulled people who, in spite of their best intentions, perceive almost everything as an insurmountable obstacle; they learn to eschew responsibility on substantive work and avoid the challenge to grapple with the system's maintenance and process obstacles. More effort is expended on protecting positions, scrounging funds, defending office space, hustling materials and equipment, explaining what one does to other people who do not have real jobs, and keeping a growing file of protective documents than on direct action on a public problem.

The behavioral norms and other influences of the system are stronger than the individual's initial, internal impulses to autonomy. Little time must be spent in the bureaucracy before most individuals succumb to a prevailing genotype.*

In the bureaucracy most people fall into one of two groups: those who understand this facade and use it for personal promotion and those who unwittingly, or because they cannot exercise another option, play the game. In recent years there have been growing numbers in a third group: those who are well aware of the sham, refuse to be lulled by the rhetoric, yet instead of joining the manipulators try to expose the inconsistencies of the system.

The people in the first group (the *cynics*) are successful or at least resigned to their fates. Many of them become addicted to the routine, the production of papers and the attending of meetings that feed their nervousness. The second (the *careerists*) are naive and coopted, although frustrated at their inability to exercise greater self-control. Many of them, after years of believing the system is valid, without question assume "it" must know what "it's" talking about and begin to devalue themselves, accepting its "put-down judgments" as valid. These people plod on doing what they are told, and do nothing when they do not have specific instructions. The low morale begets poor performance and a vicious cycle sets in that lasts 20 years, many of them devoted to pursuing personal interests of family, sports, investments and the like on office time. But surprisingly these people officially also say they are satisfied enough with the system not to rock the boat. The third group (the *critics*) suffers both internally and externally. They reject and are rejected by the aware controllers of the system, yet they are moved by a sense of justice to continue to struggle with the system's inequities. They believe the myths of the *careerists* ought to be made real. They think that equity, due process, and effective procedures are both necessary and possible. They fight to make things work the way they ought to.

---

*A conversation I had with a Greek aristocrat who had been in his government's service less than two years exemplified the difficulty even people with external supports have in avoiding becoming a bureaucratic personality. Given this, it is easy to understand how malleable young people of no standing fall easy prey to bureaucratic socialization.

They are frequently used as pawns in power struggles. Ultimately rejected by the *cynics* who see them as a threat to their personal power, they are also rejected by the *careerists* whose mental stability is threatened by their calling into question the shibboleths which have been internalized as reassurances for one's belief that in the long run the right thing is being done. From this group come the "whistle blowers" who cannot contain their discomfiture at seeing "bureaucratic facts" not square with "reality."

All three categories are dysfunctional in that they detract talent and energy from the tasks of public work. They all represent a degree of unhealthiness that inhibits both individual growth and interpersonal and performance effectiveness. They keep people from focusing on the real world and work to be done and divert attention to the unreal chimera of the personnel management system and its games.

That is why I have chosen the term "bureaucratic personage" to describe the typical employee. It connotes an individual who has ascribed characteristics, with little to support them. We have managed to create a situation where people fill positions with responsibilities in substantive areas but know little of the substance required. People make scientific decisions who are not scientists. International policies are set by people who know nothing of other cultures. Social welfare questions are resolved by people who know nothing of conditions in a poor family. Most bureaucrats see their job as dealing with managerial or policy questions and not natural or human ones.

When there is this separation of decision making from actual experience one gets a personality that focuses on form instead of substance; that which was unreal becomes the new reality. It is analogous to unwed priests making pronouncements on the principles of marriage. An EPA scientist was told how to research the effect of pollutants on the food chain by a supervisor who did not know anything about the food chain and who only wanted to satisfy a demand that something be done, even though it was scientifically indefensible.

By the nature of the bureaucratic reward system, one who is good at actually doing something does not generally have any power. Only those who can easily manipulate the symbols of the bureaucratic system get ahead. Those who keep their human experience and hearts in the forefront of thought and action remain in non-leadership roles. Consequently, all those who are motivated to progress up the ladder quickly learn the route. And that route is suppression of feeling and social concern in favor of praise for the fine-tuned phrase and the malleable personality.

One way to study the "bureaucratic personage" is to observe how he behaves at home. That day-to-day behavior is described by Dan Miller,[2] professor of psychology at Britain's Brunel University, in a survey of the effect of a man's working life on his family life. Miller did a comparison study of bureaucrats and entrepreneurs. He describes bureaucrats as doing one small job in a big organization, controlled by a long chain of authority, and having no responsibility for and remaining ignorant of the rest. In this situation they learn to subdue their independence and initiative, always deferring to authority, never muscling in on anyone else's department. This, Miller says, is strikingly reflected in their behavior at home. In the family they are uncertain and vacillating, less involved with spouse and children, more remote, liable to defer to so-called expertise or push the responsibility off. "Children of (these) fathers . . . are far more likely to be disturbed." The fathers rely more on commands, punishment, bribes—bossing, rather than leadership—to evoke good behavior.

Alistair Mant of the Tavistock Institute of Human Relations who was quoted in the same reference characterized the whole British society as debilitated by its dependence on authority and the covert rebellion bureaucracy has inflicted on it. He found that bureaucracy builds up aggressions which result in destructive infighting.

The situation is no different in the United States where despite all the contraindications that they possess the requisite disposition and skills, bureaucrats appear driven toward achieving positions that carry the symbols of status and control. The entrepreneurial spirit has been smothered and people choose the security of a niche. Even when their unique skills or ideas could earn an excellent living, people opt for selling them to large organizations that can provide a security cushion.

The net result of the organizational system is a personality type in which the bureaucratic overlay overshadows other skills and traits. The scientist's rigorous requirement for concrete data breaks down in face of bureaucratic politics. The psychologist's concern for human health gives way to authoritarian control systems. The diplomat's awareness of another culture's values takes second place to an awareness of his chances for promotion. The former farmer's concern for conservation of resources falls before the onslaught of paper associated with his work in the Department of Agriculture developing better-sounding university grants. And on and on, the values and standards of performance learned in lessons of real work are forsaken in the lure of bureaucratic rewards like titles, the perks of office, and other blessings bestowed by the keepers of the pyramid.

The government workforce is filled with people with the apparent technical and professional skills required by our society, including artists, teachers and scientists. Yet, somehow we have managed to create a social system that attracts and retains a type of person for whom the mere act of getting in is enough of a payoff that to fight against it is unthinkable. Rather than proclaiming, "I am here to help make a better society for the folks back home," the new employees state with some not insignificant degree of awe, "Aren't I lucky to get in."

If management believes the members of an organization are motivated by one set of images and makes its decisions accordingly while the employees are operating on another set of ideas, the least that can happen is that nothing positive gets done and, at the worst, things can really get fouled up. If a person believes she or he is a professional and gets treated as a bureaucrat, one is demotivated. Conversely, if one believes himself or herself to be a bureaucrat while the organization expects professionalism, the organization's expectations are not met. In either case the results are confusion and ineffectiveness. Much mediocre performance results from this kind of incongruency in the theory and practice of various units in the bureaucracy.

Such dysfunctionality can arise from two different manifestations of the lack of fit: one is differing connotations of the meaning of professionalism and the other is the juxtaposition of professional images with simplistic authoritarian concepts. Government units which have cadres of personnel who are members of recognized professions face these problems. Bureaucracy is not hospitable to the practicing of a profession and individual attempts to be professional only succeed in making everyone uncomfortable, the bureaucrats as well as the would-be professionals. At present many people call the State Department's Foreign Service a profession and most FSOs* identify themselves as professionals. Some of their behavior is influenced by that self-identification. On the other hand, it is quite clear that the Foreign Service and the Department of State function as a bureaucracy. The Environmental Protection Agency, NASA, and others that employ scientists have the same difficulties.**

In these ambiguous circumstances there are many who believe what is called for is a concerted effort to clearly define and implement a concept of public sector professionalism. But at least three options are available for government. One is to accept the bureaucratic pattern where all unquestionably follow orders in the pyramid chain of command. Another is to develop unique governmental professions. But a third is to choose neither and deny both the bureaucratic and public profession approaches. I will come back to this theme again as I consider options for new directions in government organizations.

Given the widespread existence of the bureaucratic personality type, the confusion about status, and the formal fragmentation and complexity of the system it comes as no great surprise that most of the interpersonal behavior inside the government is very superficial. The result is . . .

Interpersonal Defensiveness

Bureaucratic games epitomize the bureaucratic predilection to create an unreal replacement for anything authentic—in this case, the manner in which employees relate to each other.

In 1964 Eric Berne introduced the concept of "games" as a category of social

---

*FSO means Foreign Service Officer.

**For example, EPA scientists who, in their view, developed sound control procedures for the disposal of hazardous wastes felt their judgments were overridden by bureaucratic politics, senior officials so insecure in their own positions that they did not wish to antagonize an industry group.

transactions. Games in his schema do not equal fun. They are deadly serious and may be either conscious or subliminally learned imitative behavior patterns. Berne described a game as a "recurring set of transactions, often repetitious, superficially plausible, with a concealed motivation... (where) after the payoff it becomes apparent that these operations were really *maneuvers* (my emphasis), not honest requests, but moves in a game."[3]

In 1971 Morton Halperin[4] transferred the concept of games from the more intimate personal arena to the bureaucratic one. Writing in *Foreign Policy* and explaining why bureaucrats play games, Halperin answered the question in a manner that was too charitable and too simplistic. He wrote:

> Organizations have interests. Career officials in these organizations believe that protecting these interests is vital to the security of the U.S. They therefore take stands on issues which advance these interests and *maneuver* (my emphasis) to protect these interests against other organizations and senior officers, including the President.

Others have described additional motives, beyond a belief that one's action is in the ultimate national interest. They include career enhancement, protection of prerogatives, to cover up mistakes, etc. Games are not simply conscious, rational strategies used by bureaucrats to further their organizational or personal interests. They are the overt behavioral patterns or "scripts" that result from a complex of psychological, social, and structural factors and consequently are much more pervasive and have a more profound impact on the public policy process than Halperin alluded to.

Halperin was correct when he stated neither appeals to patriotism nor turnover in personnel would lead to change, but he is wrong when he limits the name of the game to organizational interests. That leaves the impression the route to avoiding the damage caused by games is through identification of vested bureaucratic interests and the establishment of other organizational checks and balances. Reality is more elusive and multifaceted. Games are an inseparable element of an organization's overall fabric.

Participants in bureaucratic games fall into three categories. Those who initiate the play, determine the objectives and define the tactics are *gamespeople.* (They are most often the cynics mentioned earlier, but not exclusively.) A second category is the *colluders,* people who do not clearly understand the stakes but take part on the basis of the apparent purposes of the play or as a result of personal or professional relationships with some of the players. The last group is the *victims,* those who are either knowingly or unknowingly being manipulated.

The term victim does not mean that people with this appellation are passive. They act, but are disadvantaged through either lack of valid information about the gamesperson's code which does not permit a realistic challenge of the gamesperson. The tenets of this code are: (1) Do not deal with feelings or motives. (2) Do not confront directly the stance of another player. (3) Do not question the process. They make it impossible for a player to differentiate between reality and game playing and she/he is stuck with overtly reacting to the facade. The fact that the victim today may anticipate the need to be a gamesperson tomorrow also constrains him/her from breaking the code.

The specific rules of the game set by the gamesperson deal with such things as time, place, agenda, data, procedures, and participants.

By now it should be clear that games are played to avoid facing stressful personal conflicts, to thwart efforts that pose a threat to one's own designs, to keep others in place, to minimize their impact, and to protect the *status quo*. The ultimate objective of the game is to diminish the opposition while aggrandizing oneself and it is generally thought of as a zero-sum contest.

"The Committee Game"

One of the most widely used, it is generally recognized as a means of loading the dice to ensure a desired outcome. When a person in an authority position does not wish to take the public responsibility for making an unpopular decision, or faces strong opposition, the Committee Game offers a more subtle means to get his/her way.

The attributes of a Game Committee, in contrast to the neutral committee's operation, are:
 - the membership must be biased in favor of the gamesperson.
 - the victim cannot significantly influence its make-up.
 - the mandate is primarily established by the gamesperson and cannot be modified once the project is launched.
 - the internal process is different from the public process and is controlled by the gamesperson.

The Committee must be selected to include members who already have vested interests consistent with the gamesperson's pre-ordained goals. It is helpful if these people also see the stake in question as a zero-sum game and do not wish to lose any of their perceived advantage. The more members who owe something to the gamesperson the better, even if it is only membership in the group. That token opposition which is included among the membership should be ineffectual.

Once the group membership has been determined the gamesperson must then control both the process and the flow of information. With the Committee Game it is necessary to go through the act of openly soliciting advice, even to the point of having public meetings, but the success of the game requires the absence of any systematic way of verifying whether or not and how this publicly generated data gets reflected in the committee product. Feedback and verification and weighting mechanisms are proscribed. The final drafting must be in the hands of the vested interest group.

If the committee has been stacked well enough it can be allowed to use "democratic" voting procedures, but if the pre-selected supporters are either weak or change their minds as a result of the study then the report should be reviewed by a superior authority, i.e., someone the gamesperson controls or has an accord with, before it is released.

In many government agencies, the off-site conference is often used to insure the production of a "proper" committee report. When a seminar is held miles away from Washington several advantages accrue to the gamesperson. Not only is membership in the committee controlled, but even access to the committee by outsiders is essentially cut off. Since the site chosen is usually one of several pleasant retreat-like facilities within the radius of a few hours drive from Washington, simply to be chosen as a participant is a significant inducement to do the "right" thing. Also being away from the office and together around the clock for several days permits the use of a variety of social and personal pressures in shaping the group's collective perspective. One subtle pressure is simply the hobnobbing with senior officials and hearing their cues.

The gamesperson must not only consider the tactics of where and who, but must also pay careful attention to the procedures, i.e., what papers are presented, who serves as rapporteur, discussion chairpeople, etc. If opposition is expected at the implementation or operational level it is in the gamesperson's interest to include token representation from that sector and hope they later try to convince their resisting colleagues of the legitimacy of the policy report.

■ *Short-Term Results.* When a gamesperson uses the Committee Game the short-term results are almost invariably those desired in advance, i.e., the report says what it is supposed to. If one or more participants have not been drastically misjudged and do such things as abstain or prepare minority reports, an ostensibly broad-based consensus evolves and a report is produced which is publicized as having legitimacy. It will carefully include some straw-men opposition arguments that have been set up and knocked down, thereby giving it "balance." And the participants will be vociferous supporters among their peers.

■ *Long-Term Impact.* Where there is considerable opposition to the findings of the report, and such is usually the case when the Committee Game is used in the first place, its unveiling generates additional hostility. To the already strong emotions of opposition are added feelings of betrayal or foul play. Feelings of distrust between the victims on the one side and the gamespeople and colluders on the other are heightened, thereby not only reducing the effectiveness of relations on the issue of the moment, but also on future issues. This deterioration of long-term mutual respect is of profound importance in the organization's ability to continue solving problems. The hostility may even reach the point where personnel changes must occur in order to maintain a minimal level of cooperative working relationships. This has its price in terms of discontinuity.

Expertise which has been built up over time is lost. And given the propensity to playing games such personnel turnover only gives a transitory impression of togetherness, soon to be shattered by a few games among members of the new team.

"The Hidden Boss Game"

One other game which is useful in covering up one's own role in decision making, whether to be less vulnerable to confrontation or to project a misleading impression to one's peers or subordinates, is the Hidden Boss Game. To play it one has to be in a position to control access to the boss. When this is the situation a gamesperson can declare he or she is a neutral channel, simply providing the pros and cons to the boss who makes the final decision, while actually making the decision oneself and informing the boss or while acting as a decisive advocate with the superior. This game permits someone in the chain of command to appear to be all things to all people, and at the same time enable the person to get his/her own way more easily by covering up his/her role. This game works best in rigidly hierarchical traditional government organizations.

The way it typically works is as follows. The gamesperson desires to see a certain policy chosen and his view is not fully shared by interested peers and subordinates and he is not in a position to impose the policy. He or she takes on the role of conduit to the person who, by virtue of position or other authority, can make the decision. The gamesperson is then free to play the role of recommendation gatherer, on the surface including options covering the differing views, and to assure others that a full and fair presentation is being made. The victims and colluders take the game at face value, unaware that a separate oral or even written advocacy case is being made by the gamesperson.

After sending the recommendations forward, everyone waits until the gamesperson one day returns from a meeting and announces "the boss has decided." He or she may even embellish it with such statements as, "I was surprised that a decision was taken, just like that." This kind of statement is particularly called for if there has been some general expectation that there would be further discussion of the issues before a decision. The gamesperson may say, "The boss' mind must have been already made up," neglecting to mention his or her own role in influencing the decision.

The only way one can become aware that a game was being played is to have "the boss," at a later date, describe the role of the gamesperson. In my interviewing in some cases where this game was played, the "boss" would later say something to the effect, "(the gamesperson) really convinced me that such and such was necessary and assured me there was general agreement."

■ *Outcome.* This game can work to the advantage of the gamesperson as long as it is unlikely that the victims or colluders can or will verify the actual mechanics of the decision-making process. As long as others either believe the gamesperson or feel constrained by the bureaucratic norms from probing the gamesperson can enjoy success.

If it occurs too often players become suspicious and the quality of cooperation deteriorates. And if the game is uncovered even quasi-effective working relationships are destroyed. The recipients who have been "had" turn around and start looking for a way to retaliate, or at least manifest passive resistance. Consequently, as in all games, the viability of the institution is seriously undermined.

"The Reorganization Game"

Reorganization is a way of redistributing responsibilities, formal authority, and communications channels. One of the most effective ways of mustering support for and eliminating opposition to one's policy objectives is the restructuring of the relationships in the decision making process. If studies result in the "wrong" conclusions, if policy forums end up voting the wrong way; if decisions taken are not carried out as desired, in other words, if the gamesperson is blocked in achieving his aims, then he or she is led to consider changing the players and/or positions on the team. Reorganization is almost always seen as an easier method of getting one's way than the more time consuming and complex process of education and consensus building. When the gamesperson's opposition is rooted in deep seated substantive differences that are not likely to be changed, the reorganization option is even more appealing to a gamesperson convinced of the rightness, or even righteousness, of his own goals.

In the Reorganization Game the stated motives are not the real ones and the players are led to believe other purposes are being served. Since the real reasons can never be expressed there is apt to be considerable confusion when the new public explanation is pushed by the colluders who, while left in the dark, still have their jobs to do.

One interesting example which I studied was a double-header. While an Assistant Secretary position was vacant, a senior Deputy Assistant Secretary attempted, through the good offices of one Department Principal, to reshape the bureau in such a way that his power would be enhanced at the expense of the new incoming Assistant Secretary. The suggested reorganization was proposed to the Deputy Under Secretary level and was almost approved, but the incoming official recognized what was happening and stated he would refuse to move into the job if the change was made. The new appointee had the support of the Secretary, was personally picked by him, and therefore was able to prevail. (The Secretary was unaware of the reorganization by-play.)

Then for the second game—upon taking office the new Assistant Secretary determined to by-pass the gamesperson in the previous game. The victim became gamesperson and a reorganization plan was announced, with great sounding statements of justification. Most people in the bureau never caught on, and if the victim did, he never publicly admitted it before he quietly retired several months later.

Immediately following use of the Reorganization Game the gamesperson and colluders have a sense of euphoria. The highly visible aspect of structural reorganization creates a heady sense of power and gives rise to a high level of expectations. In fact, simply the breaking up of old patterns may give rise to some initial creativity, but the shattering of regular operations makes it impossible to quickly carry through the planned schemes. The rupture of personal ties and loyalties requires time for healing. Many of those necessarily left behind continue their commitments to the exiles and may even purposefully subvert the new efforts. The successful accomplishments of the new team are likely to be limited to ringing descriptions of a new day that is heralded, but in reality never materializes.

One might assume that in this game it is possible to identify the gamespeople and the victims by watching who moves where, but such is not the case. The careful gamesperson will make sure that enough decoys are also launched to cover up the real agenda and in any large reorganization irrelevant by-standers are shuffled as well. Sometimes the person doing the reorganizing is only a colluder, being moved by a skillful gamesperson who is concurrently also making use of other games. Some of them are the Expert, the Deadline, the Cocoon, and the Classification Games.

In organizations many of the activities to which I have added the word game are consistent with their stated purpose. It is this valid mirror image that gains the active participation, or at least the acquiescence, of many players in games. Often participants are unaware of the gamesperson's purposes and see their behavior as contributing to the staged objectives.

Games may be engaged in as a result of a conscious decision or simply as a resort to habitual routines learned as mechanisms for coping with either active opposition or passive resistance to one's efforts to work his/her own will on the organizational fabric. They are the products of traditional behavioral styles learned as a result of interaction between psychologically insecure humans and defectively designed organizational systems that perpetuate the vicious cycle. The weaker individuals perceive themselves to be in their work environment the more prone they are to play bureaucratic games.* Operating from the disadvantages imposed by the bureaucratic culture individuals believe they cannot take the risk of being open and sharing the little bit of control they do retain over their own destinies: hence gamesmanship.

Games are not the only characteristic of interpersonal relationships in a

---

*Sigmund Freud wrote to Josef Breuer on September 1, 1886, "An officer is a miserable creature, he envies his equals, he bullies his subordinates, and is afraid of the higher ups; the higher up he is himself, the more he is afraid."

bureaucracy, but they sum up the pervasive distrust, defensiveness, and selfishly-oriented actions. Markedly absent is commitment to an open, cooperative, publicly-oriented approach to the job at hand. These interpersonal factors stand in the way of direct, effective work activity; they are continually highlighted and reinforced by the acting of other bureaucratic elements on the individual. Many of these games are used vis-a-vis the public as well. The nature of the system is such that reform among gamespeople is unlikely to take root from within, and gaming is not susceptible to eradication by simple training sessions conducted by outside experts.

Bureaucrats are conditioned to abhor innovation and a fine set of evasive behaviors has been developed to insure that initiatives for significant change never get "a full day in court." This is not to say bureaucrats inform others that new visions are unwelcome, quite the contrary, nor to imply that conscious deliberate obstacles are routinely set in place, but the world of action speaks louder than the glowing public rhetoric.

Officials hardly ever take overt negative positions on new proposals. In fact, so much has been said about the need to encourage creativity that you get frequent statements from managers calling for new thinking from their subordinates. (Remember everyone is "subordinate to someone else.") Therefore the smothering process is an indirect one and follows these stages: (a) No specific feedback is given while the innovator discusses his/her idea in the germinal stages. (b) Vague encouragement ("Keep up the good work!") is given and the would-be innovator can draw upon some minimal resources, e.g., time to work, travel money, computer time, access to data, etc. (c) Agreements to review and comment on the proposals are made by managers. (d) Compliments and awards are given. (e) No follow-up actions are taken. (f) The innovator's energy and time are diverted to "safe" tasks. (g) Concrete feedback and/or decisions are avoided, unless the innovator is bold enough to force a settlement.

Principles (a) through (e) are illustrated in the following case which was related to me:

> *Senior:* Your memorandum is filled with good ideas. I'll keep it and study it carefully. I'm sure they will be helpful to me. Keep up the good work.
> *Junior:* Good! Does that mean I can go ahead and change the procedures in my office?
> *Senior:* No. You had better hold off on that for a little while. I want to see what Mr. A thinks about it. I'll let you know.
> *Junior:* (Still waiting for a response three months later).

The use of principle (f) is demonstrated in the following case:

> *Junior:* We've developed this new computer model that will make our trade projections so much easier. Once we test it and get the bugs out it will

free our analysts enough to do that in-depth policy analysis Mr. Y
requested.

Senior: I'm glad to hear that. I've really encouraged you to develop it, but
I'm afraid we'll have to wait for implementation while we get the Project
X study done for the 7th floor. In the meantime, have your people give
number one priority to Project X.

Junior: (On his third re-write of Project X). I really don't think it makes
sense to try to conclude this until the Red Division finishes its input. We
could be doing more important things. Maybe I could get back to that
computer model.

Senior: Well keep at Project X anyway. I want to be the first one to hit the
Secretary's desk when the time is ripe.

When the innovator later pressed for approval to go ahead with his new
computer program he never was given a definite rejection. He never found out
what his boss really thought about it and the change in priorities it would
facilitate for his office. There was no way for him to confront his supervisor's
logic, whatever it was. The superior's response was too vague:

> Well it sounds good in principle, but I don't see where the funds would
> come to play for the added equipment costs. It would also take a lot of time
> to collect and prepare the data. I don't know where we would get the
> personnel to prepare for start-up. Why don't we think about putting it into
> next fiscal year's budget request and that way we could get specific
> Congressional approval for it.

The junior office director, not wishing to jeopardize his position by taking it
up in the Assistant Secretary's weekly staff meeting, which was the only
bureaucratic recourse open to him, simply dropped the idea. Perhaps he had
learned from the experiences of his colleague described below.

When the innovator does not accept the polite, subtle hints of his nominal
supervisor and brings up an issue in a larger forum, he may find sanctions taken
against him. An officer participating, along with his boss, in a group considering
an AID program change had developed some evidence that the change was
unlikely to actually accomplish the purported objectives without some
modifications to bureau grant approval criteria. Although he had been told his
boss and others did not want to change the criteria, he brought up the idea in the
next group meeting.

> *Researcher:* What happened when you presented the data that indicated
> the proposed change was unlikely to be effective?
> *Officer:* Very simple. I did not get invited back to another meeting of
> division heads when that issue was being discussed. My formal access was

completely cut off and I was not even informed when the meetings to
approve the new instructions and criteria were held.

Another way the would-be change agent finds himself deflected is to be
assigned a special project before he can carry through on his idea. One officer had
discovered a way to simplify the clearance process for military sales and save an
officer's position when:

> *Supervisor:* I know the work you are doing on the reorganization of the
> bureau for better use of our people is an important one, but right now
> we've got to have somebody to go out on that group to Southeast Asia.
> There's a deadline and it's crucial that the work be done on time. You're
> the best man for the job. It'll be good for your visibility with the front office
> too.
> *Officer:* Well, I can suspend my study and get back to it when I return.
> *Supervisor:* No, I'll give it to Sam to finish.

The final study report, my respondent indicated, did not include his proposed
improvements and manpower savings.

Concrete feedback and/or specific decisions on new ideas is avoided; the
appearance is one of a failure in two-way communication. It is difficult to
determine how much is "feigned misunderstanding" and how much is a selective
filtering out of the innovator's suggestions at a preconscious level, rejecting that
which is threatening for the more acceptable. There is the genuine problem of
various obstacles to communication, but certain kinds of behavior appear to be
endemic among defensive bureaucrats: subtle attempts to shift the focus,
interjecting extraneous considerations into the exchange, and a revising of what
the initiator indicates he or she wants to accomplish. These behaviors take place
if the bureaucrat cannot avoid the meeting. The bureaucratic setting provides
other aids for defensiveness if protocol makes it difficult to postpone the contact.
The meeting will start late, the telephone will be allowed to ring, the next
appointment will be waiting, and the need to "put out some fires" will provide
an excuse to avoid seriously addressing the issue and to defer further
consideration to a future meeting.

One of the more serious and direct ways of discouraging too much "creativity"
is through the use of "code words" in performance evaluation reports and job
recommendations. These are words which ostensibly bear no negative
connotations and may even appear complimentary to the naive observer, but
within the context of the organizational tradition they are damning. Here is a
personal example given to me by one officer:

> *Officer:* I always tried to express my thoughts openly so he would have the
> benefits of my thinking. In one case my evaluation of the need for a change

in the bureau's reporting requirements led me to push by demonstrating how irrelevant field post cable traffic was to our needs. He apparently didn't appreciate it. He wrote in my performance report that I was "bluntly honest."

Author: And the promotion panel knows what that means doesn't it?

This large measure of disregard for the new ideas of junior employees is probably a result of several factors. One is obvious: a career service by its very nature assumes that years of experience and promotion up the ranks is synonymous with increasing qualifications to deal with any issue. Given the soft nature of the social theories on which most government programs are based, university-trained new employees or those with outside experience are not perceived as bringing anything new to the field. Senior members of the civil service believe that competence only comes with participation in the specific area in the bureaucracy—a surprising assumption given the track record of the bureaucracy. The newcomer is expected to adapt his technique to the traditional process, not vice versa. In addition, the formal personnel system with its supervisor, top-down, evaluation and promotion process and the compartmentalized, rigidly layered hierarchical responsibility and control system are crutches for personalities threatened by dissonance, even if it is only an apprentice thinking new thoughts.

But in spite of this climate, frequently risk-taking managers in the bureaucracy do hire creative and qualified people into the career service for the avowed purpose of innovation. What happens to these people after they are on the inside, but still see themselves as seeds for significant progress toward more effective governance? So few ever get a hearing in the highest levels of federal agencies and fewer still get any sort of testing before they are discarded by the wayside. There are no statistics. No records are kept of possible good ideas that are nipped in the bud.

Although we would like for it to be otherwise, experience indicates our bureaucracies do stifle most creative thinking and innovation. This appears to result not from a malevolent·hierarchy, but from the defensive tendencies discussed earlier that manifest themselves in Washington and elsewhere among career officials. When access to the top depends on successfully piloting through the shoals of demanding superiors over long years of apprenticeship, the disinclination to rock the boat on any given day is very strong and the hint of a restraining hand is all that is necessary. When eventual fame is more likely to accrue to one who has escaped the charge of being different than to one who pushed an idea whose time had not come, the price for taking a risk is too great.

Personnel(less) Systems

One of the central, if not single most important, structural influences on the attitudes and behaviors of bureaucrats is the operation of a mechanistic personnel system. The counterproductive role of the personnel system in terms of time and resource use was touched on in Chapter 2. It is now necessary to study its impact on the attitudes, feelings, and behavior of government workers.

One test of my hypothesis about the debilitating role personnel systems play in government organizations would be a comparison of the assumptions of the personnel managers with the behavioral outcomes rewarded and/or reinforced by the actual practices of the personnel office. In other words, does the functioning of the personnel system effectively lead to the desired results? Let us look at some of the State Department's Foreign Service images of the kind of people it wants and the personnel system's contribution to fulfilling them.

Some of the expectations are as follows:

- Individuals in the Service must be able to fill successfully a large number of jobs around the world.
- They must be able to shift effectively from one to the other at a moment's notice.
- Long experience is required for the real work of the service.
- An independent professional, i.e., not partisan, service is required.

Now let us look at the system's implementation of these concepts and see what they actually produce in the Department. We are able to locate the linking mechanism in the personnel system that helps shape reality to the idea. We should then look at the side-effects or undesirable ramifications of this process on important organizational outcomes. Therein lies the value test for the operating system. Do they give what is needed to meet the external demands levied on the organization?

Interchangeability

Most traditional jobs in the Foreign Service and in the State Department have become routinized and superficial, i.e., "carry on like your predecessor unless new legislation or an executive order mandates change." Even in the latter case one is expected to modify the "standard operating procedures" only to the degree necessary to bring about minimal superficial compliance. In other words, roles are defined in such a way that any relatively quick learner can become operational in a matter of weeks. Whether you are a political specialist in Latin America or Asia does not really matter; the work is the same. You talk to a few already established contacts, read the papers and the standard texts, and carry on the internal Embassy process of meetings and paperwork, filing routine reports and responding to Department queries. In Washington an employee slips into the slot in a manner that hardly causes any reverberations to occur in adjacent activities. The result is that jobs are seen as maintenance of the *status quo* at a superficial level. One is rewarded for how well one turns over the same function that was given to him or her upon arrival.

This approach to roles has a significant impact on the quality of work in the overall organization. Internal job changes are not made to keep up with changes in the environment. Assumptions that were valid yesterday are not re-examined in today's light. Problems which require in-depth study and profound responses do not receive them. Activities of marginal utility are not eliminated and new issues which require attention receive little, if any. And finally, no attempt is made to cope with the barely discernible future.

Why does such a simplistic level of actual performance persist? *An important part of the answer is that if you assume people have to be interchangeable, then the jobs have to be made interchangeable too.*

The personnel system then functions to insure that these two ends of the log—interchangeable people and equally homogenous jobs—meet. How is that accomplished?

(1) It moves people around so often that no one can build up sufficient expertise either to change the nature of the job role or to modify significantly his or her knowledge and skills.

(2) The individual is supervised and rated by someone with equally shallow perceptions and skills in the area.

(3) Bureaucratic processes impose similar standards for the form of the job products—"take out last year's file and up-date it"—and the incumbent's relations to others—"don't do anything to jeopardize our relations with so and so."

So the personnel system is not producing passive caretakers because that is what it sets out to do; it reinforces those dysfunctional behavior patterns because of the simplistic way it tries to meet expectations about generalists.

Instant Mobility

A similar flow of expectation, implementation and unintended side-effects exists with the Gunga Din concept: individuals can and should be transferred anywhere at a moment's notice, like soldiers filling in the breach.* In order to make sure that everyone keeps on his or her toes the system uproots a certain percent of employees without advance notice each year. It is justified by the claim that such discipline is necessary to fill all the less desirable jobs in the world.

While an argument can be made that providing for rapid job changes is

---

*It is interesting and significant how many military concepts have been incorporated into the Foreign Service's thinking about its own operation, despite the fact the functions are totally different.

necessary in a few cases, it is clear that in most instances less disruptive assignment procedures would work just as well. But the central office attempts to keep the initiative by controlling information about job openings and new requirements. The laissez-faire market place approach to filling jobs has never really been tested. The individual most often is left at the mercy of the system and is not encouraged to think in terms of career planning for oneself. In this instance the personnel system simply carries out the mobility concept and it cannot be blamed for the fact that employee performance does not meet the needs of the society.

As a result, officers will not attempt to initiate and see through a demanding and untested new policy or program, even if it appears called for. After all, they do not expect to be there long enough to make a difference, even if making a difference were rewarded. Consequently, policy analyses are made with a shallow appreciation of history and recommendations are made or actions are taken with a very short future perspective.

Seniority and Previous Experience

Comparable to the above examples is the criticism that the Department is always "focusing on how to win the last war." One hears the personnel system being called upon to teach people to anticipate, to look ahead; but Central Personnel, like the other formal structures and processes, is simply carrying out the mandate of the philosophy which asserts the important work of the organization cannot be done by people who did not fight in the last war.

The career grade structure and the pyramidal hierarchical model provide the frame within which the personnel office carries out the tenure-based assignment and rewarding processes. Preparing to fight the last war is therefore not a symptom of poor training or other personnel programs; the latter is only the handmaiden of the organism's dominant ideas or myths about the benefits of a closed ladder system.

Partisan Introversion

The reality of life in the bureaucracy is that people are encouraged to look out for themselves at the expense of the public. The basic structure of the selection and reward system ensures that. The problem of public servants who do not serve the public cannot be remedied by seminars and procedural gimmicks. The personnel office cannot establish, in the current bureaucratic context, a set of rewards that will sufficiently reinforce the desirable kinds of behavior. The closed system, by its very nature, makes partisans of its members, but partisans of their own causes. The incentives to serve the organization are greater than those that would lead one to put the public interest in the first place.

Mismatches

Similar career and system assumptions break the same laws with people's lives in other Washington departments. These examples illustrate how the actual inner workings of an institution differ from the public rhetoric. The personnel system is an integral part of the organism and can do no better than the whole. This is not to say that the practice of public personnel theory by so-called professionals does not cause problems; it does. Its potential for harm is greater than its benevolent properties. The following paragraphs look at why that is the case.

Personnel systems are continually being made more complex to gain more control over the federal workforce. But it is often said that the happiest supervisor and employee are those who manage to circumvent the personnel system to find each other and design the work to be done.

I would not cry for more energy to be spent in trying to "make the system work." I was the instigator of and an early participant in just such a computer-based effort in the Department of State that collapsed under its own complexity. Yet many believe we can weigh and measure people and keep jobs fixed in concrete with enough certainty to justify a centralized rational system of personnel management. By trying to make that dream into a reality we have set up a number of pressures that curtail human creativity and limit an office's potential for adaptation. What are some of them?

First of all each job has to be written up in such a way that it justifies a particular salary and label. Although most of them are fiction they nevertheless inhibit the way the various participants perceive of their roles and responsibilities. Of even more concern is the fact that since certain standards are set for each grade level, supervisors and subordinates conspire to make sure enough "classifiable" functions exist to warrant the highest possible salary. Make-work is devised; this is particularly true where supervision is concerned. Supervision is an important factor in the job classification system so everybody tries to grasp as much as possible; layers of supervision are invented. We have already seen how that diffuses what should be concentrated and sustained efforts.

Since the central personnel system is incapable of directly assessing the quality of an individual's performance, some such substitute grading system has to be used, hence all the various performance evaluation techniques that have been tried—and found wanting. With the acceptance of a superficial grading system, public bureaucracies perpetuate a major fault of the school system, that is, failing to produce achievers because of its technique for measuring achievement. As Charles Peters of the *Washington Monthly* wrote in October, 1976:

Today's young achievers are achievers in terms of grades, in terms of others' views of them, not in terms of their own view of themselves—as they go forward from the academy to work, they still need someone to grade them.

The effort of an individual in a bureaucracy is focused on getting good grades—whatever stands as evidence of recognition—and the behavior that is rewarded by those grades will take precedence over the behavior required to meet the person's internal standards for excellence, which are usually more consistent with the job requirements.

The evaluation system which is maintained to justify pay and promotions has a net negative impact on morale and performance. It has a little value as a means for an individual to obtain feedback from others on what they think of his or her performance, but that could be gotten much more easily another way. The evaluation report actually reflects the idiosyncracies of the personal relationship, yet is placed in official files as a matter of objective judgment.

The sum of the requirements of the formal personnel system are perceived by employees, in both supervisory and non-supervisory positions, as obstacles to be circumvented. They are seen as necessary evils if one wants to work for the government. But of even greater detriment to the overall institution than the unnecessary work and emotional energy consumed by modern personnel management practices is the disdain they engender for the ideals of a competitive merit system. Because of the obvious sham involved, people tend to discredit the whole idea of open and accountable competition. Not surprisingly most people begin to develop very strong attitudes of self-interest and skills in manipulating the complexity for their own ends.

The sheer complexity of the system is so great that daily inequities, real and perceived, are clearly visible to everyone. There are many people like one black woman who once worked for me. She had genuinely been discriminated against by an arrogant, upwardly mobile supervisor, but she was able to tie the system of reviews and investigations into knots and spend half her time on it for two years. Unfortunately, she was spending no more time looking out for her future than the self-aggrandizing boss who pretended to be God's gift to the organization.

By developing a system in the name of merit and quality performance that so miserably fails to deliver we have created a backlash of contempt for the values it ostensibly promotes. People know the reality is one of favoritism and gamesmanship and find it hard to believe that the ideals of personally motivated growth and public accountability could actually work in a social institution as big and as impersonal as the bureaucracy.

Two-Dimensional Triangle

An important part of the justification for the personnel management function, and a primary reason for its failure to serve well the public interest, is a simplistic mental image that has gone involate too long. Of all the ingrained perceptual patterns that 20th Century well-educated Americans carry around in their heads one of the most bedeviling, and certainly the most inhibiting as far as government organizations are concerned, is the two-dimensional, triangular schematic concept of formal organizations. The large-scale, cumbersome, inefficient governmental apparatus that is fragmented and inappropriately staffed and managed, is haplessly rooted in this ill-conceived model. *The artificial requirement that the people and tasks of government be organized to fit a triangle is responsible for an incredibly large portion of the ineffectiveness described in this book in terms of product and individual behaviors.*

The usual image does not even have the sophistication of a pyramid, which is at least three-dimensional. Max Weber would most certainly be surprised to see how Americans have taken his descriptive concepts, derived from certain organizations, and run amuck with the pyramid approach to creating all categories of public organizations. Even modern German bureaucracies have managed to avoid many of the "refinements" we have added. Americans who have internalized this image are unaware that they limit their vision of organizational alternatives.

The reason for the pervasiveness and force of the triangular image is its simplicity; all such primary patterns are simplistic. The basic faults are not only its over simplification, but also its lack of a way to describe the multifaceted reality of social organisms and its misleading implied linearity of individual relationships. If this conceptual pattern existed only as an academic tool, and had very little social impact, it would be of little concern to us; however, it has infected us all and has had negative implications for all public institutions. What follows is an attempt to identify how the bureaucracy-as-triangle idea shapes the public personnel system.

Grades

Given a triangular type of structure with an apex at the top, some means of differentiation is needed to sort out the levels from the apex on down. The result

. . .

FIGURE A

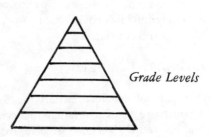

Grade Levels

The more levels, the more degrees of refinement are needed. The Civil Service has 185: eighteen grades with 10 steps each and five executive levels on top of that. Since the selection of 18 levels is purely arbitrary, one has to devise equally artificial criteria to operationally define the different levels. One arbitrary act leads to another and pretty soon you have (as in actuality the government does have) volumes of paper describing minute differences among the various degrees of knowledges, skills, abilities, traits and responsibilities that are applicable for each grade level. It is an exercise akin to the Reformation era debates on how many angels could dance on the head of a pin.

Specialization

If grade levels are used to distinguish where individuals fall between the apex and the base, then some other taxonomy has to be invented to place people on the continuum from one side to the other. *Voila . . .*

FIGURE B

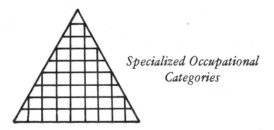

Specialized Occupational Categories

If a case cannot be made that there are many different special requirements in function, then the door is left open for the managers or taxpayers with legitimate concern about duplication to raise questions about the numbers of employees. Therefore, it is necessary to devise vertical groupings or specializations to clearly indicate where people fall on lines from left to right. This and other bureaucratic pressures cause us to refine the different categories far beyond the realities of work tasks and individual qualifications. Following the Adam Smith pin factory model mentioned earlier, we have assumed that things work best if a person specializes and does the same thing all day every day. Although we are now beginning to realize that this may not even be a valid assumption in manufacturing, we have applied it unquestioningly to public agencies—even in the complex and abstract areas of analysis and program and policy development.

Career Ladders

Since the squares or tiny triangles described by the intersection of grade and specialization lines are static there has to be some way to provide for movement of individuals from square to square. Such a device has been invented and has been labeled "career ladder."

FIGURE C

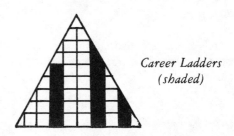

Career Ladders
(shaded)

Career ladder defines an entry point on the triangle, the specialization column, and a height to which an individual can expect to climb. In the Department of State, promotions are restricted for middle-aged officers because to do otherwise would cause the middle of the pyramid to "bulge" too much.

Career Patterns

A career pattern, on the other hand, shows a variegated series of moves over time.

FIGURE D

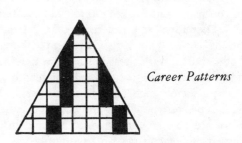

Career Patterns

This experience is usually reserved for either leaders or failures, an exception to a model specialized career.

Seniority

Since there are ladders and tracks that imply movement over time in the triangle, on which everyone has to be in some pecking order, the concept of promotion as climbing the rungs is inevitable. Seniority or time spent in the bureaucracy becomes a surrogate for other reasons that might more appropriately be used to allocate increased authority and responsibility. Unfortunately such seniority is not positively correlated to the quality of performance in government jobs; the better people usually do not stay in long enough to accrue it. In fact, due to the parallel, but retrogressive, influence of other factors seniority very often is negatively related to quality of performance. This does not mean the experience that generally comes with age is not valuable; however, the almost inescapable molding that occurs with years in the bureaucracy limits rather than broadens.

Top-Down

The apex is supposed to equal power and since it is on top, the power and control is believed to flow downward; notwithstanding Chester Barnard's brilliant 1938 book demonstrating that power resides in the will of the individual to act.[6] The top-down power flow tenet leads to all kinds of systems and procedures which would not be seen as rational by many were it not for the unthinking acceptance of the triangular image. Four of these are briefly described here.

■ *Symmetry:* Every unit has to be forced to conform to the triangle, like billiard balls being racked on the table in preparation for the break. This means that for a set number of workers there must be a layer of supervisors, more or less equally dividing the subordinates, and then above them another layer of chiefs, and then directors, all the way up to the single superchief. Even rule-of-thumb span of control formulas have been established, despite lack of similarity among functions and no empirical data to validate the particular standards. (Recall Chapter 2 discussion of too many actors.)

Paradoxically, at the very top levels of the triangle a superordinate can apparently "supervise" fewer people. I say surprisingly, because one would assume that the more sophisticated managers are nearer the top and would need a smaller percentage of an executive's time. The only rationale for the current practice seems to be the triangle; you have to get smaller spans the nearer you get to the top—in order to fit in neatly.

■ *Top-down evaluation:* The performance evaluation system is based on the superordinate's view of the subordinate, even though the superordinate generally knows less about what the employee does than that individual's associates in other parts of the organization, and much less than that individual's subordinates.

■ *Downward instead of two-way communication:* Although information flows up and down, the most important is generally considered to be the guidance from on high, rather than analysis from below. The vertical focus also means that lateral communication flows are undernourished, in spite of the fact that in most situations lateral coordination and integration are crucial to effective operations. If it does not come down in his chain of command the bureaucrat does not do it, despite indications that it should be done from some place else in the institution.

■ *Pushing upward resolution of differences:* Due to the tendency to look upward, in a straight line, for control, there is a reticence to resolve strongly held differences at a level where the participants have enough knowledge of the issues to resolve them effectively. A difference gets pushed up until it reaches an individual who is considered by both parties to be equally in control of them. This process may force an issue through several layers of "supervision" before it gets resolved, and by that time the arbiter may be dealing with such a level of abstraction that the operators with the original differences do not know what to do with the final decision. In this process very few real issues get definitively resolved.

Nearer the Peak Equals Greater Generalization

It is another tenet of the model that the higher a position is situated in the triangle, the more global the perspective of its incumbent. This is based on the assumption that higher levels have greater access to a fuller understanding of a particular issue, but this assumption is faulty. Each individual can cope with only so much information and that coping is influenced by attitudes, experience and other factors. In fact, the superordinate only can be said to have information different from that of the subordinate. Whether it is more comprehensive and realistic is debatable. There is no inherent structural reason why a lowly desk officer cannot bring to the task a perspective that is as truly global as the President's or the Department Secretary's. But the myth prevails in all pyramidal bureaucracies. It is said that the Roman Curia believe of themselves that only those in their roles have the overall view of what the church is "all about."

Climbing Rungs Equals Achievement

Perhaps the most poisonous implication of the triangular pattern, with its crisscrossing grid, is the expectation it sets up that good work will be rewarded by movement up the grid, and that upward movement is the appropriate, natural and necessary reward for satisfactory performance. Height on the ladder has come to be equated with degrees of "goodness," i.e., more important, useful, respected, etc. This narrowly focused and limited channel of satisfaction and reward influences the motivation of all employees, and control of the grid equates to control of behavior. It is not surprising that pretty soon most performance becomes superficial too, i.e., one does the visible thing required in order to get the next title on the grid. In the Foreign Service where the ultimate title is Ambassador, many individuals will engage in almost any kind of ingratiating behavior to remain in good standing and accumulate enough good grades to get the title. The fact that triangle grid climbing is a zero-sum game, because the slots get scarcer the closer you get to the peak, means that at any level there will be more disappointed aspirants than satisfied achievers. In effect the whole organization is frustrated because there is not enough to go around.

By setting up a system which has only a higher spot in the hierarchy to reward people for being good, you have to keep expanding the hierarchy to satisfy enough of those who are good year after year. There is no other acceptable option in response to these pressures than continually increasing the size of the pie. To use a current social analogy, we have to keep upping the fix to keep the beast under control.

Even when there is a continually growing pie, people recognize that its distribution is often unfair, which leads them to become disillusioned and question the legitimacy of the whole system. The prevailing attitude becomes one of trying to maximize one's own return and results in powerful demands for "grade creep" (raising the average level of all employees grades).

Since promotion is the primary way people get rewarded and, according to current theory, motivated, and since everyone wants recognition the pressure to assign higher grades to existing jobs—and to their incumbents—is practically irresistible. The struggle over grades consumes countless work years of personnel specialists and many more hours of individuals at all levels wrestling with the problem each day. Competition for and haggling about grade levels and other external signs of achievement undoubtedly consumes more energy in government than any other single function. As we created this merit badge approach to motivating quality work, we took the intrinsic substance from jobs. How can those on the top expect anything other than scheming on the part of all below to succeed them?

After years of observing my own behavior and that of colleagues in many government agencies, I believe we could not have done a better job had we deliberately set out to undermine the ethic of excellence, pursued by individuals with visions of personal contributions to a larger good. We have transformed **that** motive force into a nit-picking preoccupation with an overly complicated system of make-believe. The basic approach was created by a not very perspicacious group of elitists who have assumed:

- people cannot take the responsibility for their own destinies.
- people cannot be trusted to adequately perceive and respond to institutional needs.

- a central organism, staffed by the best, could know better what was best for the rest.

A good example of this lack of faith in people by those in charge of personnel systems is the case of the Assistant Secretary who classified and prohibited distribution of his proposals to the Secretary on how to improve employee performance. What the employees thought of the proposals and how they would react to the changes did not count. A similar secretive approach was used during the final stage of formulating the Carter Administration's civil service reform proposals.

The primary purpose of the personnel system is to ensure that appropriately qualified people are available to do jobs that need to be done. All of its selection, evaluation, training and promotion procedures are designed to accomplish that objective. In the world of actual practice most members of the bureaucracy endeavor to maintain a freedom of choice that does not depend on these efforts. In most Departments any manager with "chutzpah" can get the individual he wants to work for him and conversely any energetic employee can obtain a position of choice, regardless of personnel file and the best manpower planning efforts of the central office. In other words, the personnel system exercises control only on the weakest or most naive parts of the organization. Perhaps it is time we question the very existence of such a complex function that cannot meet its objective except in those instances where the opposite of its medicine is required, where people actually need to be empowered rather than controlled.

This chapter and the last have taken us, with selected illustrations, through the first four layers of our onion-like model. I have not attempted to be totally definitive, nor have I pretended that all individuals and units in the bureaucracy fit the characterizations I have drawn. However, I do believe they are close enough to the overall reality of the current American national bureaucracy to warrant further study and confirmation. The same claims *and* caveats apply to the following syntheses developed from my observations and personal experiences in the three inner layers.

4
A Hollow Officialdom

> The revolution of the twentieth century will take place in the
> United States. It is only there that it can happen. And it has
> already begun. Whether or not that revolution spreads to the
> rest of the world depends on whether or not it succeeds first in
> America.
>
> Jean-Francois Ravel

The formal personnel system, though a primary medium for its development, is not the origin of the bureaucratic personality and its propensity for gamesmanship. There are underlying psychological influences and, at an even more profound level, certain basic assumptions and images. These underpinnings of the bureaucratic culture hold the keys to needed change, but we must first see how they impact on all the other elements of the "bureaucratic problematique."

Psychological Set

A difficult to discern, but primal force in the shaping of our federal institution's public performance is the composite psychological set of the dominant members of bureaucratic units. The psychological set is the unarticulated, but ever present and active package of emotions, attitudes, and feelings that relate to an individual's membership and performance in the organization.

Why are citizens concerned with the psychological perspectives of employees in the bureaucracy? The basic reason is that they affect the quality of the policy and program produced by those public servants.

Their impact is often more deleterious because their influence is not always directly observable. The bureaucratic perspectives also affect interpersonal norms, and therefore the ability of the organization to monitor the environment, learn, and act. The manner in which it shapes or constrains that performance is of legitimate concern to citizens. If the performance is inadequate or inappropriate, deformed by a misshapen psychological perspective, then we have an obligation to inquire into its nature and why it is so. *The psychological paradox of the American public bureaucracy is that a system which was intended to create independent, altruistically-oriented professionals has produced outer-directed, and frequently anxiety-ridden, superficialists.*

Bureaucrats generally share a psycho-cultural set with their fellow citizens, but the focus here is on how the bureaucratic culture differentiates its members from the larger societal context.

Before getting into specifics, I would like to illustrate how the process works—how prejudgments of a general nature affect the specifics of policy analyses and decisions. If an Ambassador overseas or a federal official in Washington thinks in stereotypes then that which he sees and believes may be more formed by those attitudes than by the "realities" of the given situation. If one believes himself to be more advanced socially and intellectually than his contacts, the flow of communication is likely to be more one-way than reciprocal. In that situation there is little new learning and inadequate testing of interpretations against external perceptions. Programs coming out of deliberations of that genre reflect Washington's perceptions of needs and not indigenous ones. Yet to be successful, government programs must correspond with the perceived needs of the people who are going to implement them and integrate them with other ongoing activities in the local society. This sounds awfully simplistic and anyone when asked if he or she agreed with that observation would say, "yes," but that same person would probably be surprised to observe how often internal biases cause us to misdirect our actions. It occurs not because we are intellectually unaware of the process, but because we think it applies to others and not ourselves. Being unaware of how our "irrational" attitudes affect our "rationality," we cannot compensate for it in our judgmental behavior.

Perhaps even more important than the inappropriate specific decisions that come out of such one-way elitist relationships is the overall mode of the relationship that is engendered. The principle is comparable to television programs when content is less important to the personality development of children than the fact that sustained exposure puts them in a passive-observer, recipient mode that has a pervasive impact on their style of interacting with daily events.

One of the great ironies of most of our development assistance programming, both internationally and with domestic groups, is that the nature of the process perpetuates the very dependency syndrome which we are seeking, allegedly, to overcome. The nature of that process is not determined by the character of specific decisions, but by the underlying assumption about the state of reality which we call "developed" and "underdeveloped." These principles apply not just between "haves" and "have nots," but in every relationship which involves groups interacting on the basis of artificial categorizations: democracies and communist states, Muslims and Jews, Catholics and Protestants, majority-minority, white-ethnic, etc.

In our U.S. government service people generally now perceive of the inanities of conflict based primarily on religious differences but we do not recognize the blinders imposed by equally powerful social attitudes about self and other people.

Cold war or detente are products, not of armaments and trade patterns, but of the attitudes which shape the decisions to build fortresses, or open doors to personal contact. One act is based on a sense of insecurity and mistrust and another is based on a willingness to experiment. Whether one view or the other prevails in a government depends upon the most widely held psychological perspective.

Since the bureaucracy has evolved into such an inner-directed society, with its own selection and reward mechanisms, the elitist perspective described above exists throughout government. Whether it is the State Department overseas or the Department of Education and the Department of Defense in the U.S., the attitude is one of "I know what is best for the people we serve." The communication is essentially one-way and more shaped by what is already felt by the official than by the realities of his work world.

This sense of being "chosen" is probably the most pervasive and most counterproductive facet of the government bureaucrat's psychological makeup. The internalization of this mind set by the bureaucrat means he or she accepts the notion that one has a "license" to act, one is a "defender" of things of value, and one "must protect" something. Ironically, what is protected is really the bureaucratic entity instead of the public.

This feeling of being a select few is underscored by needs for both power and security. In general, the kinds of people who seek out government service have a strong need to influence others and exert control over events, but they desire to do so with a minimum of personal risk. Without getting into the chicken versus the egg argument, it is clear that the bureaucratic climate nurtures this personality type; it provides the symbols of authority without the constraints of real responsibility. The effective mode of behavior is that of transient laborers (instead of the entrepreneur that combines manager and laborer) who avoid risktaking and personalized decision making and make little investment of self. They become rigid, mercenary and only concerned with their internal accounting. Having been organized to react on demand, when the control is relaxed nothing is volunteered; the routine of most offices goes into neutral when the boss is away. (One can always tell by the gatherings of secretaries, the length of lunches, and the slackness of professional meetings.)

Consequently, the bureaucratic psychological set is a maze of internal contradictions: the sense of self-esteem arising from being part of a select group is undermined by considerable insecurity and self-doubt; the ego is a hollow shell. People find themselves in positions requiring poised and purposeful behavior, and at the same time believe themselves surrounded by a system and colleagues that lack integrity and in which they cannot place confidence. The resultant psychological perspective is like an inferiority complex. Big, strong, arrogant men I have known have broken into tears from fear that a desired position would not be offered. (I am not criticizing the crying, only the shallow basis for it. The same people would never cry over starvation, bombing victims, and the violation of human rights.)

In a context in which successfully relating to other people is a necessity, there is relatively little need for affiliation, as psychologist David McClelland[1] defines it. Bureaucrats are inured to the lack of close human relationships. It often appears that gestures of friendship are motivated more by a fear of rejection than a genuine concern to get to know and be intimate with someone else. The competition perpetuated by the system leads more often to keeping one's guard up than engaging in cooperative behaviors.

One can easily validate this perception of others as "objects" instead of human beings by looking at the approach managers take to personnel system changes. They are all designed to make the mechanics of management, i.e., control, easier, with practically no regard for the system's impact on human feelings and behavior. One of my unsuccessful struggles with the Department of State's management and the Carter Administration Reorganization Project was an effort to convince people to take into account the behavioral implications of proposed personnel system changes. Their reactions can be summarized as, "Well of course you are right, but that's too big of a problem to tackle, and if we can make things work a little better (by reorganizations) we ought to go ahead." (This is another example of the "take the easy way" syndrome.)

Where leadership and public policy roles require public employees to understand the perspective of others, we find bureaucrats with little empathy for the viewpoints of their colleagues and fellow citizens. It is impossible for them to empathize with people they distrust and disdain.

One typical experience comes to mind. People in one office gave a former colleague a copy of the final report of a study he had started. When that was discovered by a senior official whose pet policy was undermined by the findings he called for an internal security investigation. Its purpose was to find out who leaked a copy to the professional who was still a member of the organization. People present at the meeting said the comments of the official and several of his subordinates sounded almost like some of the Watergate tapes that dealt with the "need" for a "national security" coverup. Fortunately, cooler heads prevailed. This case illustrates to what absurd steps we have gone. An extraordinary attempt to unilaterally avoid any effective criticism which might show up one's mistaken judgment even though it was a small internal issue, is considered normal.

Another manifestation of this defensiveness is the tendency to take out the beating one gets from above on one's co-workers. Those who have to administer the unadministrable administrative procedures are particularly prone to coping with their frustration by "trop de zele"—too much "by the book behavior." Much of what they demand in terms of compliance is totally unnecessary and the manner in which it is demanded (shouting, anger, and officious behavior) elicits reciprocation; the result is a vicious cycle of recriminations among bureaucrats, which also spills over into the public.

Another important element of the bureaucratic psychological make-up that contributes to poor performance is the time perspective. Given the long-term implications of many policy decisions made by public servants, the bureaucratic time horizon is of critical importance. Elliot Jacques,[2] a British psychologist, has written about the concept of a time perspective that individuals develop, within which they are able to conceptualize and act consistently. The length of the time-frame possessed by any individual depends on the conflux of various developmental factors: the nature of formal education, experience and psychological attitudes. The nature of one's work experience over time influences and reinforces this psychological time span, to the extent that one's horizon becomes fairly well fixed.

A person with long experience in the bureaucracy brings its time perspective to a new task in a number of ways. In the understanding of problems and the forces that bring them about, one tends either to look in the recent past or to take a more historical approach, depending on his underlying sense of time. This time sense also determines the approach chosen to solve the problems. The plan of action that is formulated to accomplish significant results may vary from a quick fix to a setting in motion of subtle, long-range systemic efforts that will only show results years later.

At least two significant institutional factors tend to reinforce a short time perspective among bureaucrats. One is unique to those who rotate among jobs; the other is endemic in our Presidential system. The average length of assignment in the upwardly mobile sectors of the bureaucracy is two years or less. This means, for the most part, an individual spends only two years at a time on the problems of a given issue, country, region, or function. One year is spent getting well oriented and competent in the job, six months in focused work, and six months anticipating and preparing for the next job. When a problem arises, the tendency is to do one of either two things: consider the factors that have been obvious during the incumbent's presence on the scene or make judgments based on personal past experiences, which may or may not be relevant to the current situation. Since it is difficult to dig up a revealing historical record the easiest way out is to depend on one's own knowledge.

The same short-time horizon works in the other direction in developing program recommendations or looking ahead for other purposes. Bureaucrats find it difficult to think beyond their own possible reassignment or promotion date. The incentive is just not there, regardless of the intellectual understanding that it should be. When one must recommend changes in policies and programs, the tendency is to settle on those that will materialize before the end of one's time. The performance evaluation and promotion systems also encourage bureaucrats to claim bits of progress in their work in time for the annual report.

If the problem is out-dated, inefficient industrial sectors, instead of getting a government strategy that deals with the societal issues of what should be done to protect and retrain U.S. workers for the long-range competitiveness of the nation as a whole, we get a short-term emergency import quota or tariff bail-out for the shoemaker or the color television technicians (or a loan guarantee for an automobile manufacturer). The basic problem of how to cope with necessary social adjustments to maintain long-term national strength is left untouched, and maybe even set back by the bureaucratic mode of behavior.

The Presidential cycle imposes another set of short range time pressures. One frequently hears, "We have only one year (or six months) to go on this term, so let's show results." No credit is expected or given for contributing to organization-building activities; individuals must stand out from their predecessors by doing something new, or at least new for the current generation of voters.

The short-term bureaucratic perspective is exacerbated by a cultural factor. We have caught ourselves in a bind in our modern economic approach to work. As E.F. Schumacher pointed out, "modern" thinking looks at work as a commodity.[4] Thus, work—the individual's means to earn a living—is presented as a mechanistic commodity to be bought; organizations try to get the most for the least cost. Efficiency is the by-word in organizations modeled after Adam Smith's fantasy of a piecework, assembly-line pin factory that is the epitome of job simplification, requiring only the most rudimentary acts from any individual. Under these circumstances the natural tendency for the worker is to react by trying to give the least for the maximum pay. Under such a contract it is no wonder that people loathe the exchange and psychologically escape from it even while engaged. The prostitute using her wiles to shorten the contact with a customer, while dreaming of how she is going to use the money, is not an irrelevant analogy.

This egocentrism is reinforced by the view we seem to have developed which perceives of education and stages of experience as "investments," something acquired which then can be exchanged for a "good" (position, salary, status). In this context our selves become commodities, to be bought and sold. We no longer see our potential as a birthright, a bequest to be used judiciously, but as a certificate with coupons to be periodically clipped. The bureaucracy is simply a place to cash them in. Consequently, we continually bargain for a more "rewarding" spot in the hierarchy.

Unfortunately, when a high level is reached, the individuals are not then satisfied and able to treat those below as the human beings they, the senior managers, consider themselves to be. The evidence is pretty strong they believe themselves to be self-vindicated; they approach all believing they can do no wrong. In one among many poignant examples, an official who had a falling out with a fairly senior woman employee over an earlier policy dispute later forced her retirement when he achieved a higher position of authority. He felt that the symbols of power validated his own personal prejudices and that their implementation was therefore good for the system.

Because people tend to believe in the validity of the process that rewards them, they act to perpetuate the system without questioning the consequences. It is a rare person who will pause and ask whether or not it is best for the larger good to be where he or she is. The egocentric assertion in the phrase, "What's good for General Motors is good for the country" applies to bureaucratic thought processes as well as corporate ones. This drive to reach higher positions on the chart by the most expedient route is a central element in the motivation of the public employee.

Consequently, people who do not get promoted develop a pool of hostility and anxiety which floats just below the surface and is easily provoked. The hostility derives from the incongruities of the system and the anxiety is caused by a lingering suspicion that perhaps the system is right in devaluing the person; the individual is often unsure about the validity of the process and questions his or her own worth. The structure of the pyramidal system (described in the preceding chapter) ensures that almost everyone is afflicted with this unease.

Assumptions

A force equally important and complementary to the psychological set in shaping the life of a social organism is the mix of basic assumptions its members hold about others and the external environment. In an attempt to account for the federal bureaucracy's behaviors, we must try to identify and analyze the nature of the primary assumptions that shape the thinkings of its members. Whether they are valid or not makes no difference; the impact on thought and behavior is the same. What follows are descriptions of several themes that run through the bureaucrat's set of unquestioned assumptions; they form the starting point for mentally handling information received in the course of work. These themes are generally implicit in the bureaucratic folklore and would probably be denied if one directly asked a bureaucrat whether or not they were valid. Nonetheless, they are close to the surface of informal conversations and can be reasonably inferred from internal reactions to and decisions on citizen initiatives.

"Those Other Folks"

People on the outside are seen as lesser lights in all kinds of ways: intelligence, energy, ability, ethics, and motives. Members of the general public are on the lowest end of the scale and even other bureaucrats outside one's own circle are relegated somewhere in between.

The bureaucrat assumes almost any act of a citizen regarding government is motivated by self-interest (obviously many of them are). The bureaucrat assumes he knows best, that he has the bigger picture in mind and that he is more knowledgeable about the question at hand, any question. He sees outsiders (except his personal friends) as deviously trying to get a job, a favor, or a contract from the government and considers it his role to protect the public interest against the interested members of the public.

"Competitive and Fickle Bedfellows"

Other units and agencies of government are seen to be in unjustified competition for resources and favorable public recognition. They are seen as fickle and only interested in protecting their bureaucratic interests. Each unit believes its mandate is unique and sees any overlap as poaching by the other party. Where the overlap cannot be eradicated, as it cannot in most instances, the bureaucrat assumes the other agency is the interloper and relates to it as such. Conflicts must then be resolved by higher authority.

The knowledge about other organizations upon which bureaucrats act is most often collected on an irregular basis, depending upon the crisis or conflict of the moment, and with the phenomenon of continually changing personnel it appears to insiders that their competitors are erratic—even more reason to distrust them.

"Hostile, Static World"

While the immediate environment of other agencies, political bodies, and a few relevant private sector actors is generally seen as competitive, the world at large is seen as downright hostile. The national or global milieu is seen as challenging the existence and *raison d'etre* of the bureaucratic unit. It is seen as a disorderly and disordered panorama of forces that require the imposition of pattern and routine by the bureaucracy, which will resolve the problems and get things working correctly.

In contrast to the perception of the immediate environment as fluid, the larger world is more likely to be seen as relatively static. This is more than just a matter of being able to see more movement in the nearby trees than in the distant forest. Perturbations are perceived in the larger context, but they are attributed to local variations on the basic unchanging and threatening nature of society. Hence mutations to traditions or new trends are not perceived as such until they have long been exerting their influence.

The assumptions about self, role and others also have corollary assumptions about the process of governance. The paired concepts of being "anointed" in a "hostile world" make it very easy to accept literally the artificial dichotomy between things official versus things public.

"An Officialdom"

*One of the most dysfunctional concepts in American government is that of
"officialdom":* a domain that sets public servants apart from the public they
serve and anoints their acts with a quality that permits them to be kept secret
from the citizenry. It is a vestige of another historical period when it was
accepted that kings had divine rights. It is a paradox that this mentality still
exists, two hundred years after it was declared by our founding fathers that the
powers of this nation's government should derive from the people.

For millenia career governing groups have been more or less synonymous
with the natural, evolutionary elite of societies—Egyptian, Roman, British
Empires, and the early colonies in the new world—but as the new nation of the
United States grew into its institutions the traditional relationships got all
mixed up. We had leadership groups who stayed out of government and resented
the newly liberated masses' representatives assuming such power. Intellectual
elites have often opted out of involvement in the government. The growth of
new houses of economic power also created leadership groups. The result has
been a fragmentation of power and ideas within which it was necessary to
develop a matrix of special interest groups, politicians and career bureaucrats.
Over time these nexuses developed mutually exclusive spheres of influence that
allowed each to grow, as long as they did not detract from each other.

What is now required is some way to override these inbred triads and expose
the relationships to the general public, describing their benefits to the people
involved. The only progressive option is to finish the enfranchisement of all
citizens through a radical opening of the government to public scrutiny and
involvement.

There are those who would argue that we already have too much openness,
that the people already have enough impact on the government. A Trilateral
Commission report entitled "The Crisis of Democracy" states that there is "an
excess of democracy" in the United States and that there are "potentially
desirable limits to the indefinite extension of political democracy." The report
compares us unfavorably to "either Europe or Japan, where there still exist
residual inheritances of traditional and aristocratic values" and states
"democracy is more of a threat to itself in the United States." The report
suggested several ways in which things could be tightened up, notably including
greater restraints on the press.*

This perception that permits "officials" to justify the manner in which they

---

*Maybe the Loyalists have won after all; at least they are alive and in charge of significant parts of the
bureaucratic structures in Washington. As the Jefferson/Jacksonian thread of democracy goes too far
these threatened people push for a return to the rule of elites. Such a course of action has been
facilitated by the myth of "merit" bureaucracy. Fortunately, for all of us, in practice it has a strong
propensity to stumble over its own feet.

treat citizens, described in the last chapter, is buttressed by such assumptions. In addition, it is facilitated by the general view that if something is labeled "official" it is *ipso facto* out of the public domain. Even simple facts about the business of the nation are cloaked with this rubric. Ninety-nine percent of the time the real motivation for its use is the security of the bureaucracy, not national security.

Information equals power, not because of the inherent value of it, but because of the nature of the bureaucracy that uses it. Information is ammunition for bureaucratic games, pawns in internal bureaucratic power struggles, barricades for self-defense, and a commodity for obtaining and giving rewards. If the government did not have these attributes then information could be treated like the air and water, public resources. Until the bureaucracy changes its stripes, our public employees will label information "official," then scramble for it, hoard it, protect it, and manipulate it.

The most blatant taking advantage of this concept is the system of document classification that ranges from above "Top Secret" to "Limited to Official Use" (meaning government employees). The principle of "need to know" not only keeps the public at a distance but also aggravates the problem of compartmentalization and fragmentation within the bureaucracy. The abuse of this system is unconscionable in State, DOD and other foreign affairs units. Here the fact that the American public has relationships with other publics is the basis for keeping things classified. The myth that foreign policy is inherently different from other policy dies hard. Alexis de Tocqueville in the 19th century questioned how the U.S. could work out its conduct of foreign affairs with an open approach to government. He said:

> Foreign politics demand scarcely any of those qualities which are peculiar
> to democracy.

Many in our government still cling to this idea without considering other options. They do not understand that such a closed mode for relationships, which is required by authoritarian regimes, undermines the continued development of democratic institutions which we espouse.

The attitude which says "we can do such and such in our official capacity and the individual or public in general does not need to know" was most dramatically manifested in the episodes of the Watergate coverup. But the frightening aspect of that situation is that the specifics were more the tip of the iceberg than real aberrations. The basic problem is more than just "illegal acts," contraventions of criminal laws; it is a simple disdain for principles of openness to public review and accountability for one's behavior. The post-Watergate administrations have worn the same cloak.

Unfortunately this barrier to public access to and involvement in the work of government bodies is most often overcome by personalized, confidential relationships or special interest groups with financial clout. The official membrane is permeable, but only to certain people. An example at the time of this writing was the Department of Energy's practice of providing advance copies of draft documents to the American Petroleum Institute while other citizens had to wait. In fact, many of these special relationships with senior political and career executives are made "official" through the use of consultancy or advisory roles.

The assumptions treated here and others held by the bureaucracy are considered to be "knowledge," regardless of whether they are based on fact or fantasy, about other people, the organism's work, its immediate environment and the world at large. This so-called "knowledge" becomes *de facto* "reality" and has impact beyond its mere existence; it also serves as an *a priori* filter through which all new data, both about the organization itself and its external *milieu,* is sorted and interpreted. Where the realities of new information are at variance with the existing patterns, it is the former which are distorted; the latter are not adjusted. And where the inconsistent reality persists there is a conscious bureaucratic response to make the facts fit the preconceptions. "People are not really against the war, they just don't want to be drafted personally," is an example.

Now we peel the onion back to the innermost layer, those visions of self from which all else flows.

Self Images

Each agency or significant unit has a set of images about itself that relate to role definitions: law enforcement, education, banking, safety, conservation, budgeting, national defense, etc. There are also self-images that relate to location in the Executive Branch: President's staff, independent regulatory agency, community service, unique statutorily mandated operations, etc. But underlying such unit differences are images relating to the nature of public service in general, and to the bureaucrat's standing vis-a-vis the public at large. Some of these have already been alluded to: "We are the 'officials' of the land." "Our being here is obligatory—we must exist for the good of society." "We are the protectors of the country against the vicissitudes of partisan politics." *But undoubtedly the most troubling is the bureaucracy's self-perception as a meritocratic-elite.*

Despite the fragile base upon which the elitist images are built, they are internalized by a disturbingly large proportion of all bureaucrats. The zeal with which they are accepted in certain units has given impetus to many of the prevailing problematic attitudes and behaviors, and their corresponding performance; it has insulated the bureaucracy from social reality, changing circumstances, and the interest of its taxpayer-employers. Elitists believe they possess the "right" answers, know more than anyone else about the job to be done, and should be left alone to do it as they see fit. They want no independent confirmation of their beliefs and behavior and seek to avoid monitoring or oversight by others, who are by definition lesser lights.

In American society the elitist self-images of many bureaucratic groups are reinforced by outsiders who accept the public claims for the selection processes and behave as if those who get in government service must really have been the best candidates. Only recently have the attacks of minority groups on the inherent biases of the so-called merit system caused a variety of people to ask what have been the real criteria for selection.

Among certain obvious examples of the exaggerated self-image of elitism in the civilian part of the federal government are the FBI, the CIA, the Federal Reserve System, the International Finance sector of the Treasury Department, the Office of Management and Budget, the Civil Service Commission,* and the Foreign Service of the State Department.

The problem for the larger society lies not with the existence of this image *per se*,** but with its implications for internal organizational effectiveness and overall institutional performance.

By definition the "elite" see themselves as a cut above other groups and everything they do (performance, analyses, policy recommendations, etc.) is viewed from that prejudgment. Anything that is important can be done better by the "elitist"—from his perspective. The "elites" generally have *disdain* for the members of other groups, *distrust* their motives and rationale, *disparage* their performance, *devalue* its worth, *distort* incoming communication, and see themselves as being on the *defensive* against encroachments. Paradoxically, when faced with overt conflict the D-mode of behavior appears weak; the elitist cannot effectively cope with circumstances outside his protected environment.

FSO's refer to State's Civil Service employees and other Washington-based non-FSO personnel as "locals" (drawing a comparison with foreign nationals hired in our Embassies abroad) and label them as "support" for the Foreign Service; they are "bureaucratic" and "specialized," unable to participate in the FSO "generalist" policy-making function. There is even a caste system within the FSO Corps based on functional specialists. It is quite similar to the caste system of Naval officers, related to the likelihood of achieving line command positions. The elitist attitude is communicated very clearly to others, and those others respond accordingly. Little trust is evident, cards are held close to the chest, and manipulative games make up the dominant interpersonal style. This same behavior pattern holds for interagency relations as well. Other agencies and the Congress are seen as "parochial or provincial" and their initiatives are seen as "meddling" in one's own policy.

*Now the Office of Personnel Management.

**We need some of the best in government, but being there now does not mean one is the best.

One could write a comparable discussion of the elitist self-image and its ramifications for each of the groups named above and for any number of other government units and the main points would be the same: self-perpetuating bureaucratic groups turn inward and over time become less and less relevant to the purposes for which they were created, in their isolation form takes precedence over substance, self defense becomes top priority for time and resources, general public interest and priorities lose out to special interests, and the most important problems of the day are left unattended, if noticed at all.

There is also the other side of the coin: the non-elites who perceive of themselves as being in the trenches. For individuals who see themselves in that category it is very difficult to keep their attention on serving the public in face of the fickleness and fantasy world of the game playing layers of bureaucracy who should allegedly be leading them. They seek shelter in routine and petty protectionism of status and turf.

The group dynamics of a career service are not dissimilar to other groups with long-standing ascribed elite status: the leading family in a small town, royalty, or a priesthood. All have certain common characteristics:

■ *Seniority orientation.* There is obligatory deference to the elders of the group who set behavioral standards and define boundaries for the young.

■ *Personal loyalty.* The assignment of roles to young members and their upward progress is based more often on personal ties and demonstrations of loyalty than on merit.

■ *Perpetuation of status quo.* As a result of the above two principles, the socialization process through which the young grow to be in the group serves to perpetuate the status quo in terms of values, behavioral norms and performance standards.

■ *Black sheep phenomenon.* Those individuals who commit an indiscretion by choosing other than the group's standards are ostracized from the group and labeled misfits. The group closes itself against them.

■ *Family protection.* On the other hand, anyone who goofs up vis-a-vis the outside world, but has not also breached the internal norms, is protected. The group will go to great lengths to cover up such misdeeds.

■ *Form over substance.* As a corollary of the preceding two categories, more importance is attached to the form of one's behavior and work than the substance. It is not so much what you spend your day doing, but the way you do it that concerns the group's members.

■ *Avoidance of external testing.* As long as the group can perpetuate its ascribed role in the larger society it tolerates no external mechanism for testing how well it is doing. Because of its unique ascribed status there is no place for competition with outsiders.

■ *Outmoded entry criteria.* As time goes on the formula for admission to the group may become irrelevant to the group's changing place in society, but the group remains rigorous in its exclusion of those who do not fit the traditional mold.

Both the Foreign Service and the Civil Service-based bureaucracy see themselves as the cream of the crop, or *la creme de la creme,* as FSO's are prone to enthuse when talking about themselves. The explicitness of such a self-applied label varies from the FBI's "We are the top" to the General Service Administration's "We are the logistics folks who make it possible for the rest of the government to function." The image goes beyond pride in oneself and one's accomplishments to apply generally to the group and to the single fact that one has achieved membership in it. It says that because we have been selected, we are *ipso facto* the very best this country has to offer, the most highly qualified in all the nation to carry out these responsibilities placed on our shoulders. It gives rise to a kind of paper and pencil-based sense of *noblesse oblige;* the problems of the resulting insular, self-perpetuating and paternalistic behavior are self evident. The long-standing axiom of Vatican politics holds true: "Popes (politicians) come and go, but the curia (bureaucracy) remains."

Given that the impact of this self-image clearly appears to be more counterproductive than beneficial in the government institutions of a democratic society, it behooves us to analyze the dynamics of elitism and how they interact with the other aspects of organizational performance. How does this central image detract from individual and group behaviors appropriate to the public institutions of a democratic society? What are the realities that underlie this self-image? Do they substantiate it? Taking the Foreign Service, which is similar to other closed elitist groups, as a case study, it is possible to begin to see how such a concept relates to other elements in a social organism.

Given the general social principles sketched out above, the culture of the Foreign Service is predictable. The nature of working relationships is determined on the basis of age and grade (which are generally synonymous), with the senior practically always carrying the day. The old-boy network is still alive and well in Foggy Bottom and the process of obtaining assignments remains a highly personalized one. The seniority orientation, with one's success dependent upon pleasing one's superiors, is perhaps the most important factor in promotions and thereby helps to ensure perpetuation of the *status quo* work style.

The ultimate "black sheep" designation in the Foreign Service is to be selected-out. Knowledgeable people in the personnel system attribute most selection-outs to personality differences that get reflected in evaluation reports rather than to objectively defined substandard performance. Once a person has been blackballed by one superordinate and it is spread through the corridor system of passing on unsubstantiated gossip it becomes very difficult to escape. The bureaucrat's arrogancy toward unworthy outsiders is turned equally on the wayward insider, particularly by those in gatekeeping roles in the system. As a person gets treated as an outcast, a vicious cycle of rejection, paranoia, and hostility sets in between the individual and the informal system and eventually the individual's effectiveness within the system is permanently lost.

On the other hand, as long as a person does not break the "rules" of the Service he is protected. Officers can make gross errors in professional judgment, but if they do not breach the code of the club they are quietly assigned to a new post.* The code is one of unfailing loyalty to the system and its leaders, suppressing differences of opinion, inhibiting internal criticism, and emphasizing maintenance of the Corps prerogatives.

A particularly ironical example of the latter occurred in the State Department during the period leading to the establishment of full diplomatic relations with the People's Republic of China. Officers in the U.S. Consulate General in Hong Kong (our China watching post for almost 30 years) and the U.S. Liaison Office in Peking were charged with trend reporting. A Foreign Service officer in Peking predicted the outcome of internal leadership struggles in the Chinese government in a manner consistent with U.S. aspirations and administration policy. An FSO in Hong Kong assessed the situation differently and in fact turned out to be correct. You guessed it, the officer in Peking was given an award for creative dissent.

Another norm is learning the system's style rather than striving for improvement in one's professional skills. Since challenging current practices is *verboten,* there is no positive incentive to improve the quality of the system's performance. Rather than inquiring of well-qualified young professionals what their knowledge and experience indicate should be done to handle a particular problem, they are informed, "This is the way the Foreign Service does it." In the bureaucracy such set movements have become a substitute for action. If you are moving yourself on paper properly, or being moved around by someone else, then it is considered that you must be accomplishing something.

As long as such a closed system sets its own standards, informally and depending on the personalities involved, inspects itself, and has no direct external competition there is no pressure to validate its approaches or techniques.

One can take out the words "Foreign Service" from the above paragraphs and have a good description of the internal dynamics that determine the behavior of any bureaucratic group with ascribed elite status. I have used the term ascribed status because the so-called elite groups within the bureaucracy, due to the nature of the bureaucratic personnel selection and reward processes, cannot be considered elites by objective standards and therefore only enjoy the status ascribed to their roles. They are therefore *ipso facto* not necessarily the most appropriate individuals available in a democratic society for the task at hand.

We have been led to believe that the requisite "objective" instruments exist

---

*I am not implying that an institution should not protect its members in the performance of their duties, but I am raising the question of what they should be protected for. For example, the Department of State should have protected its China officers in the execution of their established responsibilities during the McCarthy era.

for a true meritocracy and have accepted the fact of differential scoring on written tests as evidence that we are sorting out the wheat from the chaff. We have not paid enough attention to probing deeper and asking whether or not the things being measured by the tests, and the other steps of the selection process, particularly the oral interviews and personal contacts, are relevant to the essential skills needed among permanent employees of our system of governance.

Why has the elite myth persisted without serious attack from within or without? As long as a unique and relatively isolated role can be maintained for a group with ascribed status and at the same time let it have self-control of access to membership, those on the inside will never question the validity of the selection process. Continuing with the Foreign Service example, it is assumed that one is qualified to play a foreign policy role because one was decreed to be an FSO. Most outsiders, as well as insiders, unquestioningly accept the ascribed symbols as real. Due to the fact that almost 100 times as many people apply for the Foreign Service examination each year as are actually hired, it is assumed that only the "best" are finally selected. Few question in which ways they are the best and what they are the best for. (The same holds for other units with test-based selection procedures.)

Given the current selection process there is no way to test whether or not the top one percent of the original pool of applicants, in terms of qualifications necessary for a truly elite group of foreign affairs professionals, has been selected. In fact there is some independently gathered evidence that there is a negative correlation between scores on the written exam and the presence of these traits. In other words, it may be that to possess the detailed factual knowledge necessary to answer the multiple choice questions used requires a much more passive, studious, introverted disposition than that which is best suited for the active life of what should be a fast-moving world of ideas, problems, and programs.

So in essence FSO's in each new group are people with refined verbal skills who possess enough academic book learning to answer even the esoteric questions and whose personalities are adaptable enough to present themselves as the mirror images of three interviewing career officers whose implicit aim is to duplicate themselves.

If the required traits are not necesssarily present in the new FSO's it is unlikely that they will appear over time, since there is no constructive development of them. Given these realities there is little basis for the all-encompassing "elite" label in either the FSO selection process or career development system. Years of work which result in people who speak more languages, have lived in more countries, and talked to more foreigners than the average American citizen (except for officers in ICA, AID, CIA, DIA, FAS, and a few other agencies) do not by themselves create a superior foreign policy type.

To perpetuate the myth is dysfunctional to the larger needs of government and is counter-productive to efforts at self-renewal and reform from within the Department. As long as career members of the Foreign Service are isolated and defensive, distrusting of the outside, convinced they have "the answer" as the chosen "elite"—all based on invalid premises—it is unlikely that the future performance of the Department of State can be any different from its recent past. One female official who graduated from a mediocre university, but had been fully socialized by the elitist mentality, was heard to ask, "But where will you get your quality talent?" while being briefed on plans to recruit minority and women applicants. Such is the significant and largely retrogressive impact of the myth of "elitism" on the people who conduct our foreign affairs.

But if this description sounds bad to you, the Civil Service system is even worse. At least the FSO Corps, but not the other pay plans used in the Department of State, in the lower levels where most officers enter is free of politician or individual bureaucrat patronage. All the deficiencies in the Board of Examiners process notwithstanding, it is not very susceptible to direct placements of personal proteges. That is why politicians have used the Foreign Service Reserve appointment system for patronage, since it has no competitive controls.

On the other hand, the Civil Service system of evaluating qualifications, conducting "merit" selection procedures, and awarding jobs and/or promotions is wide open to the most blatant manipulation. Its various channels for potential abuse were clearly illustrated in the so-called Malek Manual* of the Nixon years which provided advice to the President and his staff on how to circumvent the ostensible merit system processes. The bureaucratic personnel system is a formidable obstacle to the sometimes 100s of applicants for each federal vacancy, but is easy to manipulate by those on the inside with enough bureau-cratic clout and/or knowledge about how the system works. I use the term bureaucratic clout instead of political power because the collaboration or at least the passive accommodation of the bureaucratic gate-keeper is required for subversion of the system; ultimately the control or willingness to acquiesce is in his or her hands. This means that just not any politician can have his or her way with placing people in the bureaucracy, but when the bureaucrat is also amenable the politico's interest is used to internally justify a non-merit placement. On the other hand, the bureaucrat who so desires and is in a position to work the system can use it to protect his own personalized selections. In either case, the objectives of an independent merit system are aborted and there is no mechanism for public monitoring. The red tape obfuscates the patronage whether it originates from a politician or bureaucrat. The paper record of evaluations of experience and qualifications, review panels, interviews,

---

*The manual or guide was produced by the White House Personnel Office during the period when it was managed by Fred Malek.

rankings, etc. will be in order, by the book, but nonvalidatable against objective job or performance based criteria.

The end result is a self-perpetuating workforce that replenishes itself through personal ties, thereby engendering an insidious form of loyalty that acts as a barricade to public exposure. Getting in, and the process by which that is accomplished, requires that one consciously collude and assume part of the responsibility for keeping the code secret. (It should perhaps be made clear that there are some truly competitive selections, and particularly at the subprofessional level, but what I am describing here prevails in the system.)

One might rationalize this process if it truly resulted in the best performance for the country, but the personal-contact selection process militates against the subsequent questioning, innovative behavior that we need from our public employees. These circumstances make it in every insider's interest to keep the myth of elitism and meritocracy alive, despite its counterproductive institutional influences.

The End Result

The cells of our metaphorical bureaucratic onion are really individuals. Our ultimate concern is how the social organism affects each one and their endeavors as a whole.

The Individual

What is the accumulated impact on the individual personality of the bureaucratic environment described in these three chapters? Theodore Roszak, in writing about the effect of the urban-industrial reality on people, captured, perhaps fortuitously, the essence of being a person in a bureaucracy:

> . . . this painfully intense experience of being a person in a world that despises personhood, a world whose policy is to grind personhood down into rubble, and then to remold the pieces into obedient, efficient, and, of course, cheerful personnel. It is the experience of being shown what we are told is our image in a mirror society holds up to us, and then discovering that this is no mirror at all, but a crude, mass-produced composite photograph bearing our name . . . or perhaps our number.[4]

The government employee sits amidst tall buildings and modern furnishings, surrounded by electronic equipment and an overflow of information, and with money to spend, yet feels and is impotent. The bureaucrat has everything about him and can do nothing.

In the unnecessarily complex bureaucratic thicket we have created the employees become so harassed by the phone, people, paper, and pressure that they no longer promise anything. After having been made into liars so often by a system that they cannot control they refuse to take responsibility for anything. The result is an inability to decide, even to give an opinion which they will own the next day. Afraid to make commitments, they blame administrative and regulatory prohibitions, conflicting public demands, and time constraints. The paralysis is hidden by a flurry of rushing to meetings and shuffling papers. Behind the frenetic screen is a mediocrity that feeds on its expectation that failure on anything of significance is inevitable. When a course of action is the least bit risky, they refuse to take the option.

One of the greatest tragedies of government service is to see the metamorphosis from an energetic, motivated, innovative, strong young person to a cautious, hesitating, vacillating, scapegoating bureaucrat—to see the very attributes for which a person was hired squeezed out. We have trained a whole generation of public employees to be disillusioned cynics. And our professional schools have followed suit and are training many of them in advance only to work their way through a discredited system.

We cannot expect these citizens to be humane to their fellows outside if the experience they have inside government is anything but humane. We cannot call for cooperative, caring behavior as long as the internal structure rewards game-playing competitiveness.

Wendell Berry[5] clearly perceives what we have done to ourselves. He writes that while we use people as machines, we have used our animals in a better fashion—they were at least considered fellow creatures. We depended upon them and took care of them as ones of us. Now we see people as robots on an assembly line. Such work is not unifying nor healing. How can we expect anything else other than misplaced pride or despair?

With our Newtonian-Cartesian logic we have created a rigidly segmented organizational world that has ended up fragmenting the personalities of our employees. We have created institutions on a massive scale to face the problems that are so complex despite the fact that the more complicated things are the simpler the problem solving organism has to be. By swallowing ideas that have been distorted visions of human reality we have in fact created something less than the best possible institution and the most effective individuals to people it. We have given Freud's libidinal burden to everyone and created a system to keep it under control. Our psychological theories about what human nature is have led us away from an approach to work and learning in government that emphasizes responsibility for self and one's actions. Masters and Johnson's enlightened view of the nature of the drives that Freud called libido, with its demand for a whip-wielding superego, came too late to influence post-war personnel systems.

Just as we have used government to treat illness instead of developing health; to pile on resources instead of removing obstacles to community self-determination; to increase the size and number of technologies instead of finding appropriate technology; and to punish criminals instead of eradicating conditions that spawn them, we have applied the same misconceptions to the internal management of government. We have tried to focus on the weaknesses of employees, to pay increasing amounts of money to improve performance,* to buy complicated hardware and systems, and to establish tighter controls on behavior.

This has given us people who undervalue their real selves, accept the superficial reward system, depend on externals to solve the problems under their purview, and learn to circumvent constraints only when it serves their own purposes. They are lacking in zeal and obsessed with form. They learn to focus on their personal career interests and the makework that keeps them visible, but safely so, to the keepers of the keys to movement on the pyramid. What we have in sum is a system that creates personally insecure and inhibited individuals and compensates for those weaknesses by a patina of power symbols. The latter leads to an arrogance that is in inverse proportion to the competence underneath.

But when it is all over, the retirement ceremony and words uttered by those leaving and those left behind all have a hollow ring. The bittersweetness of unfulfilled human potential and the release, finally to be oneself, leaves an unsatisfying aftertaste. The promise of opportunity offered by public service does not materialize and the satisfaction that should be there is not. There is envy among those who see a colleague go free, tempered by a sad recognition that when the time comes their lives too will not have counted for much.

The Whole

I have spent three chapters on material that is often obvious to anyone, and much of which has been written about by others, because I have not seen a comprehensive, holistic approach to defining the problem. Even among those of us who have worked as internal analysts and change agents in government there are few who are able to visualize and articulate the overall, interrelated nature of the beast we have tried to domesticate. I am persuaded that until large numbers of people, both inside and out, can easily and quickly conceive of the multifaceted social organism with which we are dealing, we will continue to take potshots in a willy-nilly fashion that leads nowhere. The result is a lumbering on of incoherence.

We have seen how there are fragmented, isolated and weak bureaucratic responses to any particular problem of significance. Choose any problem and the

---

*This has been despite considerable research evidence that beyond a certain threshold money is not a significant motivating factor in performance.

quality of government reaction will probably be the same. There are of course short-term economic and political interests at stake which cause powerful groups to try to protect the status quo, but that is insufficient explanation for the failure of the so-called "independent public service" to develop and present an effective national strategy for public debate and Congressional and Presidential review.

It is important that we take another look at the symptoms described earlier and restate them in an integrated way. By doing so I believe it is possible to provide a useful analysis and to see a way out of our predicament.

The images of elitism and officialdom and the general sense of being above the public that defines society-at-large as mediocre, self-aggrandizing groups that need control, contribute to a sense of arrogance, defensiveness, and disdain for those on the outside. The self-selecting and self-rewarding systems reinforce the insularity. The seniority system with top-down control of power and opportunity ensures that new entrants who wish to open up the system are either shaped up or shipped out, or relegated to a corner if they persist in staying in. The inward focus and the authoritarian control of opportunities and rewards lead to minimal innovation and risk-taking. The confusion that reigns in the overlapping assignments of roles and responsibilities, and the cautious mentality give us the least common denominator product. Hundreds of thousands of our potentially most capable citizens who are theoretically organized in government behave in the most disjointed and disorganized way.

The failure of a department to produce a comprehensive, well-developed set of proposed policies and programs that would lead to the (let's say) maintenance of lower and middle-income housing in renewed city neighborhoods—whether they would be approved by Congress is another question—is illustrative of the bureaucracy's failure to perform. Why is it impossible in a bureaucracy to produce a report that would command the respect of experts and lay citizens, clearly articulate the arguments, set forth alternatives susceptible to public discussion, and identify its own biases? Probably the institution has within it some people competent to the task, but they are interspersed with layers of supervisors, gamesmen, and other competitors for a piece of the action. Guidance given through the many layers of hierarchy is distorted. Other activities concerned with space, materials, administrative reports, organizational relationships, and other diverting substantive tasks reduce significantly the time and energy available to devote to the main project. Discussions and joint work on the project are filled with extraneous behaviors: games, defending turf, and seeking recognition in the grading game. The formal role definitions which divide responsibility among several units add to the in-fighting. The various groups have only limited responsibilities and they are not well defined. The cumbersome structure discourages the mid-level professional who does not have a facilitating work environment; he or she sees the inequities of the complicated reward system and naturally decides that one must look out for oneself. All of the elements are part of the bureaucratic structure and they, in their circular relationships, act in concert to give us the national bureaucratic problematique.

The result is an excessively costly operation, involving too many people, but with no one able to be in charge of anything. It is an institution that is self-centered and takes the easy way. These traits are caused by outmoded concepts of humans and their motivations, by inappropriate and too rigid organizing structures, and their resultant impacts on attitudes and behaviors.

Our national bureaucracy is in such a state because the elements of the organism are disconnected from the external reality of our 3rd Century world of knowledge about people and their social relationships. Conceived in a former time, they collectively have evolved to serve primarily the purposes of the bureaucracy, which are not consistent with the current needs of our nation and globe. The organism's goals have become self-survival ones, even at the expense of the larger national good. Such are the laws of integral social units, and it does no good to deplore their natural predilections.

Bureaucracy in America today is a perfect example of actions taken for good reasons leading us awry: we wanted to ensure equality; we set out to reward merit; we believed in the efficacy of rational attacks on society's problems; we wanted to protect different aspects of our society; and we strongly believed we could make a logical system work. But our limited organizational understanding, combined with certain social, economic, and cultural conditions, has resulted in the denial of opportunity, the smothering of creativity and the loss of individual initiative and responsibility.

The central institution of government does not appear today to be capable of initiating or even nurturing the possible revolution Revel sees for America.

An Historical Perspective

The cumbersome, pyramidal bureaucracy has been identified as a prime culprit in the destruction of human talent and the wasting of society's resources and a first impulse may be to deride those in leadership positions as simpletons who ought to know better or engage in hortatory calls on them to change their ways. But this state of affairs results from no conscious, malicious intent. It is simply a result of the process of our society's mirroring back on its human community the externalities of its mechanistic philosophy. Man's invention of machines and their subsequent impact on his conceptual patterns have evolved to the point where he tends to see himself as the machine Wendell Berry contrasted so eloquently to what might be.

When people talk about human life in a bureaucracy, how do they describe it? It is a pressure system, a black box with inputs and outputs, dominated by individuals who have access to levers of power. Frantic workers in it are described as crashing. They get wound-up and must let off steam. When the components get out of sync they must be regulated and tuned in order to get them running smoothly. Similar phrases would be used by a mechanic talking about an engine.

Such a vision has led man to believe that he had boundaries and had to subdivide himself and his activities into very narrowing squares of thought and action. It is ironic that man (three centuries or more ago) who saw science as God's creation, composed of simple laws, and imposed the same mechanistic ideas upon himself is now faced with a much more complex reality, but finds it difficult to escape his own estimation of his simple nature. Society reinforces that limited vision of the individual in its compartmentalization of science, education, government and community; the Pied Piper of specialization and professionalization leads us in ever-narrowing circles. In the public sector the ineffective communication and decision-making processes and the uncoordinated internal procedures that impede progress are all ramifications of this specialist paradigm.

We are now prisoners of that bind and find ourselves in the ineffective government morass described in Part I. This mechanistic view of man has supported the myth which asserts that pyramidal bureaucracies are the natural habitat of modern persons and, even with all their shortcomings, are the most reasonable way to cope with complex public problems.

To accept that modern bureaucratic principles, developed in less than a century, result in the highest form of purposeful social structure is to show little appreciation for the lessons of history. Today we no longer have a few educated elite and large masses with limited perspectives; our education programs have produced populations of aware, broad-gauged minds whose bloom is stamped out if they are placed in little boxes and told to follow the mazes.

While both the tasks and workers have changed dramatically, we still attempt to force them into the same old frames. This perpetuation of a utilitarian/degrading social structure can only be explained by the lag in philosophical or conceptual development; our behavioral assumptions have not kept up with the pace of changing reality. But the problem is not just one of ideas. Vested interests have developed. Just as in religious institutions, public organizations of governance have developed an appendage which retards the necessary adjustments required for continuous renewal: a priesthood of "bureaucratic experts" who only know how to "administer" and "manage" people, processes, and papers and could not produce a product even if required to do so under the pain of death. They obtain positions, aggrandize their role, and take on proteges to help them carry out the "tasks" they have invented and which continually expand their bureaucracy.

Universities have seen it as a means to exploit government funds and are rushing to give the "field" academic respectability. The proper role of universities, i.e., to study and teach about the phenomenon, has given way to training or producing larger and larger numbers of people who can only be middlemen; the rate of graduate professional school production is a national travesty, both in terms of misuse of valuable intellectual resources and in the constraints it places on the creation of productive organizations. Everyone knows you do not need "specially trained managers" to use small units of workers, so if the ever growing cadre of "bureaucratic administrators" is to protect its future, the bureaucratic model of organizations must be continually expanded. No group that I am aware of consciously seeks to work itself out of a job. So we cannot expect innovative alternatives to come from this sector of society. They hold conferences to discuss modern trends and new developments, but we can be assured that nothing which strikes at the very heart of their "religion" will be given much of a hearing. Those who started out as administrators for the public now perceive of themselves as administrators of the public.

How can this hold on our lives be maintained? Because we continue to believe, or at least acquiesce in, the myths that lead us to accept their self-defined role and its interference in the real work that needs to be done. These myths include fallacious assumptions about the nature of people and work and the dynamics of scale that support the bureaucratic model.

But hierarchical, segmented "paper and policy mills" are a development of the last 50 years, based on military and automobile assembly line models. The conflux of modern medicine and technological innovation, neither of which came from bureaucratic sources, permitted large massings of urban populations and gave rise to a demand for public services that could only be met with large numbers of public employees. In the absence of alternative models and in the typically Western search for rational ordering of life's activities, the Weberian paradigm was chosen. The interchange between German and British and American academics in the late 19th and early 20th centuries left its indelible mark on U.S. patterns of intellectual thought.

The Henry Ford praise for the fragmented conveyor belt system of industrial production and the success of specialist-oriented European armies offered practical examples to those trying to provide governance for a rapidly modernizing nation. In the early part of this century, science, which had spewed forth such power for gaining control over the physical environment, also promised administrators the tools to harness large numbers of human beings. All that had to be done, many theorized, was to treat them like machines and organize them along the lines of a factory. In the 1920's and 30's Frederick Taylor and others fine-tuned this perspective into what became known as "scientific management."

In fact, such theories only codified existing practices in large industrial units of the time.

In the late 30s Elton Mayo and Chester Barnard attacked the overly simplistic concepts of the scientific management school, but the New Deal reformers had already opted for them as harness to drive the bureaucratic vehicle. Then World War II came along with its pressures for mobilization on a mass scale and much of the production and troop deployment effect seemed to be susceptible only to the regimentation of the Taylor/Weber approach.[6]

After the war, when Herbert Simon and Dwight Waldo attempted to expose the shallowness of the facile and over-confident tenets of scientific management and point out that such models were not suitable for all types of organizations, it was too late. Successful participants in the machine that had given the allies a military victory were now in positions of leadership in government, universities, and industry. They knew only one model and it was applied to every new challenge of the post-war world, to be epitomized by the Great Society mentality of the mid-60s. Faced now with greater global ambiguity they can only resort to the ineffective textbook administrative remedies.

Now we have a generation of officials, managers, and academics who have known no other alternatives. The myths have been ingrained from childhood and we seem only capable of rearranging the pieces on the chessboard, unable to conceive of another framework.

Given what had earlier happened to government and business institutions, society's only hope in the second half of the twentieth century lay with its institutions of higher learning, but they too fell into the trap of the "factory model." Formal learning became more specialized and fragmented; the work of producing graduates and/or other visible products became the goal of most institutions. Layers of degrees and titles became overt symbols of progress and ticket punching became the standard in the universities as it was in the military officers corps and the Foreign Service.*

As Dwight Eisenhower warned in the late 50s, the overly-specialized administrative paradigm is firmly in place among (1) the business-industrial technocrats, (2) the public bureaucracy, and (3) the social science academics. The latter is a clear indication of the depth of our problem—we have now so socialized ourselves that even our best and brightest intellects do not perceive of other alternatives for their own self-actualization and confirmation, much less that of society. Our social scientists now spend their time describing the status quo, looking through a darkened glass at a marred landscape, unaware that by simply turning around they could behold a whole new vista.

The pleas of Simon and Waldo, and Charles Perrow more recently, for different approaches to organizational management for different categories of organizations were always ignored, but they are even more pertinent today. The kind of organization that is appropriate for deploying an army is not suitable for producing perceptive analytic insight into international problems and

---

*Our early industrial society encouraged workers and new immigrants to move up, to be a success, but somewhere along the way the symbols of progress became less and less related to real achievement. Then the merit badges became something to fight over.

stimulating creative new strategies for coping with them. A global perspective is not developed by a series of narrow assignments looking at different small parts of the globe. The process used to assemble an automobile is not amenable to developing a coherent strategic options paper for Presidential decision making. The need for change is recognized, but the alternatives are not easily visualized. They exist, but we are blind to them because of our mythology.

The process of institution building in the federal government has been largely an unconscious one, where the few initially well thought out concepts were added to much in the same way that most social myths grow: accretion of small, apparently compatible, but misleading ideas and practices. A sound historical perspective requires that we go deeper in our analysis than the what and how of current government activities. Such an analysis will be required if we are to overcome the bureaucratic problematique described here which daily saps our society.

Part II
Breaking
the Cycle

5
Abortive Reforms

> So stubborn are the defenses of a mature society against change that shock treatment is often required to bring about renewal . . . In the final stages of . . . senility there is a rule or precedent for everything . . . (but) written rules are the least of the problem. More perplexing is the straight jacket of unwritten rules that hems the individual in.
>
> John Gardner, *Self-Renewal*[1]

The malfunctioning of the bureaucracy described in the preceding chapters has been evident for some decades now. Many reform efforts have been initiated, by both public groups and internal managers.[2] Each new Administration brings on a wave of "fresh starts," from Presidentially launched projects to individual appointees attempting to master the units for which they are responsible. A profitable business giving advice on coping with organizational problems has developed for consultants. Many others, including writers, make money off the market demand for ideas on how to improve the government bureaucracy. One would think that with so much attention and effort there would be noticeable improvements in our institutions. But the record is very clear. Little progress has been made in the understanding and the conscious reshaping of our bureaucratic institutions. Bureaucracy and misguided inefficiency remain synonymous. Employees of the bureaucracy are well aware of it and the public cannot escape the evidence. A 1978 Harris poll showed less than one-third of Americans had confidence in their government institutions and that number has fallen lower in the last two years.

There is widespread agreement that no study, commission, or book, nor any combination of them from the 1947-8 Hoover Commission to the Carter Administration's Reorganization Project, has had significant constructive impact on the federal bureaucracy. A few of the commission or task force studies have received prominent but superficial attention; they have not, however, been sufficiently relevant or durable to overcome long-standing institutional flaws. Obviously some new programs have been started and a few have been terminated, but the organizational sluggishness and piecemeal approach remain endemic. The reform efforts spawned by some of the studies have come to naught despite the large number of people involved in them. The most that can be said is that some small units touched by individual reforms or innovative managers have become more efficient and better places to work. Those isolated and limited benefits have not occurred because of an efficacious theory of institutional reform, but as by-products of a process with principles that were implicit and largely unintended; employees were recognized as co-creators of the institution and encouraged to take charge of themselves. Most informed observers now believe that the government's organizational capability is less adequate to its challenge than was the case 30 years ago.

Their concern is deeply felt by many and it is accompanied by a high degree of frustration, a sense that nothing but limping along and making the best of a poor situation seems possible. Even by those on the inside, the problem is perceived as too complex and overwhelming to be coped with. In response to questions the bureaucratic responses are: "we'll just have to do the best we can," "we try to improve parts that we can have some influence on," "we are doing a study to make recommendations to the President," or "we are introducing this or that new technique."

The record of our government's continuing false starts cannot be attributed solely to the fact that we elect a President every four years. It is surprising how many members of the policy level establishment remain in place through the periodic changeovers, or return after a short hiatus. And, of course, the career bureaucrat leadership turns over very slowly. Given that much stability, we must look more deeply for answers.

In the face of seemingly intractable problems, it is understandable that observers inside and out seek to pinpoint blame. Given the human need for explanation, coupled with the emotional resistance to searching within for causes, it is not surprising that politicians condemn the bureaucrats, that employees accuse managers and vice versa, and that individual citizens find fault with everyone in government. Line managers criticize personnel systems and personnelists reproach supervisors. Brought together to study the problem they end up agreeing the difficulty is either human nature or the intractability of our necessarily large organizations.

After coming to believe answers are beyond their competence many practitioners turn to outside experts. Unfortunately, the "experts" are prisoners of most of the same perceptual patterns held by the managers and employees; they are products of similar cultural and educational experiences. The only difference is that the experts do not have responsibility for seeing things whole and actually getting the work done. But they do not hesitate from marketing limited tools as panaceas, nor do managers pause to question before applying their untried prescriptions to whole organizations. Onto the stage are paraded PPBS, MBO, ZBB, Theories X and Y, Decision Analysis Techniques, Management Information Systems, etc., etc.

The modern management techniques and organization development fads they peddle frequently exacerbate the problems that are inherent in our large social entities. The artificial grafting on of alien "systems" to organic social structures is counterproductive more often than benign. And we seem doomed to repeat only variations on the same themes.

Some of the inability to break new ground must be attributed to the lack of relevant analytic concepts to collect and evaluate data about the underlying reasons for the failures of past reform efforts. Most individuals who participate in such so-called reforms see only the obvious reactions to their own part of the action and their reporting tends to be on the symptomatic level, with little attention to the intellectual and psychological dynamics. The initiators of change efforts tend to blame political, personality, or turf problems for the negative reactions to their attempts.

The basic reason, however, for the lack of progress is that the institution's leaders and most "experts" do not understand the nature and the magnitude of the task of bringing conscious change to large social units. A simple but fundamental fact has escaped most would-be reformers:

> The federal bureaucracy is not simply an organization. It is a social organism, a society within a society that has its own internal dynamics which isolate it from society at large, and like most closed societies it places self-interest and self-perpetuation as its highest priority.

Consequently superficial efforts at reorganization, rearrangement of inter-agency relationships, and system/procedural changes only stir up the muddy water, not redirect it. The basic product—public policies and programs—is little affected.

What is also not well recognized is that the expert explanations for lack of progress are just as off-base as are the intervention techniques; the critics of specific attempts operate from the same mechanistic, input-output patterns as the method's proponents. The critics come out saying things like: "they don't take into account sufficient quantity of variable X," "the structural modifications had XYZ gap," "counterforces weren't minimized," "the next steps weren't ratcheted into place," and "leverage wasn't high enough."

In other words the critics accept the basic concepts and appoach, but fault the change agents for poor tactics, lack of perseverance, and limited application. It is reminiscent of one 18th Century physician criticizing another for being too sparing in the bloodletting of an anemic patient given to fainting spells. Executives take organizations that are low in morale, fragmented, overwhelmed with useless paperwork and bureaucratic exercises, filled with individuals who have sorted out some kind of compensating identities and relationships for themselves and then force them to submit to (1) filling out questionnaires, (2) giving interviews to naive newcomers about what they do, (3) rewriting of the social rules of the game, and (4) telling anew of how screwed up the system is. The latter they have known for years, the first two they have done *ad nauseam* and the third they suffer through with each change of administration or unit manager.

Because the bureaucratic model so shapes the perceptions of managers, even those appointed fresh from the private sector after an election, they cannot conceive of nor seek out new approaches to resolving organizational problems. Faced with resistance the knee-jerk reflex is to give out louder and more detailed orders, shuffle people around to put friends in charge, or launch some new clean-up or shape-up program.

This chapter critiques the various types of attempts that are most often made to improve governmental effectiveness. There are a half-dozen different general routes people follow in these attempts: (1) placing the "right people," (2) introducing comprehensive management systems, (3) training programs, (4) reorganizations, (5) amending the activities of the personnel system, and (6) modifying basic structures. There is another one that is hardly ever used, introducing new primary concepts into basic patterns of thought, but more on that later.

My purpose is not to deride all other ideas that have been tried in attempts to improve the performance of our bureaucracy; some have been truly counterproductive, but most are simply more of the same fighting fire with fire approach. The latter is best exemplified by the Commission on Federal Paperwork's October 1977 recommendation that a Cabinet level Department of Administration be created. So-called professional public administrators hailed this innovation, with the expectation that it would be staffed by members of their guild. An apt analogy might be asking the starving to take over the rationing of food.

The criterion of success in all institutional interventions is whether they bring about more effective and constructive behavior in the governance and public service functions of the government. If there have been any significant success stories they have escaped public notice. The fact of the matter is that no currently used tactics have been capable of overcoming the deficiencies of our government's bureaucratic organisms. They either strengthen the inherent destructive elements of bureaucracy, although perhaps unwittingly, or when intrinsically useful they alone are unable to redirect the distractions already hobbling our public employees. In the former category are most of the personnel and management systems interventions and reorganizations. In the latter category are some of the structural change and training efforts described below.

Right People

The simplistic belief that "a few good people can make the system work" remains one of the most powerfully deluding siren songs in Washington. Every new wave of officials just cannot believe that a rational creation of the American society such as the federal bureaucracy could be that bad; they believe the state of affairs must be due to the incompetence or warped priorities of their predecessors. All that is required, from their view, is to get right-thinking people in there and they can shape things up in no time; they only need the right vision and willpower to get things back on the right track.

The American mystical faith in the "rugged individual" is enduring and non-incumbent politicians appeal to this hope, but there is increasing evidence that citizens are beginning to understand that a few substitutions at half-time will not change the nature of the game. The fallacy of the "right people" approach was brought home in the summer of '79 when President Carter replaced one-half the Cabinet leadership. There was wide recognition that the new appointees would be no better able to rein in inflation, make more energy available, shore up faltering social institutions, build a more efficient transportation infrastructure, or ensure justice any better than their predecessors. In fact, due to the perturbations throughout the bureaucracy caused by the manner in which the changes were made, the entire bureaucratic organism became more sluggish and less well-focused on the tasks at hand.

A good example of the right people perspective is I.M. Destler's[3] recommendation that the President get his personally selected support team in a particular network of positions in the bureaucracy if he wishes to really control foreign policy. The point here is not that a few individuals do not make a difference, but that their impact is much more incremental and transitory than an outside observer would expect to be the case. There are a number of reasons why this is so: complexity of the flow of events, differing perceptions and difficulties of communication even among members of the leadership group, time constraints, and personal lack of competence, but the primary obstacle is the relatively impregnable nature of the bureaucratic organism. Its internal dynamics and inertial force are simply not susceptible to the manipulation of one or a few individuals acting within its membranes. A significant change will occur only when we develop a new type of leadership that observes different principles about human nature.

Management Systems

New managers, when confronted with what appears to be a group of runaways on whom they must depend, seek sets of harness to corral and bring employees under control and provide means to drive them in the desired direction. They search for more effective ways to control the flow of information, to provide for evaluation, to manipulate decision making and in sum direct all actions of the organization.

Large scale examples of this approach are the Program Planning and Budgeting System (PPBS) of Lyndon Johnson, Management-by-Objectives (MBO) of Richard Nixon, and Zero-based Budgeting (ZBB) of Jimmy Carter.

When the Nixon Administration attempted to push MBO as a technique to enhance government performance it was characterized as a way to increase rationality and accountability. But it was also billed as a mechanism to ensure joint goal-setting, or building of program objectives from the bottom up as well as top down. The idea was to have it appear that the political and career employees were engaged in a gigantic collaborative effort to get the best possible performance out of the old buggy—the carrot and stick were woven together in the "page of agreed upon work goals."

The ideal system would have had each agency with its Congressionally-approved objectives, each bureau with its Cabinet approved sub-objectives, each office with its Assistant Secretary approved subsidiary objectives, etc., on down to the solitary individual, with no one to supervise but himself, and his goal statement. All of these bits and pieces would be accumulated upward and fall together as in the running in reverse of a motion picture reel of a house being blown up. How much more logical and rational can one get? The idea just sounds great—all of us doing our bit in the great jigsaw puzzle. Well, why didn't it work?

The simple answer is because it was one new concept introduced into a very complex living organism without an understanding of what factors had to be taken into account for a successful grafting to occur; there was no provision for developing congruence between the network of existing elements and the new formal process.

MBO was both a concept and a formal process. As a concept it had both an implicit human image and an assumption about bureaucratic work: knowledgeable individuals freely setting work priorities for a well-defined task that was susceptible to logical subdivision into small individually managed components. As a process it was the periodic negotiation of individual and/or unit performance objectives and priorities in terms amenable to evaluation.

The MBO ideal bureaucrats were employees who had substantial knowledge of general organizational purposes and priorities, who accurately understood their ability to work within the larger context and could predict the likely success of their efforts, who accepted the responsibility of a significant degree of autonomy, and were able to control their own activities and the environment enough to reasonably follow the agreed upon course of action long enough to prove their mettle.

The MBO concept assumed the agreed-upon contract would make sense in terms of work content and time-frame in relation to the realities of the overall organization, that the work could really be cut up that way and brought to a conclusion during the agreed upon tenures of the contractors, and that other parts of the organization would perform in concert.

The MBO format was very simple: a short list of work goals set forth for an agreed period of time and acceptable to both supervisor and subordinate. It could be used as the basis for evaluation of performance or for the allocation of resources.

Now let's compare these descriptions of the ideal to the typical government office into which the MBO idea was introduced.

The key relevant beliefs in the real world of bureaucracy are that the employees are getting paid to do a job, but have no power to determine what that job will be; that innovations are reserved to the Congress and the political executives; that one does only what needs to be done to respond to demands from above; and that traditional divisions of labor and working relationships cannot be overridden.

Relevant characteristics of the formal bureaucratic structure are: (1) Particular individuals or units are not fully responsible for the totality of a task; production of the project or program is fragmented. (2) The tenures of participants are keyed to political terms, tour lengths, promotions, etc., instead of the task requirements. (3) Although successful performance is dependent on the group, it is the individual who is evaluated. (4) Control of resources is not coterminous with task control.

Even such a limited review of other elements of the organization indicates something of the obstacles faced by a would-be implementor of the MBO idea, but an overview of the totality of the organism leads one to the conclusion that "twas pure folly" to have seriously expected the successful incorporation of such an incompatible pattern into the existing fabric.

The mismatch was almost total. The kinds of role conceptions necessary for MBO did not exist in the heads of most bureaucrats and the countervailing organizational constraints were too much for the few who did have them.

To confound the problem even more, the psychology of most bureaucratic units is completely antithetical to MBO principles. With the willingness to be risk-taking at a minimum, no new or untried departures are articulated. People are too cautious to go out on a limb and spell out objectives explicitly that are not safe, i.e., easily achievable. The least that can be said and still fill up the space on the form with high-sounding jargon is what is finally written down and filed away. And caveats are neatly tucked away in dependent clauses, just in case some inspector or auditor decides to take a look at actual performance in the future.

The bureaucratic interpersonal mode with its distrust and limiting of self-made commitments to safe obligations reinforces the banality of goal-setting negotiation sessions. In addition, the actual and perceived manipulative power of the supervisor discourages the subordinate from believing that any leeway exists for exerting personal influence on the definition of the work. The individual tends to "just go along with the boss' suggestions" or conversely, if the boss does not know much about what the person does, writes up a statement that will sound good to the boss and simply gets his signature. In neither case is there a serious discussion of possibilities, alternatives, and priorities.

Even when reasonably useful plans and schedules fortuitously result from the unlikely matrix of circumstances described above, the prevailing behavioral tendencies toward reacting to the immediate "crisis" overwhelm the fragile forces supportive of the long-range focus called for by MBO.

The fact that the performance evaluation and promotion processes are little related to actual work activity and the degree to which the MBO process is seen as just another "paper exercise" isolate it from reality. So the outcome of a change strategy that was launched to improve the overall performance of a government entity is a charade, a production of pieces of paper for the record that modifies no attitudes, individual behavior, or group products.

The same general pattern has been the experience of innovators throughout government with a variety of prescriptions. The introduction of PPBS in the Johnson Administration had already suffered the same fate.

One could have safely predicted that the outcome of the Carter Administration's effort to introduce the concept of ZBB into the management of the federal government was to be very similar—long on rhetoric and reams of paper and short on enhanced government.*

Everyone believes that you cannot be honest in dealings with other layers and units of the bureaucracy, that you must try to second guess what the market will bear today and cater to it with the appropriate program descriptions and justifications. Since the bureaucrat's continued security is dependent on preservation of his turf, the motive force in the budget process is to do whatever is necessary to ensure that one's programs at least are spared the knife, if they cannot be increased. Therefore no stone is left unturned by the determined bureaucrat in making efforts that will compensate for the formal paper exercise. Myths and other public assumptions are called into play, including impassioned pleas to the Congress and maybe even the press, *sub rosa*. Biases of key players in the review process are pricked and orchestrated. All the rules of the bureaucratic culture—avoid conflicts, cover issues, mutual protection, etc.— conspire to keep fundamental questions about priorities and beneficiaries from being raised and much less resolved. The inherent weaknesses of the organization, little knowledge about program realities at the budget decision making level and pieces of an activity scattered among several units, make it impossible to make real trade-offs among discrete programs. The diffuseness of the responsibility and the ambiguous nature of the product, and the almost total lack of measures of effectiveness for them guaranteed that ZBB decisions would devolve from considerations other than concrete public service criteria. The ongoing processes of the organism closed around the ZBB injection and neutralized it. A few specific decisions were perhaps taken within the ZBB context that would not have been taken otherwise, but they will have been ultimately affected for reasons external to the data generation and analysis called for by the new system; they could just as easily have been made without it. The ZBB approach in those instances only served as justification for a covert rationale.

Consequently, the end results of such overly complex, so-called scientific

---

*The fiscal year 1979 budget preparation exercise clearly spelled its demise before it got started.

decision-making approaches are (1) the generation of excessive amounts of paperwork, (2) successful defensive measures by the bureaucracy, and (3) further disillusionment among those who are not already completely cynical.

Training Programs

When management systems like those described above fail, many attribute it to the lack of proper knowledge or skills on the part of employees. The next logical step for them is training in the use of so-called managerial or organizational skills. The training processes cover a wide spectrum of development activities from very cerebral management philosophy seminars to personality oriented T-group or sensitivity training sessions. The purpose of these courses is to teach people how to plan, to communicate, to manage others, to manage oneself, etc. They are offered by universities, consulting firms, and the training sections of bureaucracies. They may be within the organization's spaces or in pleasant, isolated off-site environments. Much of the $1 billion plus the federal government spends on employee training is devoted to such activities each year.

The courses are short and focus on specific elements of the bureaucratic organism, such as formal structures or procedures, interactive processes like interpersonal effectiveness, technical theories, etc. They present employees with slightly different patterns of thinking about the organization, but they hardly ever improve bureaucratic performance. The introduction of the course lessons by a few individuals in a larger system, and without the support of complementary changes in the outer elements, is inadequate for them to take root and flourish. Very significantly, most of such training only treats the surface of the social organism and ignores the implicit elements and therefore encourages the trainees to think only about symptoms and not causes.

This kind of change strategy suffers then from two basic faults: conceptually it is flawed because it does not include an intellectual understanding of all organizational elements and their interrelationships and its application is also too limited in terms of actual acceptance throughout a formal system. People who receive this training become quickly frustrated when their post-school efforts back in the office fail to bear fruit, but after a while they rationalize their failures by blaming the unresponsiveness of the larger system of human nature. They seldom, if ever, question the premises on which their newfound techniques were based.

The activities that fall on the other end of the spectrum (towards the psychological away from the purely intellectual) tend to be doubly injurious to the individual, while equally ineffectual in bringing about increased effectiveness in the larger system. Courses or training in this area primarily treat the behavioral element, providing alternative interpersonal models. They may also touch slightly on self-image and the psychological set, but the compelling influence of these two usually unarticulated influences on overall organizational performance is not well treated. Neither is there a direct relating of the explicit performance problems to what should be the object of treatment, the organic, bureaucratic life style.

Employees in the courses learn new behavioral patterns quickly, being rewarded by the warm embrace of their fellow trainees, and go back to the office with great hope for change there. Their new alien norms are immediately rejected by those prevailing in the bureaucratic organism and with no reinforcements from the formal systems and other people any remaining glimmer of hope soon fades. Here too the result of using partial measures is total failure. In addition, the new converts suffer psychic pain at the hands of the home environment because they have been affected emotionally by the training experience, not just intellectually as were the management theory or systems trainees. It is much more difficult to cope with office rejections when one has become so deeply committed to new visions and new emotions.

Such institutional training courses alone, even if they were conceptually on the right track, can never lead to profound organizational renewal. As long as they are only efforts at better control of existing defective structures and procedures they lead nowhere. Some courses, treating such problems as poor communications or lack of analytic ability, which do have intrinsic value also more often than not lead to little progress. Their practitioners find themselves in a hostile environment, with well-established traditions and formalities set against different ideas and practices. The new skills and approaches do not get rewarded, even when not negatively reinforced. People continue to get recognized, supported, and promoted by the same bureaucratic standards.

Infrequently the concepts included in some training courses are truly revolutionary: dealing with basic issues such as the foundations of power and control; looking at individual, organizational and public rights; questioning accepted views of social purpose and motivation; and proposing alternative visions. But these concepts find themselves in a *cul-de-sac* without a mechanism to transfer their implications into the formal, larger organism. Training is not expected to lead to such large ideas, and when it purports to, the bureaucratic leadership considers it presumptuous.

A reasonable conclusion to draw from the past experience of government with these types of organizational development activities is that they are at most benign and often counterproductive. The fact that they are recognized as benign by many institutional leaders, who would otherwise be threatened by interventions leading to fundamental change, makes it possible for interested employees still to get time off and financial support for the consultant/academic entrepreneurs who push this approach.

Reorganization

If one cannot place a new harness on them or train the horses to change their gait to meet new expectations, from the traditional leader's perspective, it is reasonable to shift around their relationships to each other. That process is known as reorganization. Most of the so-called post-war reforms fall into this category.

Obviously reorganization can be a bureaucratic game as described in Chapter 3, but it is often undertaken as a serious and conscious attempt to resolve problems of bureaucratic performance. Reorganizations on anything more than a very small scale are doomed to failure from the outset since they only deal with the most superficial element of an organism, the formal communication structure and unit interrelationships. Reorganization has become a misnomer; instead of implying that one is going to go through the process of building a new organization, with all that means for the conception and integration of all elements in a new form, it indicates only partial realignment of certain relationships, perhaps changes in roles and some reallocation of resources. Real reorganization can only follow the reconceptualization and repatterning of the primary images, assumptions, and structural principles of a social entity.

The Carter Administration fell in a big way for the easy, relatively speaking, lure of reorganization as a substitute for reform. It surveyed users of the products of bureaucracy (although the data gathering was light in the average John Q. Citizen sector) and identified high priority problem areas. They were briefly described in Chapter 2.

A relatively large staff, the President's Reorganization Project, was assembled to carry out the campaign promise made by Carter when he accepted the Democratic nomination: "It's time for us to take a new look at our own Government, to strip away the secrecy, to expose the unwarranted pressure of lobbyists, to eliminate waste, to release our civil servants from bureaucratic chaos, to provide tough management. As President, I want you to help me to evolve an efficient, economic, purposeful, and manageable government for our nation."

The approach of the Reorganization Project, housed in the Office of Management and Budget, and its largest subunit, the Federal Personnel Management Project that had been in existence for several years under the Civil Service Commission, was almost exclusively devoted to the formal framework. The basic assumptions underlying the strategy taken inevitably led to its lack of success. The philosophy of the Project was limited to the view that most of the bureaucratic problems that concern Americans result from fragmented, overlapping, uncoordinated responsibilities among organizational units. The energy area was the first to be diagnosed in this fashion. No one would deny that these conditions are problems, but they are only symptoms and unless the root causes are eradicated, a rearrangement of the fragments will not add up to the promised bureaucratic reform.

In 1977 President Carter stated, "The legislation (creation of the new Department of Energy) I am submitting . . . will bring immediate order to this fragmented system." The reorganization was to meld together the Federal Energy Administration, the Federal Power Commission, the Energy Research and Development Administration and other entities into an integrated unit that had both broad authority and dealt with energy problems in a comprehensive way.

The public saw clearly by the summer of 1979 that not only were the energy problems not being systematically attacked, there was not even an overall analysis of them that the government could convincingly communicate to its citizenry. The history of the first three years of the new Department clearly indicates that restructuring the organization chart does little to overcome basic analytic and policy development deficiencies.

The Project, as the principal mechanism for the President's reform strategy, suffered from the same pitfalls that beset the bureaucracy it was to affect: it worked through the already discredited bureaucratic communication and decision-making channels.* Its decision makers were too far removed from the realities of the work-a-day world they wanted to change. It was vulnerable to bureaucratic games. It fell prey to the myth of centralized managerial power. It adopted the bureaucratic norms and procedures, arrogating for itelf the ultimate bureaucratic authoritarian role. Succumbing to the quadrennial song of bureaucratic power, the architects of the Project opted for a strategy of imposing change from the top when what was needed was an effort to facilitate change from the basic conceptual glue outward through a public process.

The reason for this contradiction is easily understood. An elected official who wishes to make a serious reform attempt is caught on the horns of a dilemma if he or she does not already have a well thought out change strategy. Coming in as an outsider the electee believes the people who know most about the realities of the problem to be attacked cannot really be trusted. Those who are trusted by the leader do not know much about the day-to-day substance. Therefore, the inclination is to turn to simplistic, arm's length techniques to "get those folks out there doing what we want them to do." Members of the Carter Administration began to recognize the inefficacy of chart shuffling upheaval among agencies as an approach to reform too late in the game.

Let's take a quick look at the first agency reorganization effort handled by the Project as an illustration of the above weaknesses.

Two conceptually related but operationally distinct government activities had

*A leader in the Project stated he saw this involvement of the permanent bureaucracy as a virtue. But there is a crucial difference between token involvement of bureaucrats and approaching the reorganization with the insights of people who have lived within the bureaucratic perspective.

been housed in two different agencies for 25 years,* but certain parts of the administration of one program were carried out by the other agency under a cost reimbursement relationship. The activity in question was the primary *raison d'etre* of one agency, but only a small part of the other agency. For a number of years there had been a fair amount of public discussion of the purposes and effectiveness of both agencies. Because of the existing public reports, and Congressional interest, this area was seen as an easy target for early reorganization action.

The early reorganization initiative came from the independent agency; in the larger department housing the smaller relevant unit, early reaction was largely superficial and did not involve the pertinent professional staff. Since it was to the independent agency's advantage to focus on the administrative dichotomy and play down questions about the substance of what was being done, the early draft papers dealt exclusively with organizational chart boxes and lines. Taking the lead in the bureaucratic in-fighting the one agency largely set the agenda for the subsequent proposal writing. For a variety of personal, power, perception, and attitudinal reasons the senior hierarchy of the larger agency was not interested in raising questions of purpose and effectiveness. They focused on the administrative division. Efforts of the professionals involved in the programs to get questions of substance raised were politely shunted aside.

When the White House and the Reorganization Project got involved, the discussion still did not treat basic issues. Power plays began with various Executive Office personalities weighing in on bureaucratic questions. The final action memorandum to the President gave him no sense of the program and performance issues, reflected no consideration of the various substantive questions, contained no direct references to the view of people actually involved in and knowledgeable of the concrete operations and their impact, and provided no real alternatives for his consideration. In effect it was the product of the most superficial approach down the path of least resistance, which offered the least hope of significant change, yet it was billed as reform. The individuals, who actually make the agency's policy through the manner in which they set priorities, allocate resources, including their own time, and make the day-to-day decisions that have impact in the real world were left out of the basic decision making process. In fact, they were even excluded from knowledge about the deliberations. Information was so tightly held that only three people in one Agency were privy to the various documents on which the President made his decision.

This is a clear example of why the tool of reorganization, as it is now practiced in the bureaucracy, does not lead to reform. Although engaged in as a mechanism for reform, ostensibly leading to improvement in delivery of services and greater

---

*The United States Information Agency and the Department of State's Bureau of Educational and Cultural Affairs.

effectiveness, reorganization at most results in a shift of a few power relationships but has little lasting impact on daily bureaucratic life. It is the latter which determines most real priorities for government time and resources and the approach taken to deal with them.

In addition to being ineffective, the reorganization approach to reform has many undesirable side effects: Morale sinks in a majority of those involved. Even routine work is disrupted. Valuable institutional memory and experience is lost. Substantive personnel and their energy are diverted from creative tasks to bureaucratic games and unnecessary defending of turf.

Personnel System

Perhaps the most important influence on the government's performance is its personnel system. The indisputable role of personnel practices as a linking medium between the raw material of employees and the finished organizational product is slowly being analyzed; having gone unrecognized its contribution has more often been that of spoiler than facilitator. People are beginning to ask probing questions about the policy consequences of personnel systems and their impact on the formulation and implementation of policy alternatives. A sense of this key role motivated many to support the ill-fated Civil Service legislation of 1978.

But personnel managers and academics are unwitting obstacles; the difficulty is an inappropriate conceptualization of the personnel process. Personnelists are being urged to become more proficient in their human engineering skills: developing, managing, and socializing. Much is being said about the perceived need for an upgrading of "personnel systems," an expansion of their mandate to include more and more influence over employees and their work. To do more of the same genre of things from a strengthened position in the bureaucracy seems to be unquestioningly accepted as the school solution.

An illustration of the imperialistic impulse of the modern public personnel professional is the following paragraph from a reader for students in the field.

> Recognizing that the problems of managing the human resources of an organization must be approached comprehensively, an increasing number of personnel departments . . . have begun to take an expansive view of their mandates. Instead of viewing the personnel function as simply that collection of disparate duties . . . they assume their appropriate missions to be the maximum utilization of their organization's human resources.[4]

This view must be radically revised if we are going to reform our public institutions.

Such misplacing of faith is almost analogous to giving the keys to the burglar.

The personnel system is an integral element of the bureaucratic organism. It conforms to the same pressures toward the organizational mean as do all other elements of a living, social entity. As it cannot be studied in isolation, neither can it act directly and exclusively on particular problems such as behavior patterns of work performance.

In general, the actual impact of a personnel system reflects the primary images and attitudes that persist and dominate perceptual patterns of leadership groups. The selection, reward, and career progression functions all work in sync to insure the perpetuation of the ethos the dominant members believe in. So the real issue is not whether the personnel system works or not, but for what purpose.

The Civil Service, Foreign Service, and other so-called "merit" systems were created to do away with the "spoils" system in public organizations. Fear of the evils of a patronage or some other less rigid personnel system has served as blinders and prevented creative innovations in the field of facilitating human growth.

As we have moved from handwritten ledgers of personnel transactions to computer-based manpower information systems, we have, in a parallel vein, tended to think of the people themselves in rather mechanistic terms. Personnelists spend half their time making people fit the system and the other half trying to justify making exceptions for those who do not.

The formal personnel system of an organization is generally charged with the following functions: selection or hiring, evaluation, promotion, training, and other areas of responsibility such as medical care, morale problems, grievances, etc. These are basically control functions, "to make sure the right person is in the right place at the right time," to carry out the wishes of management in a way that keeps the troops satisfied that due process is being followed and that everyone has a fair chance. Elaborate charades are constructed to give the appearance of equity, rationality and relevance of the personnel processes to the real purposes of the organization.

I do not castigate the current personnelists; they did not invent the function. They can only be criticized for aggrandizing it beyond the realm of plausibility. In that sense they are no different from any other vocational group in our society with its pressures for "professional status." The personnelists have simply taken a leaf from the book of the public administrator, the college professor, the military officer, i.e., the bureaucrat wherever he or she is.

Riding the coattails of "rational managers" and "behavioral scientists," the public personnel manager has carved out a niche in government organizations that has now assumed the proportions of an almost unbridgeable chasm between human potential and human performance. That unfortunate development was aided by the late 19th Century impetus towards an independent, "merit" civil service system, the later "scientific" theories of psychologists and rational political scientists.

In addition there has been the nationwide hook-and-sinker swallowing of the "pyramidal myth" of organization theory that requires such specialists to guard access to the sanctuary.

Essentially primitive research instruments have been applied wholesale in the management of real people and real organizations, without regard to the fact that they were originally created as experimental aids to academics in measuring little bits and pieces of human differences. The urge to differentiation seems to be a strong human motive and it is not surprising that people in a rational "scientific," technological society could produce multiple categories in which to place themselves. When you have developed thousands of skill categories, grade levels, pay groups, hierarchical titles, etc., and must at the same time ensure fair distribution of them, more and more complicated systems are needed to manage them. In a society where people are judged by the labels they wear and the overt status symbols they enjoy, it is not surprising that a system which purports to hand out "merit badges," grade levels, and occupational titles on an equitable, objective basis would enjoy support. Consequently, we have evolved an overly complicated system of labels and rewards that are inherently beyond rational management, and we delude ourselves that our superficial manipulation of them contributes to positive human change.

Since the personnel system's superficial "paper" procedures are relatively easy to change we find that they are often modified in *ad hoc* responses to specific problems. But if the "paper" changes are incongruent with the primary ideational and attitudinal elements then informal practice will make a correction and ensure the "new system works the way it ought to," i.e., just like the old system.

For example, in the Department of State it was decided that the assignment process should be more objective and effective, with the impact of the informal, personal-network system being reduced. So a written change was made in the standard-operating procedures to implement the decision. When it did not seem to be working, management decided that new personnel officers, not wedded to the old system, should be assigned to implement the new policy. How were these new officers identified and assigned? Because of their personal relationships with the managers. Needless to say it was not long before the *status quo ante* old-boy system was in full swing again.

In all instances where superficial, structural or procedural changes are not compatible with the prevailing concepts they never become effective. The exclusive and self-perpetuating traditions prove to be stronger than innovative paper system changes. Many examples like this serve to illustrate why isolated new techniques interjected among the traditional personnel office functions have a "flash in the pan" character and never ignite a larger metamorphosis. Changes conceived within the framework of the personnel function, even though containing many details such as the legislation of the Carter Administration's Personnel Management Project, cannot revitalize atrophying organisms.

Let's take a look at that 1978 Civil Service Reform Act. It included nine merit principles that should govern all personnel practices and ten prohibitions. While salutory, they will have impact only to the extent individual officials feel committed to carry them out. The complexity of procedures and regulations remain such a thicket that any "guerilla" who wants to subvert the system can find cover for his or her deeds. The following paragraphs describe the most important elements of the legislation.

The division of the Civil Service Commission into two agencies, the Office of Personnel Management and a Merit System Protection Board, will keep the policy making and adjudication functions separate. A new Federal Labor Relations Authority will administer the labor relations program and investigate unfair labor practices. But merely changing the labels will not make offices any more effective; an entire system of legal, and, more importantly, customary practices will have to be changed before the political and bureaucratic inequities will be reduced substantially.

Middle level managers and supervisors will be placed in a system that reduces their annual cost-of-living (comparability with private sector) salary increases by one-half and eliminates within-grade longevity step increases. Some of these managers will receive the total overall savings from these cuts, divided among them on the basis of performance evaluations by their superiors. The Act requires that all agencies develop formal performance appraisal systems to implement these principles, notwithstanding the fact that no agency in government today has a workable approach which can be used as a model. Once again we have set up as a precondition a personnel tool which has proved illusive during 30 years of government and private sector research.*

Approximately 9,000 senior executives will be placed in a new service category that makes it possible for management to reassign them more easily within their agencies and to move executives among agencies, with their consent. The Act also provides for a performance bonus of up to 20% of base salary for 50% of those career officials in this Senior Executive Service. Each year up to 5% and 10%, respectively, of this Service may receive special awards of $10,000 as Meritorious Executive and $20,000 as Distinguished Executive.

Do these changes attack the crux of the problem? A bit of reflection indicates they do not. The 3% of incorrigible employees, the crooks and the misfits, does not keep the other government employees from doing a good job. The 12% with less-than-average competence is not responsible for the incompetence of the whole. The fact that annual salary increases now are almost automatic does not demotivate employees. There is no evidence to show that incentive pay will elicit better public service or policy formulation.

---

*It is difficult to understand how such an extensive change was implemented on the basis of so little evidence that it would work. Few pointed out this fallacy. Michael Maccoby was an exception with a small Op-Ed piece in the *Washington Post.*

What is likely to be the impact of this legislation? Its proponent, Alan Campbell, Director of the new Office of Personnel Management, reportedly stated that perhaps 10 percent of the problem may be remedied by it. Given the elements of the bureaucracy which it leaves untouched—the fragmentation of responsibility, the overcomplicated salary and grade structures, excessive hierarchy, the bureaucratic mentality, internal protectionism, and the susceptibility of the system to special interests—the situation five years from now will be worse than the current stagnation.

- Elaborate criteria and procedures will have been developed to insure "justice" in passing out the "productivity" salary increases. No performance evaluation system will be generally accepted as valid. Charges of favoritism will be widespread.* Morale will be low. "Safe" behavior will continue to be the norm and no increase in innovation or public responsiveness will be evident.

- A similar climate will exist in the Senior Executive Service.* Bureaucrats at that level will scramble to be on the right track, and it will be a politicized one, but with the President unable to keep them all responsibly accountable directly to him. The arrogance of elitism and its officious behavior vis-a-vis the public may even be worse.

- Personnel rules will be more complex and require more union and management time patching them up.

- Obtaining significant government jobs will become more a function of who you know than at any time since 1883.

- Instead of moving the career system toward simplicity and greater public control, the changes will only complicate management and further remove workers from a sense of obligation to the public.

This package of symptom-oriented fixes is a clear demonstration of why we have to look to different people for reform; we cannot ask the beneficiaries, despite the most noble of intentions, of a closed society to open it up. The personnelists (in government, academia, and consulting firms) whose profession is based on the bureaucratic system will not de-bureaucratize government. Union leaders whose existence depends on complicated personnel and management systems cannot be expected to promote simplification. The Congressional sub-groups, bureaucratic fiefdoms, and special interest groups who form mutually beneficial triads have no incentive to expose and replace them with more publicly accountable arrangements. That is why the legislation which passed will require more personnel specialists, enhance the power of senior bureaucrats, and broaden the role of government unions; they reflect their designer's aspirations. Even the media who make their profits from describing the sensational symptoms are unwilling to engage in weighty education of the public about the dynamics of social organisms that need attention.

*The first year's awards have resulted in just such internecine charges.

The confluence of these forces with the 1978 election, politicians needed to claim they passed the Act to take a whack at the bureaucratic monster, insured that no one shouted "the emperor has no clothes." All the principal actors had an interest in maintaining the fiction that a few bandaids were "the greatest reform since the Civil Service Act of 1883." Unfortunately the public will see no improvement in bureaucratic performance. It is clear, therefore, that reform of the public personnel system is too important to be left to personnelists and public officials. The following are examples of why we need to turn elsewhere if our objective is improved government.

Selection

Early in this century personnel offices were charged with processing the paperwork for putting on the payroll new people that the boss had hired or with interviewing lower level employees that management had no particular interest in. As bureaucratic structures multiplied and their management became less personal the personnel office began to have more influence. This was particularly true in the public sector where the mandate was to maintain a politics-free merit system. The number of applicants necessitated expeditious mechanisms for sorting them out "objectively" and by World War II the testing business was well underway. As the calls for more sophistication placed greater pressure on the personnelists, they did the natural thing. They said, "We've got it." From measuring mechanical skills they moved to claim success in predicting interpersonal effectiveness, leadership, analytic ability and a whole host of other intangibles. As the demand increased for better selection tools, they met it with jargon, statistical validations, and sleight of hand. Their products were not too critically examined by managers, who were simply looking for something to take the responsibility off their backs, and if a little hocus-pocus would do it so much the better, particularly if there was still room for the exceptions in which the managers had a personal interest. But a little leeway was a dangerous thing. With more scope and public credibility, derived from being dubbed professionals, the personnelists began to do organizational studies that allegedly showed the need for better selection devices and not just for entry, but for periodic assessments at various rungs in the career ladder.

In this area a great overselling job has been done. Two factors are ignored: (1) We do not know what our organizational needs will be 10 to 15 years from now. (2) We really do not have simple tools to measure current human effectiveness in organizations, much less predict it for the future. By being blind to the magnitude of our ignorance we are seduced into accepting partial answers to whole problems and palliatives for our doubts. We accept the superficial labels given as a result of selection machinations and many people are stuck with them for life. Even if all the psychometric tools were much more valid than they are we should question their use simply because they *ipso facto* absolve organizational leaders and individuals from assuming responsibility for their own acts.

One of the manifestations of this perspective is the behavior sampling in the assessment center technique. This approach has individuals engage in a variety of activities which may include role playing, problem solving, communication scenarios, planning sessions, etc. All these activities allegedly relate to job requirements, although the exercises used by experts vary little from one organization to another. Long term promotion, placement, and training decisions are made on the basis of the score cards collected from observers.

The central assumption in this approach to enhancing institutional performance is that one can clearly identify personal traits and skills for future performance and discern their existence or the potential for them in people through the use of psycho-social tests. Inordinate faith is placed in our ability to isolate these variables. To relate them to a few personal behaviors manifested in a hypothetical setting shows little regard for the influence of different environmental and co-worker factors on future behavior.

This current hot sales item also has the invidious effect of placing another device for self-replication in the hands of personnelists and managers who are inevitably the current products of the ineffective institutions that bedevil us all.

By believing in the selection-system labels we set up a series of self-fulfilling dynamics on the part of all involved that insures the "picked" safe people will get the choice opportunities that lead to the top, and no one can ever know whether some of the "left-outs" would have done just as well or better. This phenomenon occurs throughout the government service where people are selected into "tracks" or other special treatment categories. As the world changes around this system, it is unlikely that the organization's leadership will be able to adjust, since the selection process is one of self-perpetuation, and the opposite of the objective of the personnel system occurs, the wrong kind of person is most often in a crucial position at an important time. The person molded for the job has been shaped to fill a need that has already disappeared.

Evaluation

Evaluation is a function related to selection, but in the public sector it is also a "periodic appraisal of performance." On each employee there is a file in which at least once a year the supervisor's, and possibly other, comments on the individual's work and potential for the future is placed. I am aware of no study of an agency which indicates this type of evaluation system is worth a damn.* The reports are invalid as measures of different qualifications and experience. Consultants and study groups engage in a cyclical process of trying to improve and make them useful to management and employees, but the result is always

*See earlier comments on this aspect of the 1978 Act.

the same: employees resent them and management ignores them when real personnel decisions are made. They are filled out by the hierarchical superordinate, regardless of whether there is a real understanding and appreciation of the work of the employee. If the supervisor wants to maintain good relationships with the subordinate, flattery is used. If the supervisor wants to defame the employee then code words to get around grievances are used to hint at deficiencies. Each system has its own set of insider code words for the negative reports.

This function persists because it is a natural corollary of our faith which says we are intelligent and scientific enough to evaluate people objectively, because it is a good authoritarian control mechanism for the careerists, and because not enough people have had guts enough to stand up and proclaim it the hollow shell it is. It has no overriding positive benefit, but it can still be used as a crutch to prop up negative actions taken by the formal system against individuals and consequently will continue to exist as long as we maintain the pyramidal model. This persists despite the tremendous psychic and time costs and the dysfunctional strain it puts on even fairly normal working relationships. Even in its most benign form the top-down performance evaluation system tends to create a dependent personality type who learns not to make new departures without prior confirmation.

Assignment

The title of this function logically flows from the perspective that shapes centralized, rational management theory, but like so much else in the bureaucracy the concept is upside down. Here is another paradox—to the extent that the central personnel office gets its way the system suffers. Only when individual employees and managers connive to go around the central system and get their own way, particularly in terms of job assignments, is there personal satisfaction and high motivation. Our concern should be to preserve the avenue for personal initiative, making the job placement process compatible with the precepts of a democratic society.

The central "assignment function" has two unfortunate implications for the healthy operation of most organizations: (1) The personnel functionary who has internalized the concept believes that he/she knows better what is best for the individual and the place to which the employee is being assigned. As a result arbitrary decisions, not necessarily in the best interest of either, are made. (2) The individual who comes to view him/herself as the object of such a system waits passively to be manipulated, to the detriment of personal motivation and its impact on work performance.

For many parts of the Civil Service individuals seek their own new jobs through an allegedly competitive promotion process, but the other elements of the bureaucratic system (competitive games and the non-performance related reward system) make that process anything but open and fairly competitive.

The purpose of this section has been to demonstrate why the realities of existing personnel systems pose more obstacles to the development of healthy, self-adjusting and effective public institutions. Instead of making a constructive contribution they have evolved into one of the most significant elements of the bureaucratic problem. Instead of raising people to new heights, they demean them and inhibit their growth. We must find ways to reverse this trend and move toward a view of personnel practices that are facilitative, not controlling.

Basic Structure

Although the basic civil service structure has become the predominant pattern for the federal bureaucracy, during the last half century or more several structural variations have been tried. By structural modifications, I mean those affecting the basic make up and character of the permanent federal work force. A recent and nationally known example of such structural change was the switch to an all-volunteer military service. The ramifications of such a change are far-reaching in their potential impact on overall institutional performance. In efforts to provide for significantly different kinds of organizational outputs several so-called "excepted services" have been established within the federal bureaucracy. They include such units as the Public Health Service, the CIA, and the Foreign Services of five agencies. In all these instances fundamental differences from the Civil Service system were introduced to meet different performance requirements. They include such principles as: (1) Rank-in-person instead of rank-in-job that permits greater job flexibility for both managers and individual employees. (2) Retirement systems that reward willingness to serve under abnormal conditions of service. (3) Independent selection systems that remove most career appointments from the general political/bureaucratic competition for entry into government slots.

While some of these latter structural differences could contribute to a better quality of organizational behavior they are not sufficient to offset or counteract the other bureaucratic elements discussed in Part I which shape so much of our institutional behavior. A flexible job placement capability cannot produce its full potential for high motivation, career enrichment, and appropriate individual growth if it is countered by limited images of individual roles, retarding interpersonal norms, and strangling work procedures and managerial systems. Independent selection processes will not improve much on the typical bureaucracy unless more valid and publicly controlled approaches are introduced into the "excepted services" entry mechanisms.

Another structural change that has been introduced into the bureaucracy in recent years, although not as a result of a conscious national policy decision, is the widespread use of outside consultants. As managers of bureaucratic units have become more and more unable to secure from their own people adequate performance, through the use of contracts and daily consulting fee arrangements, they have turned to outsiders whose performance is not hobbled by the bureaucracy. In most instances the work they perform could and should be done better by people on the inside, except that the latter have been rendered ineffective by the system. This structural innovation has not proved to be satisfactory for a couple of reasons. The outsiders are frequently not well-prepared to deal with the subject matter and spend an inordinate amount of time and energy "catching up" with the bureaucrats with whom they are working. Second, their products are then taken into the bureaucracy for use by the very organism that was incapable of producing it in the first place. There are also problems of insufficient accountability and constructive competition. Under these circumstances it is not surprising that less than optimal use is made of the consultant's products—most of them quickly begin to gather dust on shelves. This example is consistent with so many others already mentioned; potentially constructive concepts cannot be actualized because of the inappropriate bureaucratic base within which they must be developed.

In recent years Congress has been more willing to create independent exceptions to the traditional bureaucratic requirements for funding and personnel controls. Examples in the international affairs sector have been the Inter-American Foundation and Appropriate Technology International; both were created to foster innovative approaches to assisting developing countries. They were given semi-independent and independent boards of directors, respectively, relatively greater flexibility in the use of funds (including the melding of public and private monies), and almost total freedom to design new approaches to personnel management. Within less than five years of its creation the IAF had become very similar to traditional bureaucracies in terms of its internal processes and climate and its products. Although not fully operational at the time of this writing the early institutional plans drawn up for ATI would put it squarely in the bureaucratic mold. While some argue that such a course is inevitable because man's inherent nature leads him to bureaucratic patterns, I would attribute it to the paucity of alternative concepts in the intellectual repertoires of the organization builders and their psychological inability to break new ground. Even when given the freedom to break out of bureaucratic bonds people cannot easily do so without the existence and acceptance of new road maps.

Another way to radically change the structure of a bureaucratic unit is to significantly increase the ratio of political appointees to career employees. This has been done in some isolated units, but more with a view to controlling the bureaucracy than enhancing its institutional capacity. There are also other problems with this approach to structural change. The appointees suffer from the internecine constraints of partisan power politics and the intragroup jockeying for power and advantage. While recognizing the potency of this structural variation, I do not believe it offers a satisfactory alternative to the present bureaucracy. Substituting partisan politics for bureaucratic games is like changing from the firing squad to the hangman; they are both fatal.

After that little bit of sermonizing (written after a particularly trying day of discussing a reorganization plan with a neophyte political appointee and a curmudgeonly old bureaucrat, neither of which, for different reasons, wanted to reveal his real objections to an employee-developed proposal) let us now turn to consider how the six factors were involved in one attempt at institutional renewal.

Kissinger and the Department of State: Scuttle Diplomacy[5]

Each generation of politicians comes to Washington with a briefcase full of platform promises and policy objectives. These intentions lead to a process that includes preaching and cajoling by the politicos and cooptation and socialization by the bureaucrats. This engagement usually results in a stand-off, regardless of whether the issue is policy or process.

The more perceptive elected or appointed political executives realize that the accomplishment of some institutional reform is necessary if they are to be effective in influencing public policy over the long term. They know the bureaucracy has the data which shapes the framing of issues and alternatives and in its acts of implementation will determine the success or failure of those policies chosen. Henry Kissinger came to government with this kind of understanding and made some attempts to have an impact on one Department. Therefore his tenure at the State Department makes an instructive case for a review of the classic confrontation between the political executive and the bureaucracy. The fact that it is not typical, he had more power, charisma and insight than most department or agency heads, simply underlines the obdurate nature of the problem. As will be seen, he also was one of his own greatest obstacles. Nevertheless, the case illustrates the primitive state of organizational reform knowledge and skills among Washington's executives and bureaucrats.

Kissinger talked often of the need to "institutionalize foreign policy." He had written profoundly on the problems of bureaucracy prior to his entry into government service. In 1966 he demonstrated a clear recognition of (1) the inevitability of institutional influences on foreign policy decision making in the nuclear age, (2) the stultifying influence of bureaucratic processes on problem solving, (3) the large role of career officials, and (4) the rigid, backward-looking, and mediocre orientation of bureaucratic behavioral norms.[6] His critique gave a good description of the symptoms, but demonstrated no clear understanding of the causes and offered no prescription for change. Subsequent events suggest that he was more able at diagnosis than prescription, better as a critic than manager.

Personalized decision making was preordained by the views set forth in Kissinger's subsequently widely publicized and analyzed *Daedalus* article. He saw the bureaucracy as an obstacle to policy innovation, particularly when questions of changing strategy for the future were involved. He expressed the view, which he has since often repeated, that the institutional decision making process was so complicated and disgorging a policy so painful that little energy was left to later revise it when change was called for.

Given this view of bureaucracy, a view reinforced by the managerial philosophy of the Nixon Administration, it is not surprising that his approach to foreign policy did not include a profound role for the established institutions. His inclination was to go it alone instead of risking the perils of ineffective organizations.*

Decision making in the Department ground to a halt when he was away and only papers from the trunk on his plane or telegrams to it could result in action approvals. The sheer volume of decisions reserved to him insured that they could only get limited attention. Very few subordinates could speak for him. Seeming to believe the bureaucracy was not attuned to him, he tried to keep as much action as close to his personal signature as possible. While a logical short-run tactic from his secretive perspective, it may prove to have been the most significant hindrance to his effort to leave an institutional legacy. Let's now review his actions in the institutional impact categories described earlier.

Right People

Kissinger's personnel selection practices went through an interesting metamorphosis. His early appointees in the National Security Council were bright, young, energetic men of conviction (including FSOs) who gave him the capability to run circles around the State Department, yet by the time he left State eight years later most of his top advisors were disciplined career personnel.

Instead of such appointments energizing the career service, most officers at lower levels felt themselves cut off from their few colleagues in the inner circle. The appointments were not always seen as constructive examples for a Service that many perceived to be at its best when led by inner-directed professionals. There was frequently not a perception that merit had been rewarded and that the best models had been established for emulation.

---

*What he did in both the White House and the Department is well-known and needs only illustration here: (1) First trip to the People's Republic of China in July 1971 without the knowledge of the State Department. (2) On-the-spot, shuttle diplomacy decisions in the Middle East and elsewhere without reference to the bureaucracy. (3) Back-channel communications with Moscow during the SALT negotiations that left his negotiators in Geneva in the dark.

The individuals so chosen considered themselves to be either explicitly or implicitly charged with the responsibility of only carrying out the Secretary's wishes. Frequently they seemed to act because he had ordered it, not because of personal commitment of the type that stems from participating in a decision. The period reinforced the narrow concept of disciplined "professionals."*

In two appointment decisions of organizational significance, Kissinger, after over a year on the job, named new people to the positions of Deputy Undersecretary for Management and Director General of the Foreign Service. He appointed people he knew and had worked with. They were given the mandate to revitalize the State Department's general management and personnel functions respectively.

Both came to their new positions with considerable Foreign Service and Washington experiernce, but with no sigificant management expertise. They were both highly motivated and desirous of bringing about improvements in the system, but they failed to put together the type of staff required to develop an effective action program. The few well-qualified career management professionals in the Department were not used and appropriate outsiders were not called on either. The task of conceiving, designing, and implementing constructive organizational change strategies fell to persons with limited training, experience, and capabilities in the requisite fields. As a result of this lack the overall organizational response to Kissinger's other institutional initiatives was very limited.

Reorganization

Modification of formal organizational relationships was relatively limited during Kissinger's three and one-half years as Secretary. Despite a widespread judgment that dramatic changes were required in the government's mechanism for dealing with international relations, and his own statements to that effect, Kissinger failed to pay much attention to large organizational questions. He ignored a Joint Congressional-Executive study (the Commission on the Organization of Government for the Conduct of Foreign Policy, aka "The Murphy Commission") that recommended significant changes. Very little was done to adjust the organizational structure to the changing nature of the environment that Kissinger's speeches so well described: the increasing inter-relatedness of problems, the merging of domestic and foreign issues, the new agenda of diplomacy, and the changing nature of public expectations.

---

*Kissinger himself seemed to have mixed feelings about it; at times he called for individualism and dissent and yet his behavior often negated what he said.

Management Systems

Kissinger set up a Policy Priorities Group (PPG),* including the Deputy Under Secretary for Management and other central figures such as the Director General of the Foreign Service and the Assistant Secretary for Administration. Its responsibility was to review the allocation of funds and positions and relate resource use to global policy priorities. It developed a Policy Analysis and Resource Management System (PARM) which was tried out worldwide in 1977 and replaced earlier instruments designed for similar purposes. PARM was similar to the management systems discussed earlier and had about the same less than salutary impact. The Inspector General and his staff were given a role in the assessment of the relationship between staffing and policy priorities. These changes had very little impact on overall policy development and program performance; decision making on resource allocations was simply raised from the Assistant Secretary to the Deputy Under Secretary level.

Personnel System

Use of the formal personnel system was apparently seen by Kissinger as a way to have some institutional impact. On the basis of an in-house report and the advice of his career advisors, he decided to make some changes in the personnel system. In a speech to a new FSO class in June 1975, he called for minor changes in the FSO examination procedure; the establishment of standards and competitive process for hiring non-FSOs; an increase in employment of women and minorities; a strengthening of the promotion system by adding screening thresholds at both junior and senior levels; an improved assignment process; an improved Departmental training program; and provision for greater outside experience for FSOs.

Although Kissinger billed them as "reforms," they could hardly be characterized as anything but minor adjustments to the system. Not all the changes were implemented and those that were have had little impact on the substantive performance of the Department.

No one ever seriously addressed the myriad and interrelated managerial, experience and reward factors that would require modification to effect a change in the general quality of overseas and departmental performance.

Training

Little was done in the formal training area, but Kissinger did attempt to

---

*The concept was developed by the author as part of his role in the departmental task force on institutional change.

enhance the ability of officers to recognize the interrelationships of events and to place them in a global context through a career development change. Kissinger recognized the need for greater skill, but too quickly concluded it was caused by too many tours in one area. The result was GLOP (Global Outlook Program) which was the establishment of a percentage formula to insure officers moved around the globe in a series of assignments. Whether in fact the assignment pattern was the most important underlying cause of the analytic myopia is a question that was never adequately studied.

Structure

No formal structural changes were made under Kissinger, but his staff did start a process of revising the relationship between the excepted Foreign Service and the Civil Service groups in the Department (later formalized by the Carter Administration).

It is not possible to predict the impact of Kissinger's actions on specific issues of future policy, but it is possible to identify certain elements of institutional life that were directly affected by organizational interventions and project some of their general policy implications.

The level in the organization at which decisions got made was raised even higher than is normal for a bureaucratic hierarchy. Raising the approval level had two negative effects on decisions quite apart from their specific content: they were slower in getting made and all the alternatives were worn off in the compromising clearance process. By drawing so much to himself Kissinger reinforced two facets of the bureaucracy that he had so often criticized: the cumbersome process and the cautious outcomes of decision making.

As State Department officers came to understand that he wanted his personal imprint on policy it became more and more productive from a bureaucratic point of view to give him what he seemed to want the first time, thereby reducing the consideration given to alternatives. In these areas his managerial style had a direct impact on the substance of policy. But perhaps of more importance was the depressing impact of Kissinger's approach on the attitudes and motivations of employees, and on the amount of energy and dedication they would devote to a task.

The system innovations such as the Policy Priorities Group and PARM provided a framework for significant change in substantive outcomes, but several necessary ingredients were lacking. The introduction of a new global priorities system alone, without solid analysis and managerial will, could not overcome the outmoded geographic and largely bilateral orientation of the Department. Resource, environment, population, and social problems remain underattended and the identified need for a global perspective is yet to be translated into an organizational force.

The personnel system of the Department, which is widely described as inappropriate to today's challenges, remained unimproved during Kissinger's tenure despite the public fanfare. The few changes attempted may prove to have been more dysfunctional than constructive. Inasmuch as they did not bring about visible improvement they tended to decrease employees' faith in the system and its ability to facilitate their work.

The reasons for this failure are legion, but the lack of a clear picture of the challenge is not one of them; Kissinger articulated it very well.

His many speeches on the new agenda of diplomacy and the convergence of foreign and domestic policy have widespread institutional implications. Kissinger appeared to understand them and relate them to the need for a redefinition of the Department's role or mission. He called such a redefinition "the first phase of institutionalization." He characterized the new institutional challenge as nothing less than "reconciling the increasingly complex and interrelated domestic and foreign policy issues." Although he articulated the need well, forcefully, and repeatedly, he did not develop a useful prescription for dealing with it. Neither has the career leadership been able to relate such a new conception of need to the real world of workable and appropriate plans for organizational change. Reactions have been simplistic and superficial, taking the grafting or incremental approach instead of a strategy of profound reshaping of the organization.

It is a great irony that a leader who understood the weaknesses of modern bureaucracies and the need for institutional change found it impossible to bring about the necessary changes when placed in charge. In his attempt to avoid getting mired in the bureaucracy, he left it to its own fate and by his style discouraged those on the inside from rising to the challenge and trying renewal from within. The opportunity costs have been considerable.

An Impasse

The Kissinger case exemplifies the confluence of factors which result in the never ending impasse between reform initiatives and bureaucratic inertia in Washington. No single actor bears the total responsibility. Executives come with a clear vision of the symptoms, with determination to make progress, but without either the conceptual or personal skills to carry them out. Many bureaucrats share the leadership's desire for reform, like several of Kissinger's key appointees, and attempt to institute apparently constructive changes, but they lack awareness of the elements of effective strategies and do not enjoy the support of most of their colleagues who opt for the *status quo*. The latter engage in scuttle diplomacy and join forces, frequently unwittingly, with the few who seek only personal advantage from playing the games of the current system.

The deficiencies in the six categories of change techniques most often tried result from a lack of understanding of the dynamics of social organisms and the manner in which constructive change can be stimulated within them. They are based on general analyses of causes that are hardly more than descriptions of the problematic behaviors themselves. By not taking into account the multiple factors, including basic perception-shaping ideas, that lead to the behaviors in the first place the design and ultimate impact of any change strategy is bound to be limited.

Those who propose upgrading the personnel function ignore the impact of structure and ongoing systems that if not initiate at least perpetuate the ineffectual behavior so well documented by writers like Chris Argyris. Those who favor manipulation of the squares on the organization chart never spell out how the human resources are going to be induced to break truly new ground and carry out the higher level of performance they call for. And both groups almost totally ignore the role of self-images, psychological attitudes, and strongly held assumptions in shaping the structure, climate and performance of organizations. For example, Allison and Szanton, in their book on the foreign affairs sector[7] completely ignored the process of ideational and psychological change required to get from the *status quo* to the desired new quality of institutional performance. They and most other advocates of reforms appear to believe that it is possible to excathedrally ordain that public servants transform themselves.

To overcome the deficiencies of the approaches discussed here two things are necessary: A rethinking of the specific behavioral implications of the various recommended actions—do they in fact result in the opposite of what is desired? Adoption of a holistic, comprehensive framework that places specific changes into a total organism context.

Those in leadership positions must come to realize on a more fundamental level that significant institutional improvement will come from where the problems do, from the thoughts and feelings of thousands of employees who must cope with living their personal lives and still be able to make a contribution to the commonweal. Why does such a simple truth escape public notice? Perhaps it is because the channels for additions to public knowledge are dominated by those on the outside who make their living as experts (academics and consultants) or merchants (publishers). Both groups must sell products including tests or techniques that can be packaged, or "ideas" and "understandings that are so complicated organizations must pay the consultants to continually explain them to employees." Outsiders, who look for consultant or student registration fees, have a vested interest in perpetuating the idea that public employees are incapable of throwing off the yokes of simplistic myths, onerous rules and regulations, ill-fitted supervisors, and make-do tasks. People on the inside who try to publish must also get that work accepted by the editorial boards of the aforementioned experts. Public administrators and level after level of managers have the same vested interest in keeping anyone from calling the hand of those who deal in incrementalism within the *status quo*. And alas, I must confess, so do many of my former colleagues who have become habituated to letting someone else do their on-the-job thinking for them, while they pursue their own personal sidelines from the office desk. My subjective impression is, however, that the withdrawal symptoms would not be too great and many of them would be willing to be freed, if given half a chance.

When it was possible, in our early expanding society, to create new, relatively independent institutions politicians could exercise considerable influence on the future course of events. But the constraints of our current bureaucratic overload, in terms of both its demand on the society's resources and its ability to ensnarl and sap any new initiative, make such singular acts of leadership almost impossible. Unfortunately, it has been only dimly perceived that we are in a different ballgame. Individuals who aspire to lead our society through the travail of our 3rd Century must comprehend and learn how to redirect our existing institutional base. It will not go away of its own volition and direct action cannot harness it. Limited in their scope of action, future leaders are obliged to look inward for new alternatives.

We know what is required is a real "zero-based review," but what is currently being passed off as a modern budget process under that label does not provide it. We do not have a workable blueprint for that review, and trying to link it in to ongoing bureaucratic process is the wrong approach. We know that attempting to impose change from central management through bureaucratic channels just does not work either. It is like overloading the horse to cure his lameness. There is another thing we have learned—we do not know how to covertly change the basic way people behave in organizations. Our knowledge and skills are not sufficient to the task. And even if we knew how, we should not try. The very act would be denying our government what it needs: self-starting, independent people who are in control of their own lives, sure of themselves and masters of their own fates.

Many individuals and groups within and outside the government are motivated toward profound reform and possess the requisite energy, but at this point their efforts are inchoate and a conceptually sound and reality-oriented framework is required to focus their energy.

Even this chapter's superficial review of ineffectual, piecemeal approaches to reform or institutional renewal clearly indicates we need a more comprehensive and integrating concept of social organisms. We need to draw lessons from the efforts gone awry and assimilate their implications for breaking new ground. We must try to go below the surface, suppressing our proclivities for the linear logic of social science analysis and the straight-line correlations of cause and effect that is the stock-in-trade of organizational psychologists.

To overcome the inadequacies of our organizational theories, we must make a giant leap forward in our analytic and predictive tools. As tinkering with the bits and pieces fails we should go back to the drawing board and look at the whole. Chapter 6 is my effort to make a contribution to that rethinking.

Surprisingly what has been lacking has been an historio-anthropological trek backward, looking at the basic concepts around which the institutions were built and tracing those images and assumptions involved to their present day ramifications. Instead of a quest for the interplay of techniques and specific organizational acts we need an investigation of the images "movers and shakers" have about themselves and others. Perhaps we are not in search of a science or theory about control of organizations, but seek an understanding of how beliefs about people shape our formal social regimes. Maybe we are in need of a pattern of study that examines the fallacies and binds in current answers to existential questions about the social nature and purpose of the species *homo sapiens.* Such a journey into the seminal and thought shaping facets of the federal bureaucracy is, in my view, the only way to build hypotheses for attempting 3rd Century institutional reform.

6
Theory for Analysis and Action

> Knowledge will forever govern ignorance, and a people who mean to be their own governors must arm themselves with the power knowledge gives.
>
> James Madison, Father of the Bill of Rights

After several years of being involved in attempts to improve the State Department's personnel system, reform the Civil Service, increase the effectiveness of international programs, and strengthen internal management in many federal offices, I began to realize I had no hypotheses which made sense out of my organizational experiences. My academically learned constructs, the basic ideas with which I tried to interpret government life, left large contradictions in reality. The experiences my colleagues and I had almost led us to believe there was no order in bureaucracy, despite the office wit's comment that its order was disorder. We could not explain much of the group and individual behavior in the bureaucracy or the lack of success we and others had in coping with it through use of our conventional organizational concepts. The only way bureaucracy seemed to be definable was to ascribe to it such terms as "junglelike," "Frankensteinian," etc. While emotionally satisfying in times of frustration such labels did not point toward effective action.

We had no intellectual framework that enabled us to arrive at an actionable understanding of the frequent opposite effects of our conscious system manipulations. We needed better concepts to explain the bureaucratic personality and the games that comprised its stock in trade. We wanted to understand the reason for incongruence between a bureaucrat's espoused theory of management and his/her actual behavior. For example, how does one explain why managers call for creativity and initiative from employees and then act as if their real intentions were to stamp them out? As observers of both the initial assertions and the subsequent behavior we were left confused.

As different jobs challenged me to understand and resolve various organizational problems I began to search for alternative theories and hypotheses to make order out of this apparent chaos. I went through the textbook schemas or models people have used in research and management consulting in organizations. Finding none very satisfactory I became convinced that we needed a more all-encompassing, yet not too complex framework for viewing formal organizations. This chapter is the result of my effort to deal with that lack in a manner that seems to meet my needs.

Years in the government bureaucracy led me to understand it was not adequate to talk about it as an organization; in fact it is almost a society or culture unto itself. Consequently, instead of the typical organization model, with its focus on two-dimensional and temporary arrangements of people and functions, we need a different set of concepts if we are to better understand and guide the public bureaucracy. The bureaucracy is more than a group of people joined in a common effort, linked together by telephone wires. It is ideas, needs, and goals with a lot of activity aimed at giving them life. It is people, structure, environment, tasks, technology, etc. It is a phenomenon in time and space, yet apart from them. To understand it we need an anthropological approach rather than a "human relations" or "systems" view. We must combine the insights of psychology, sociology, and other disciplines into a perspective which sees the mammoth public bureaucracy as a social organism that is the aggregate of large parts of the personalities of its members and has a force of its own, which reciprocally has significant influence on the total lives of those involved. We must expand Philip Selznick's[1] concept of social organism introduced in 1957. Only with such a fleshed-out view finder that more realistically focuses our perceptions can we define our problems in useful terms and design more effective remedies.

Organizational Models

Ironically mechanistic computer models of various kinds have helped us more accurately perceive the multifaceted and interrelated nature of large social systems. The simple capacity to manipulate massive amounts of seemingly unrelated data in a manner that demonstrates interactions makes the complexity of real life more believable and comprehensible to us. For example, the combining of economic modeling theory with an anthropologist's case study method suggests a more holographic approach to the analysis of social organisms or subcultures. Most social science based organizational research to date has dealt with only two or three links in a complex, interactive chain of reality, and frequently those factors were not contiguous or mutually influential. Such research has been conceived with too simplistic notions about the elements of organizations.

Since Max Weber's description of bureaucracies with formal, impersonal, rational and essentially structural concepts (whose translations left Americans thinking in terms of triangles with neatly drawn lines and boxes) we have improved our understanding of their nature. But there is still a long way to go, and as we attempt to restructure the "eyeball" with which we have looked at organizations it is important to reflect on the patterns which have accumulated there. It is necessary to clarify how we have been thinking before we can think new thoughts; a selected, but illustrative review follows.

Frederick Taylor and others in the 20s who took the Weberian paradigm and assumed it was scientifically developed rather than superficially descriptive, tended to see organizations as mechanistic. Human organizations were considered susceptible to being systematized and engineered. The Tavistock School in England later developed a socio-technical model of organizations. It tried to take account of both the social context and the state of the technological environment in which the organization exists. Lawrence and Lorsch of the Harvard Business School took cognizance of the importance of both individuals and process in their definition: "An organization is the coordination of individual contributors to carry out planned transactions with the environment."[2]

Harold Leavitt in 1964 combined all these components into his organizational model illustrated below:[3]

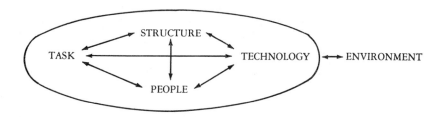

The importance of this approach in the evolution of our thinking is not its effort to cover the whole waterfront, but its indication that each organizational element interacts with all others and that any variable could be an obstacle to change. Leavitt used this model in developing organizational change strategies for industry.

Charles Perrow[4] took us further with his sociological perspective. To environment, technology, structure, and tasks, he added values, goals, and the impact of recruitment policy as important elements that define the nature of an organization. Rensis Likert and Douglas McGregor, among others, emphasized human relations variables that are crucial in determining the effectiveness of an organization. George Litwin went even further and developed a fairly comprehensive operational definition of a phenomenon called organizational climate. It included such categories as clarity of roles, goals and communications; type of rewards and recognition; performance standards and expectations; quality of organizational framework; and the nature of responsibilities.

Each of these accretions to the conceptual understanding of the nature of organizations has added more refined diagnostic and prescriptive tools to the repertoire of both the researcher and the practitioner. But all the building blocks are still not in place. Our horizons must be broader still and the magnification of our microscopes increased many times before we will be able to understand and cope with our social inventions to the degree that we can our physical ones.

Various people are now studying such things as small group dynamics and decision making. Others are considering the role of values and much research has gone into the influence of psychological needs or motive profiles on behavior in organizations. Information systems and communications theory are other approaches under development. But thus far the various efforts have been too isolated from each other.

These limited models have nevertheless shaped the course of research, the behavior of managers, and the development of perspectives people have of their own organizations. They have in effect determined how all concerned with life in modern bureaucracies have thought about them; in doing so the concepts have shaped reality. Unfortunately they have been too limited, too fragmented, and misleading as to the potential we have for conscious, effective change.

Small steps are being made toward better understanding of the multi-faceted and interactive internal dynamics of organizations, but the integration of insights from different disciplines is still lacking.

Anthony Downs in 1967, gave us two helpful ideas: the concept of organizational layers of reality with varying degrees of permanence and its implications of their related levels of resistance to change. He postulated four layers, from deep to shallow: general purposes, institutional structure, decision making rules, and specific actions.

He posited a directional character to the influence of change in the layers that is helpful, but inadequate:

> Change can occur at any depth without effecting layers of greater depth, though it will normally affect all shallow layers—but if (the organization) adopts new purposes, all the other layers will be significantly effected.[5]

We now understand that it is not a uni-directional process, but that change at any level reverberates with varying degrees of strength in all directions; stimulating further change or reinforcing the *status quo*.

Downs goes on to correctly point out, "the high cost of changing deeper layers creates personal and organizational inertia." The more profound things are the more difficult they are to change, and the most profound of all is an individual and/or organization's sense of purpose.

Now various people are writing about the reverse impact. The kind of person you are, and consequently your sense of purpose, is, to a large degree, a function of the kind of place in which you work.

Michael Maccoby[6] describes how the socialization process acts on employees, perhaps even in unseen ways such as dulling the intellect, hardening the heart and freezing the emotions. He points out that the necessity of adapting to the organization affects one's mental, emotional and spiritual health. The individual who joins an organization to affect it and its products finds the tables reversed. Maccoby labels this nexus psychostructure: the context in which the needs of the organization for work activities and the needs of human beings come together in a way that reshapes both the dynamics of character and the mode of work.

Rosabeth Kanter moves us further along by identifying specific structural and procedural variables that help shape attitudinal and behavioral factors, but she has not given enough attention to the reciprocals: self-images and assumptions. She does not explore the circular binds that afflict all employees and perpetuates the vicious cycle, but she has immeasurably improved our appreciation of the complexity of organizational reality-shaping dynamics.

Kanter, in describing this interactive process, writes:

> What I am suggesting is that the job makes the man—and the woman. People bring much of themselves and their histories to their work, but I think we have overlooked the tremendous impact of an organization's structure on what happens to them once they are there.[7]

Now that we have begun to see the circular nature of organizational reality, rather than approaching it in a linear fashion, deciding to do action "A" to bring about condition "B", we can heed Michel Crozier's advice and enhance "the ability of men to break out of the bureaucratic vicious cycle."[8]

To serve that objective is why I wrote this chapter. Its aim is to force us to look at "C" and its relationship to both "A" and "B" and their relationship to it, as well as to each other and to "D" and "E." We have been too long stuck on the idea that "A" causes "B" and have developed large numbers of explanatory equations which have structured our search for solutions to organizational problems. Until we are willing to expand some of these approaches we are doomed to continue "careening," without control of our own destinies and those of our social institutions.

Flawed Application

The essential error is not in the existence of various theories and models, nor in the elementary state of our knowledge, but in the overzealous use of them by personnel managers and consultants who call themselves "organizational doctors." Such concepts are used by people with the power as managers and shapers of human resources. And therein lies the fatal flaw. If such partial research "findings" were written only for explicitly speculative discussions, we would have no cause for concern. Unfortunately, they are taken as "truth" and enter into the never-ending circular process of co-creation by which widely held concepts shape the reality of important institutions.

One such example of the inadequacy of artificial, abstract, fragmented approaches to the understanding of organizations is David Garnham's 1975 article on Foreign Service elitism.[9] (I chose this article as an example because of its relevance to Chapter 4, not because it is particularly bad or particularly good. It simply epitomizes much of the current pseudo-scientific approach to organizational study.) After a tortuous, statistics-studded journey through arcane definitions and data he arrived at the totally misleading conclusion that "Foreign Service elitism probably has little or no impact upon the conduct of U.S. Foreign affairs."

Garnham followed the typical social science research design when he collected biographical data on a sample of officers, asked them a series of questions about their attitudes, and compared the answers of various sub-groups of the sample. The biographic factors included were region of birth, father's occupation, religion, and educational institution. Since the officers' answers to the "psychological" questions were relatively homogeneous, the researcher concluded elitism (in biographical terms) did not have an impact on organizational performance. He completely ignored the reality of the socialization process, the impact of self-concepts on behavior, and the implications of a group's psychological set for organizational procedures and products.

Unfortunately for the rest of society, social scientists have contrived a defense against this genre of lay criticism. That defense rests on the assertion that the operational definition of one variable or the other used by the researcher must be accepted. Obviously if one accepts that *a priori* assumption, *and* the validity of the instruments, *and* the validity of the methodology, then one is boxed in by the time the conclusion is unveiled. Regrettably it is so often the case that the whole house of cards has nothing to do with reality, which in this instance is the Foreign Service and foreign policy making.

Psychological Theories

During the last two decades organizational leaders have been turning more to the field of psychology for assistance in improving performance. This has been a result of the trend toward human relations techniques, away from the earlier scientific management focus. For the most part these organizational psychologists have fallen into two groups: the determinists and the behaviorists. The former is personified by Sigmund Freud and the latter by B.F. Skinner.

In the quest for constructive change or increased organizational effectiveness, the behaviorists manipulate formal systems, trying to influence indirectly employees' behavioral patterns, while the determinists attempt to control directly people's behavior. The former treat us as Skinner's white mice, rearranging the maze and readjusting the rewards, and the latter relate to us like the proverbial Sunday School teachers. The determinists and the scientific management people collaborated nicely. They set up complex systems to control unreliable man and gave us our present mechanistic approach to personnel management. The behaviorists have more or less accepted the formal system in place in government, but suggest that we rearrange the details to elicit the desired behaviors. Consultants, representing these two schools of thought, have blossomed and are engaged by each new generation of government managers to impose one version or the other. For example, in the Department of State a new outside "expert," with a different technique, has been hired [to try his hand] on the average of every two years since 1965; no cumulative progress has been made.

The two schools suffer from the same fault; they pretend a level of knowledge about the human personality which social reality does not confirm. They assume causal principles for which there is little or no evidential support. They devise training or other group activities that appear to cure one symptom or other but never deal with the whole.

Determinists and behaviorists assume people are not capable of knowing what is best for themselves. Their treatments are antithetical to people taking responsibility for their own actions. By using them, managers and the experts have convinced employees they are dependent on the system. And with that dependency goes uncertainty and fear that comes when people are not in charge of themselves, insecurity that debilitates, defensiveness that blocks creativity, and a need for approval that feeds on the "safe way" and avoids the risks of individualism. The cures end up weakening the very people they were meant to strengthen.

A third force in the field of social science, the humanistic psychology movement personified by Abraham Maslow, Carl Rogers, and Rollo May, has not yet been influential in the strategies of many public managers. But its perspective, combined with other skills, in an interdisciplinary approach offers some hope for a new era in organizational structures and operations. The views set forth here are compatible with this more positive conception of human potential and the means to social growth.

Thoughtful practitioners and profound theoreticians understand the necessity for looking at things whole, for viewing organizations as indivisible organisms, composed of interacting layers of thought, form, and behavior, inter-locked like a three-dimensional jigsaw puzzle with many other social entities. When one pauses to reflect on this reality the inadequacy of the overspecialized analytic techniques of most social scientists becomes evident.

Instead of accepting the current state of bureaucratic design as immutable, we must devise alternatives; we must reshape the playing board and not limit ourselves to simply lmoving the pieces around. Crozier, in the mid-60s made a strong case for the view that "evolution towards large-scale (bureaucratic) organizations is not so unrelenting as Weber thought." While the realities of current ineffective institutions and the inertial tendency of their members to resist innovation seem overwhelming, particularly when coupled with the misplaced emphasis of most organizational research and management education, there are some rays of hope. Insights have been made in a number of areas of research and thought. They can be applied to our thinking about the "bureaucratic problematique." In the following pages I try to pull together a broader and more integrated framework for addressing the problem of conscious, constructive institutional change. We might call it a holistic approach.

Seeing Reality Whole

A social organism is a composite like music, which is an instrument, a musician, a concept, rhythm, a scale of notes, a key, measures, tune and values. To create a new or improve the quality of an existing concerto one must take into account all the elements. So too must we approach the study and management of social organisms.

The inter-penetration and the interaction of all the elements require that one pay attention to the whole and the way the piece of interest at the moment fits into it. We cannot afford to think and act as if there were isolated fragments in organizations that can be manipulated without regard for the subsequent impact on the whole system. Consequently, any vision of organizations that is useful to analyst and practitioner must be a holographic one—taking into account all of their units and elements and the interrelationships among them.

Managers and students of organizations are caught in a dilemma. In order to think and act with conscious control we must develop abstract concepts that allow us to order reality, but any abstraction is a distortion. Our only recourse is to attempt to construct abstract frameworks that more closely approximate reality than the ones discussed earlier. Since the Western tradition of thought patterns are more two-dimensional and linear than Eastern ones, we have difficulty conceiving of models that are spiral circles that curve back on themselves and are interlocked with untold numbers of similar coils that are all meshed together so that it is impossible to find a beginning and an end or a direct link between cause and effect. The reality of life is that everything affects everything else, that there is no real beginning nor end, that the temporal is related to the infinite, and the boundary between thought and action, mind and matter, is a nebulous one.

Perhaps our difficulty arises from the fact that it is impossible to portray such four or more dimensional concepts on the printed page, which is our major medium of communication about such topics. Maybe with the advent of holographic photography we will soon become more sophisticated. In the meantime, let us try to avoid the traps of linear, two-dimensional, and vectoral thinking by discarding our conventional boxes and charts for a moment as we attempt to visualize the elements that must be included in a holographic model of organizations.

Below is a schematic representation of eight elements, with an indication of their interrelationships and the environmental context, of any relatively permanent social organism. It is an attempt to depict the integrity and interrelatedness of reality and also give a sense of the stronger influence of thought on form than vice versa, without ignoring reverse shaping flows. Other than that, no directional or force priority is intended. I am simply reflecting the fact that we do not know how to portray any better the reality which we only "see through a glass darkly." Conversely, I do not wish to imply that we are simply speculating or creating fanciful concepts. Experience in organizations clearly indicates the existence and impact of these elements. The taxonomy may not be totally discrete, and certainly there are some aspects of reality omitted,* but it seems to cover the major factors of concern to us. It is important to keep in mind that we must move to such new patterns of thought about organizations if we are to progress beyond the current stalemate.

HOLOGRAPHIC MODEL OF SOCIAL ORGANISMS

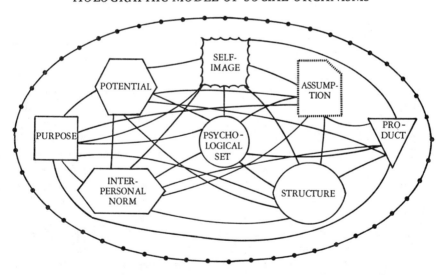

It looks like a mess, doesn't it? I admit that it is somewhat more confusing than the typical two-dimensional model of organizations, but I submit that with

---

*Such as the physical environment and the deep psycho-cultural structure brought to the organization by individuals.

a little explanation it will come to symbolize a general, yet quite useful understanding of the complexity of social organisms.

An organization starts with an idea, a formulation of purpose or objective. Then people are brought together to give flesh and blood and activity to the vision. In this early stage the vision becomes embodied in a group of people who see themselves and their behavior as coterminous with the image. From the moment the group is convened, occupies space, and starts to implement the idea (whose conception was initially an individual intellectual act) the organism is born and assumes a life of its own. The original concept of the creator remains intact only so long as all the members continue to manifest it perfectly. In reality, from the first moment of independent life an organization's members take over the process of creation themselves; the ultimate course is in their hands.

What are the elements then of this living social being as it grows and changes over time? The following pages illustrate some of the specific components of the bureaucracy in a schema that applies to any social organism.

The outer ring represents a permeable and interactive relationship with the organism's environment.

We could start anywhere within the circle, but I will start with the element which I consider the most important: the self-images held by most members of the organization.

Self Images

Some believe "self-image is the key to human personality and behavior. It sets the boundaries of individual accomplishment. It defines what you can and cannot do. Expand the self-image and you expand the area of the possible. The development of an *adequate, realistic* self-image will seem to imbue the individual with new capabilities, new talents and can literally turn failure into success."[10]

That may sound a little exuberant to some, but it illustrates the primal influence of a few key personally held visions on all other aspects of the personality. The principle is the same for an institution except that here it is a question of common self-images held by the collectivity of dominant people in it. One can identify a set of such images in any social organism with some history.

The SELF IMAGE is the group's conception of the "sort of people we are." It is built up from explicit beliefs about themselves and others that have unconsciously formed from past experiences, successes and failures, and humiliation and triumphs. The images are also the results of previous actions of the organization, internal dynamics, and the contribution of ideas from the outside that are brought in by the unit's members. When organizations have a long tradition and are relatively closed a distinctive set of images develops that delimits a unique internal perspective among its members; it in effect stands as the essence of the institution.

The SELF IMAGE includes such components as: "The things we do best"; "Our mission in life"; "The *real* objective of our organization"; "Why we are like we are." Therefore, a key quality, in terms of social relations, is the manner in which the self-images reflect class values. These distinctions have very important behavioral implications as we saw earlier in the image of "elitism."

These basic ideas do not have significant influence on the performance of the organization until they are shared by influential people—or large numbers of the membership. The critical mass in terms of behavioral impact, is achieved when enough people internalize the composite self-images to the degree that they become central to members' thought and behavior, bonded to considerable emotion and personal commitment. Over time they may even become articulated and sustained in oral and written form.

To use them as a SELF IMAGE in organizational analysis one must be able to demonstrate that the images are (1) persistent over time, (2) shared, and (3) vested with high personal value. Whether they are based in any sort of objective reality is largely immaterial. Just as the human nervous system cannot seem to tell the difference between a "real" image and an "imagined" one, the impact on organizational behavior is the same. In fact the phrase "real image" may be a contradiction in terms.

Assumption

The ASSUMPTION is composed of dominant, collective assumptions held by members of an organization; it is almost the social organism's equivalent of the individual consciousness. I have treated the conscious views about self separately in the SELF IMAGE but all the rest is subsumed by this element: the knowledge or beliefs about others, the organism's work, its immediate environment and the world. The ethical principles of the group are also a part of this element. It includes both valid information and untested assumptions. Although on an empirical level one may distinguish between fact and fantasy, as far as the social organism is concerned, as long as the dominant members believe in the ASSUMPTION it does not matter which it is; the impact on the institution is the same.

Components of this element include assumptions such as: "People are all......" "The world is going......" "What is really needed is......" "If you do.....then....will happen." "....are the real causes of....problems." "This is the way ....really works."

The ASSUMPTION has been an element of social organisms since man first settled into groups, but up until the last 5,000 years it was comprised of folk knowledge. Beginning around 3,000 B.C. we began to accumulate written data about the ASSUMPTION. And within the last 300 years[11] we have entered an era with a scientific approach to improving it. All three types of knowledge and beliefs now coexist in our federal bureaucracies, but the folk lore and literary aspects still far outweigh the scientifically based component. The reason is twofold: the immature state of the social sciences and the predominance of myths in bureaucracies which are antithetical to systematic self-study and evaluation.

Yet two developments have occurred which impel us to better understand the ASSUMPTION. Within the last two hundred years man has become conscious of the interrelationships of his local social organisms with all the other organisms that make up the planetary social system. (More recently he has begun to recognize more clearly his interdependence with the physical systems of the total biosphere.) He has within this century, realized that the very act of accumulating and manipulating the knowledge about the social organism impacts upon its own evolution. The potential for conscious influence is there and will materialize for good or ill; the choice depends on man himself.

The existence of myths does not mean that the ASSUMPTION components are all invalid. Some of them are and some are not. Those that are valid, congruent with reality, contribute to the overall effectiveness of organizations. Just as with the SELF IMAGE the ASSUMPTION is the product of tradition and the socialization process. It is inculcated and accepted at face value by each new generation until some discordance leads a few to question it. A few individuals may mature and reach a level of psychological autonomy that permits questioning as a matter of course, but for most people a jolting personal experience of incongruency between an ASSUMPTION's myth and an important reality is required to stimulate rethinking. Myth makers are institution builders and myth breakers are institutional revolutionaries.

Psychological Set

It is impossible to precisely rank the eight elements of a social organism according to the importance of their influence on the overall unit character—all of them are inherent and essential—but it is certain that the PSYCHOLOGICAL SET is one of the most important. It is in effect the nexus that channels the translation of thought into action and the reverse filter that screens externalities into mental patterns. It is the emotional gyroscope by which members sense whether a given set of organizational acts or social relationships feels right or not.

There are a number of phrases which convey different aspects of the composite psychological set: emotional stance, attitudes, sentiments, inclination and disposition. What I am attempting to define is the generally preconscious emotional assessment the organism's members have of themselves and the non-rational (affective) stance they take in interacting with the physical and social world about them. It is the feeling perspective as apart from the explicit ideational interpretation of things.

The PSYCHOLOGICAL SET derives from the group's primary images, past experiences, and the input from contemporaneous interactions with the "world." Its shape depends on the diet of ideas and experiences that feed it in a reciprocal relationship that is difficult to dissect in anything more than theoretical terms. Suffice it to say that at a given point in time each member has an institutional SET that both colors his perceptions of the world about him and influences his reactions to the organizational stimuli impinging on him. Regardless of the original source of its various nuances and its intangible nature, the social organism's SET is a primary factor in shaping the realities of group action.

The PSYCHOLOGICAL SET is a value ascribing mechanism that influences the energy load attached to any event. The nature of the components in the SET and their relative strengths comprise a decision-tree hierarchy of response patterns. In other words, the internal structure of the SET strongly influences both the nature and strength of behavioral patterns; it gives priority to one mode over the other.

As with the other elements of a social organism, to be healthy and effective over the long run the PSYCHOLOGICAL SET must possess internal harmony and reasonable congruence with its external environment. It is probably obvious, but perhaps should be made explicit, that not all members of a large and complex organization have exactly the same psychological profiles, but the SET is composed of the dominant collective ones.

If the SELF IMAGE and the ASSUMPTION form the window frame and sash, the PSYCHOLOGICAL SET is the pane; its nature determines how the incoming rays (communication) will be refracted and/or reflected and constrains the view towards the outside. This predisposition influences the employee's approach to life and work in an organization. For example, if they believe themselves to be members of an elite group and assume that their unit is the most advanced around, their SET vis-a-vis another organization will include contempt, or at best a deploring of its dearth of sophistication, and their perception of stimuli from that body will filter through primarily impressions of things that need improvement. A group set with an inferiority complex will see others as successful *per se* and will adopt a submissive attitude in dealing with them.

New ideas influence the PSYCHOLOGICAL SET, but the group's receptivity to new thoughts is constrained by the degree of trust or risktaking that is already present. The degree of trust, of course, has been shaped by previous experience. The experience, in turn, has been limited by formally-assigned roles and basic assumptions about the outside world. And the circle continues.

Interpersonal Norm

The INTERPERSONAL NORM is the set of stylized behaviors and informal procedures within the organism. It is through this element that individuals collectively cope with and adapt to the formal structure.[12] It is where concepts get translated into form. It is the world of behavior and practice, in contrast to theory, structure, or internal mental processes.

Here one finds group standards made more or less explicit—couched in terms like "one does this in this manner"—at least to the point where they are generally understood by all members. Individual hopes are now transformed into realistic expectations—"I know that's what the regulations say, but here's what really happens." Personal, individual proclivities are molded into a general interpersonal style that fits within the formal system.

The manner in which bureaucrats relate to each other to carry on their work has become, like all other elements in the organism, a specialized interpersonal pattern that is quite different from that found in most social settings. Without some stylized mode which is generally recognized by participants as "the way you behave in the office" the other bureaucratic structural and ideational elements simply would not be tolerated. People would say, "To hell with it; this is no place for a human being."

Because there can be some degree of dissociation between "what is required to get along at the office" and what one normally does, the bureaucratic INTERPERSONAL NORM can be accepted. But there is some evidence that over time the office norm will extend itself into the bureaucrat's personal sphere—simply because it is the one used for such a significant and emotionally invested part of an individual's life.

The element INTERPERSONAL NORM is rooted in the ideas of the SELF IMAGE and the ASSUMPTION and it is reinforced by the STRUCTURE. It parallels or is a behavioral manifestation of the PSYCHOLOGICAL SET. It is composed of more or less implicit norms which people slip into as they would a studio smock; if you isolate them and describe them people can immediately recognize them and relate them to their own bureaucratic experience. The fact that they are unnamed in the formal verbiage of the organization makes them no less real.

In searching for a way to intellectually treat the experiential reality of the INTERPERSONAL NORM I settled on the learned behavior concept of "games" discussed in Chapter 3. It appeared to me that it was a term which had already established standing in the public mind and it seemed to convey the idea of special rituals, fully developed, but unrelated to the normal business of living. I therefore took bureaucratic games and used them to illustrate the dysfunctional components of the bureaucratic NORM.

The relative influence of the various elements on organizational performance depends on the particular case, but in general terms the constantly essential variable is the NORM, the behavioral patterns that directly shape organizational outcomes. Without taking them into account, no organizational description or explanation is complete, and no outcome prediction has any chance of being valid.

Structure

The STRUCTURE is the formal system and the element of the model that probably needs the least amount of explanation. In analyzing an actual organization its characteristics are the easiest to define. The STRUCTURE designates what is to be done, who is to do it, and possibly how. By its very nature it has been made formally explicit and is generally available for everyone to see.

Included are such things as the formal hierarchy, with its attendant communication channels and assigned roles; the use of technology; and, most important for this discussion, the official personnel system. Organization charts, titles, office space, prerequisites, clearance procedures, pay categories, written regulations, formal examination, assignment and promotion instruments and processes, and training programs all are components of this element.

Not only the most visible, the STRUCTURE is the most amenable to modification and hence the target of reformers who wish to show visible results and do not have time to wait for profound institutional change. This is not to imply that this element is not important. It is! It has the power to be constraining or facilitative. It may provide the framework and reinforcement for individual or collective action that leads to desired organizational outcomes or it may frustrate the participants and divert efforts to achieve the espoused goals.

In the federal bureaucracy the STRUCTURE is more inhibiting than supportive. It is set forth in tons of written codes, rules, regulations, standard operating procedures, manuals of instructions, etc.

The STRUCTURE, while the most concrete of the elements, is always in a continual state of change in our society, and always in the same direction: increased differentiation and expansion.

Purpose

In chronological terms the first element in the development of a social organism is the PURPOSE. It indicates the reasons why someone took the original creative action to form a new entity. It is the *raison d'etre* and includes such things as aims, objectives, general goals, or the principal role of the unit.

For government organizations, it is the formal charter, the legislative or executive act which authorizes a unit and states the reason therefor. The PURPOSE is fully public and more or less similarily perceived by members and outsiders. It can be discussed with a reasonable degree of certainty that people are talking about the same thing.

This is not to say that the PURPOSE does not get seriously distorted in the implementation, how and when and where it should be carried out. It becomes subject to all the perceptual and attitudinal biases that afflict all ideas, but it at least provides a starting point for creation and development and influences the initial shaping of all other elements in the organism. Later it becomes the reference point against which corrective judgments can be made. It relates directly to the product and provides in general terms its formal specifications. In the discussion of a government bureaucracy PURPOSE will be the overt justification for continuing to provide public funds for its existence.

Product

The product can be broken down into two categories: the formal and the informal, the explicitly desired products and the by-products, those that are sought and those that just happen. But for analytic and management purposes I lump them all together: the products, the end result, the output, the overall performance of an organization. The PRODUCT is composed of those tangible items or personnel activities that non-members of the organism can see and/or touch and recognize as having come from the unit in question. It may be material goods, reports, analyses, decisions, service, information transactions, or any combination of them. The PRODUCT is the sum, a collection of individual products with an aggregated impact.

The PRODUCT is supposed to be derived from the PURPOSE. But all its components form the basis for evaluations of effectiveness and efficiency. Put another way, it is the end by which one assesses whether or not the public and/or members' expectations for the unit are being met. For the owner/taxpayer, it is the bottom line.

Potential

The POTENTIAL is the overall human ability, capacity or power to accomplish the organism's tasks. Its components are the actual resources of an organization—the different kinds of people, their knowledge and skills. The POTENTIAL can be called upon to produce the PRODUCT obviously with the process of performing or producing being influenced by all the other elements. At its most simplistic level are such things as typing and other mechanical skills, the possession of demographic or financial knowledge, the use of a second language, and the ability to elicit cooperative social action.

This element in my spiral model consists of the actual learned or developed capabilities that individuals or groups possess. Here one must distinguish ideas and beliefs held about things from the experienced or confirmable expertise. What is included in this element must be demonstrable and acceptable to others, using common standards. Although all elements can be considered as part of reality, this is the one which, along with the PRODUCT, is most susceptible to external confirmation.

The POTENTIAL sets real limits on performance. Even the best self-images, assumptions, attitudes, working relationships, purposes, support, etc. cannot produce an opera unless members possess the requisite musical skills. But that is an extreme and opposite example of what generally confronts us in the bureaucracy; there the potential (which is constrained by the other elements) usually far exceeds the actual performance.

A Complex Organism

What do all the eight elements mean, taken as a composite? They identify the various aspects of a living social entity. What they are and how they interact give us institutions that can be perceived as integral units of human activity.

By now it should be clear that all the elements of social organisms are intertwined in a multicausal way. While contributing to the other elements the PSYCHOLOGICAL SET is also receiving continuous feedback from the ideational, behavioral, and work product spheres. A confused PURPOSE and poor PRODUCT in turn contribute to low self-esteem, defensive attitudes, cautious inclinations and other negative aspects of the SET but they are not the only causes. One could also make a case for them being the effect.

If one wishes to bring about a change in the PSYCHOLOGICAL SET new concepts and assumptions must be introduced and the processes of the system must be consistent with and supportive of them. If a risktaking stance is desired then the idea of individual initiative and responsibility must be accepted in the organism's INTERPERSONAL NORM, and the STRUCTURE must facilitate creativity and reward it. All of the elements of the organism must be supportive of risktaking before such a disposition pervades the collective set.

This holographic analysis makes it clear that the formal personnel system of an organization is an organic, integral part of the total entity; it is simply a formal embodiment of the organism's dominant self-images and concepts about human reality. The externalities of the structural framework and formal procedures of an organism are no more than a manifestation of the inner visions of the dominant members. In effect the personnel system cannot be out of sync for very long with the rest of the organism.

When one understands this reciprocal, inter-locking nature of social organisms it becomes clear why personnel and other management systems have not been able to serve as effective vehicles for organizational change. With this insight we understand why we cannot excathedrally prescribe a new formal system that will resolve the performance weaknesses of the unit. Any superficial STRUCTURE modifications are quickly defused and bypassed by the traditional attitudes, behaviors, and interpersonal modes known as the "informal" system.

But if the outmoded SELF IMAGE and ASSUMPTION are replaced with more relevant and viable ones, a workable system to implement them will evolve naturally and organically. This is due to the dynamics that operate among the above described elements in any social organism.

Organizations that make up the federal bureaucracy are live social organisms, with all the eight elements, and they behave over time in a predictable way. Their evolution is governed by principles developed in man's long history.

There are several such universal principles in living social units which perhaps are obvious, but should be made explicit as we attempt to create a holistic framework for study of the bureaucracy. The first is an overlapping, permeable, and symbiotic interface that exists between all social organisms and their environment.

Environment Interaction. To attempt to define the environment of an organization is just as difficult an undertaking as the grappling with the definition of the organization itself—requiring comparable time and analytic energy. Since the focus of this book is primarily on the guts of the single institution, I will not try to do justice to the environment, which is after all a composite of myriad organizational entities interrelated in a macrocosmic whole. In this view the environment is the planetary macrocosm and the individual organism, such as the Executive Departments and the Civil Service, is the microcosm. Of course each unit has its own subgroupings so that the taxonomy could go on *ad infinitum,* until the continuum is bounded by the universe and one sub-strand of an individual personality. All this simply to say that one must keep in mind the poorly perceived and unending linkages that characterize human and societal reality if being carried away by unrealistic expectations of understanding and control is to be avoided.

For our purposes here it will suffice to define "environment" as those important general elements in the outside world that most directly impinge on the federal bureaucracy: the President and the White House, the Congress, our Constitution and statutes, influential private sector groups, technology, certain social values and trends, educational institutions, and our international allies and protagonists. The demands these factors place on the organization in terms of work products and behavioral patterns are of immediate concern to the model discussed here. Any one of the eight elements is a potential channel for interaction with the environment.

Integrative Network. The internal elements discussed above are tied together with sinews and conduits of reciprocal influence that cause actions in one part to ripple or flood throughout an organism to eventually have some impact on all other parts, directly or indirectly. This means, in effect, that attempts to manipulate one sector will have some ramifications for the others or at least stimulate reactions that serve to negate or modify their influence.

For example, the values of managers will, to a significant degree, determine how they view the role of certain employees. This in turn will color any diagnosis of organizational problems and influence the shape of their proposed actions vis-a-vis the employees. Those proposed formal remedies will then be filtered through the informal system and the employees' world views before their creation of a final product. The latter may or may not be as originally conceived by the creator of the idea, but the idea has made its influence felt throughout the system as it was also modified in the process. It is like the old game of "gossip" where each person whispers what he has heard to the next one in the circle, except that in a living organization people act on those distorted communications.

Internal Complementarity. There is an essential law of social units that results, over time, in a high degree of complementarity among components within each element. A sadist living with a masochist is an oversimplified example of the kind of symbiotic relationships that must be maintained to hold an organization together. A group of teachers must have students. Bosses must have subordinates. Kings must have servants. Rebels must have reactionaries and on and on.

In organizations these seemingly antithetical individuals and groups co-exist because they all require the overall character of the organization for satisfaction of their own needs. Consequently, they engage in a process of mutual coercion aimed at homeostasis.

Although groups are used as illustrations here, the principle applies to relationships among the components of all organismic elements. By that it is meant that extreme attitudes are offset by countervailing ones, that rigid formal procedures are balanced by informal shortcuts, etc. One possible result of the operation of this principle is an organism completely filled with misfits who match each other's idiosyncracies in a manner that each appetite has its prey. (An isolated, inbred island society I have known was a good example of this phenomenon.)

Components of elements with only one leg will find other one-legged components to prop each other up, complementing their deficiencies. This means social organisms are not naturally self-correcting; they are only self-balancing. They will not necessarily reject a half-baked idea, they will only create an opposing one to offset it. A political scientist colleague was reflecting this principle when he stated our nation cannot effectively resolve 3rd Century problems because counter-balancing special interest groups keep us on our current course of societal decline. The natural evolution of a synthesis, and that is another principle which may operate, takes too long for our collective, conscious creations of government to adapt rapidly enough to cope with the rate of external change in our 3rd Century.

Congruency Principle. Because of the integrative channels of communication that tie all elements of the organization together there also exists a tendency toward congruency and mutual consistency. This means each element is engaged in a process of reciprocation with other elements where the compulsion is to meet each other's expectations, while at the same time maintaining internal integrity. In other words, a degree of overall consistency among the elements almost always exists.

Values get reflected in organizational relationships, which affect behavior patterns, which relate to the quality of work performance, etc. This omni-directional law of congruency permits us to start our understanding of an organization from any point in the cycle. We can observe the structure and predict the values and the images held by the members. We can take basic assumptions and predict the structure and the organization's behavioral norms. This principle means the psychological profile will be compatible with the behavioral element and the informal system, as well as the formal or structural one.

The existence of a relatively static congruency precludes the randomness of behavior of some individuals or groups that is necessary for creative change or evolution. As long as the fit among various segments is too neat there is likely to be little change, and certainly not from the inside.

The content of social organisms may vary, but in all instances the dynamics at work are the same: (1) symbiotic relationships with the environment, (2) omni-directional interaction and reciprocal influence among the eight elements, (3) intra-element complementarity and (4) inter-element congruence.

Self-Correction. I would add a fifth principle, one that does not exist in all social organisms but is found in ones which continue to evolve toward greater fulfillment of their own internal potential and better satisfaction of their external demands. This principle is self-correction, involving the comparison of observable products with the starting beliefs and assumptions. The process reinforces the latter two or throws them or other parts of the organization into question. A fit results in satisfaction. Incongruency leads to a tension that in turn has to be resolved. And the process which never ends starts all over again. This principle is very similar to the concepts of organizational health or effectiveness used by some other writers and may also be the continuing synthesizing process postulated by some. There is some evidence to indicate this principle is only operative at the macrocosmic level. Individual organisms, and particularly those with artificial support from the larger society, may not manifest this trait. Chapter 7 has a fuller discussion of self-correcting organizations.

The Opposite of Conscious Purpose

In taking a holistic approach to the study of social organisms, looking at the intervening elements and their reciprocating cause and effect linkages, one quickly discovers a phenomenon which has been labeled the "opposite of conscious purpose."[13] Simply put, this means that an examination of the behavioral events assumed to follow in time and in sequence from a conscious act are often quite the contrary to what had been intended. The simple, straight line "cause and effect = intention and result" equation that most of us carry around in our heads leads us to expect reality to be different than what it actually turns out to be.

Some illustrations are: A spouse who wishes to retain the love of a partner and lavishes total attention to demonstrate it is surprised to find after a number of years that the distance between the two has increased. An employer wishes to see a new employee grow and gives him daily advice, only to see him become passive and dependent. The apple polisher is usually stepped on rather than embraced. Government funds are spent to increase demand to take up slack in productivity to increase competition to lower prices, but the result is increased inflation. Land grant colleges were set up to strengthen the role of agriculture in American society and ended up weakening it.

When we see our intentions thwarted the tendency is to strengthen our resolve and direct effort rather than question our assumptions or ability to perceive reality. With the desire to protect democracy from communism we have supported the forces that are anti-communist in rhetoric but stamp out democracy in their own homelands. The real effect of this one of our national conscious purposes in the world, to build democratic institutions, seems to have been exactly the opposite: enhanced totalitarianism.

This lesson has been understood in Western society, though not widely applied, for at least 2,000 years. Jesus taught "the meek shall inherit the earth" and "whosoever will lose his life shall find it."

Why does organizational reality seem to be so contrary and out of our conscious control? Why do our organizing principles (hierarchy, span of control, assignment of rules, etc.) give us in government what everyone knows is disorganization? Why do our reward systems produce low morale instead of motivating people? Why does our merit system give us mediocrity?

The problem is not in the dynamics of reality, but in our partial perception of them. We have been unable to see the social organism's intervening elements between purpose and product, particularly the implicit ones which shape implementing steps and directly influence the final outcomes. These counter-indicated results occur because strong beliefs in simple myths prevents critical examination of the operational tenets which are used by people to carry out the espoused intentions. We must get into the murky world of myths and their tenets if we are to identify the basic patterns of thought that block effective reform in the bureaucracy.

Organizational Myths and Tenets

As we begin to move through the morass of modern government bureaucracy in an attempt, intellectually at least, to bring it under control, it is necessary to go back to first principles: the primary self-images and assumptions. In dealing with social organisms such a metaphysical (or metasocial) journey leads us back to fairly simple concepts which have been lost sight of with the accumulation of more recent layers of interpretation and elaboration.

These metaphysical elements transcend the world of acts. They are basic convictions, ideas which have become energized and have the power to move us. They cannot be proved or disproved by the academic scientific method, but they ring true in the recesses of the mind. For example, absolute monarchies with their influence on social, economic and political actions at all levels of society could not have existed so long without the myth of a godly blessing: the belief in a divine bestowal of certain rights on the kings. The paradox is that although they transcend physical evidence these myths shape the world we experience.

The holographic approach to institutions presented in this chapter highlights the crucial role played by these primary images and fundamental assumptions in shaping the reality of organizational life. They include images about the nature of people, assumptions about motivations and concepts about the roles of organizations. They shape thought and action which shape the woof and warp of the social organism. Over time the combination of these images and assumptions evolve into mythical forms—where they become traditional and no longer questioned. They assume an ideological life of their own, influencing thought and action in an even more powerful way than the external reality of the moment.

Myths in this context are assertions whose veracity is simply not seriously or generally called into question. There are some instances where the mythic assumptions may have initially been valid, in an independently verifiable way, but after a time they too are bypassed by changing realities. So our current myths about the federal bureaucracy may be the result of either initial miscalculations or changing circumstances.

For a myth to last for very long it must be reinforced by tenets and practices that appear to support it. The tenets themselves persist because they are conceptually consistent with the myth, so they too are likely to be as fallacious as the overall myth. To evaluate the impact of the myths requires a critique of the underlying tenets as well. There are untold numbers of untested assumptions which should be scrutinized when looking at the mythical underpinnings of bureaucracy.

Examples of program myths are: (1) welfare programs help dependent people become self-sufficient and (2) correctional institutions rehabilitate people. These simplistic assumptions continue to influence the thought and behavior of both employees and the general public despite considerable evidence that has accumulated to the contrary. The nature of welfare programs seems to most often perpetuate the client's dependency relationship to the government, even into succeeding generations, while the traditional prison environment is likely to serve as a training school for increasing the prisoner's repertoire of criminal skills.

One could list several types of commonly held fallacious assumptions that shape human perceptions and behavior (wearing hats causes premature baldness and cancer is contagious), but it is sufficient for our purposes here to simply illustrate their existence. Here we must focus on those that have influence on organizational life.

A simple bureaucratic example is the strong belief in the efficacy of variation in structural personnel categories. In searching for different kinds of thoroughbred performers agencies create bureaucratic personnel structures such as (1) the military rank system, (2) the Civil Service grade hierarchy, (3) the Foreign Service Officers Corps, and (4) the Public Health Service, and (5) many slight modifications to them. Their different labels obscure the fact that all are fundamentally the same, the basic principle being that the individual is supposed to be externally controlled by an omniscient, omnipotent system. The end result is the same kind of bland employees, individuals who are dependent and outer-directed.

One could probably identify a large number of organizational myths that shape the primary images and perceptual patterns of the American collective mind, but five which appear to be most relevant to our discussion of government bureaucracy are discussed below.

Myth of the Pyramid

By this myth I mean the triangular or pyramidal image of organizations captured by Max Weber and simplistically passed on to generations of American students. That the belief that it represents the most effective way to organize tasks and people to perform them in today's government is a misleading myth should be quite evident to the reader by now. While the theory may have some rational appeal it is clear from the discussion in Chapter 3 that its impact is quite different from that intended.

It is an inappropriate image for several reasons. One, it does not even hint at the interrelated complexities of social institutions. It cuts down the way we conceive of the dimensions of human personality. By portraying individuals and units in relationships only to those formally on each side of them it implies that those with such proximity are the most important. Two, it excludes or minimizes the influence of factors other than explicit formal reporting or control relationships on work behavior. An example of the unreal expectations engendered by this concept is the assurance given to me by one Department's Deputy Secretary that the chief-to-chief relationship was the sole key to better integration between the work of two agencies; he apparently really believed the top point of the triangle directly controlled all below. The pyramid concept leads us to believe in, and more importantly it leads the participants to attempt to implement (both by controlling and by accepting control) the diagrammed patterns of interaction, communications, collaboration, decision making, etc. Yet the problems with which organizations must deal refuse to divide themselves into such neat compartments. Nevertheless, we attempt to force them into the mechanistic triangle's constraining rigidities, blockages, delays, and fragmentation of vision, knowledge, and effort. In this view of bureaucracy the influence of personal factors, environment, history, anticipated futures, and cross-cutting processes are not generally taken into account, except by reference to them as exceptions.

Yet in spite of mountains of experiential data to the contrary this simple image has gained the stature of an almost immutably engrained myth in the thought patterns of this society in less than a century. If evidence of its latent potency is needed, one only has to observe the behavior of a new administration's appointees. Although highly critical of the policies and performance of the career government and impatient to make changes, they unthinkingly resort to the long discredited shibboleths of pyramidal thinking in an attempt to direct and motivate it.

The symbols of the hierarchical model (titles, grades, and positions) are shuffled as if one were dealing directly with reality. Aberrations to the clean triangular model which have evolved to better serve specific needs are abolished, seen as threats to bureaucratic order. It usually takes at least three years before the illusion begins to fade, but the myth is embedded so strongly that even then few fundamental questions are raised.

Instead of questioning such concepts as chain-of-command, hierarchy, bureaucratic roles, etc., they only believe that greater pressure or cunning must be used to manipulate them. The basic myth and its tenets form a doubt-resistant conceptual framework that rebuffs fragmented efforts to pose alternative interpretations. New political appointees and anointed careerists equally accept the tenet of top-down wisdom and authority; they *ipso facto* believe they have it. They acquiesce in the layers and rows of specialization. They fall prey to the belief that position on the bureaucratic ladder denotes value and wisdom.

In other words, the outsider's behavior after entrance into the bureaucracy does not differ in important respects from that of the insider; they both operate from the same basic conceptual pattern inculcated by our society. To be different would require fundamentally different assumptions about a number of things.

The Self-Evaluating Meritocracy Myth

We have now reached a point where the term merit system implies red tape and favoritism. It conjures up a vision of an organism that sets its own standards, maintains control of its own replenishment, and determines itself what is best for itself. There is no external provision for assessing whether there is in fact anything meritorious about it. The belief that a "meritocracy" that monitors itself can insure merit standards is one of the most damaging myths of our system of governance. It is like having this year's beauty queen pick her successor.

In the public sector the adoption of a merit system to replace the spoils system has in less than a century come full circle, to the point where favoritism is dispensed by the bureaucrats instead of the politicians—all in the name of "objective merit." The public is lulled into believing that fairness and equality are realities and the ritualistic facade of "due process," "merit selection panels," and individual evaluations is maintained to cover rampant non-merit personnel procedures.

Acceptance of the myth reinforces the use of superficial grading procedures (performance evaluations) that substitute for real merit. People who have studied the government's performance evaluation systems recognize that they reflect anything but the actual quality of the work.[14] Using bureaucratic grades as surrogates for performance has led to the development of "ticket punching" as a substitute for human development. This creation of an artificial set of balances relieves the pressure to deal with real human needs and motivations. It makes possible the creation of personnel systems that deal with abstractions instead of humanity.

This state of affairs has evolved because we have led ourselves to believe that so-called "objective psycho-social instruments" exist to grade performance potential and achievement and that their application ensures system integrity. We have accepted the "scientific" label, even though it is belied by reality. Belief in the meritocratic myth reassures the layman and acceptance of it absolves the citizenry of any responsibility for the sins committed in its name.

The myth of a self-selecting meritocracy gets additional support from several tenets. Among them are: (1) The work of government is so esoteric that the people on the inside know better what is needed to serve the outside. Acceptance of this makes it legitimate for the insiders to control the selection of their successors. (2) Pennies are the key to human motivation and manipulation of salary levels can improve personnel performance. This is still touted despite considerable evidence that above a certain level pay loses its motive force. (3) Internal competition builds *esprit de corps*. This tenet prevails despite the distrust and alienation bred by the scramble for grades in the current system's zero-sum game.

If the public good is to be served by a merit system, then the public has to find someway to re-insert itself into the processes of defining merit, finding it and using it.

The Myth of an Independent Public Service

If we pause to reflect for a moment, attempting to shed our perceptual blinders, it becomes immediately obvious that the concept "independent public service" is internally contradictory. To be asked to be both "servant" and "independent" at the same time is a mutually exclusive set of charges. We have assumed the public-at-large needs a group of employees to carry out the programs voters authorize through elected representatives. We as a society have managed to create a permanent public service largely inviolate from fragmented, indirect voter influence. I have already described the weaknesses of the Congressional oversight function and the tenuous hold the President has on the system. Most of the President's appointees become co-opted and part of the problem; they assume the attributes of the permanent elitists and benefit from the system.

From the administration of Andrew Jackson until the late 19th century the federal system of public services was beset with corrupt bargaining, favoritism and graft, inefficiency, lack of job security for government employees and political assessments on their salaries. The display of favoritism and inefficiency led to pressures for a "clean system" and the assassination of President Garfield by a disappointed office seeker hurried along acceptance of the idea of a permanent civil service, independent of politics. Since the previous situation had been so bad it was easily assumed the opposite of the *status quo* was what was required. So instead of individual hiring of known people, we substituted a bureaucratic system; instead of making public employees responsible to elected officials we placed an elite supervisory layer between the two groups; instead of rotating people in and out we gave them life-long sinecures; instead of accepting them as part of the political system we made government employees independent of it.

As with all new systems it appeared to be an advance over the *status quo ante* so it began to be eulogized, even by no less a figure than Woodrow Wilson.[15] It seemed to correct the worst excesses of the period and no one was able to predict its negative implications for the long run. That it might become in fact more of a tyrant and less effective than Jackson's "honest citizens rotating in public office" was of little concern. That this myth prospered is not surprising since it was the antithesis of another myth: all politics are dirty and politicians are crooked.

So the public began to read and learn in civics classes and the popular press that the necessary public servant was an independent person, selected on the basis of merit and part of a self-perpetuating system untouched by partisan politics. We reinforced the myth by proclaiming that the public service was concerned only with administration, while elected officials made the policies. This led us to believe the real power still rested with the people. And so the "Civil Service" quickly expanded so that by the last half of the 20th century more than 85 percent of public employees were in the "career service." As the career system grew to near current levels it became even more necessary to support the myth by the "policy is separate from administration" tenet, thereby assuring Congress, the political leaders of the Executive Branch, and citizens that policy was in the hands of people directly responsible to the electorate and that the sinecured careerists were only carrying out orders.

If one stops and thinks about it the obvious becomes clear; policy which is not implemented or translated into action might just as well not have been made. Similarly, actions which modify, even if only slightly, the intent of the policy maker in fact make a new policy. Currently "professionals" in this area do not hesitate to talk among themselves about the disappearance of the division between public administration and public policy making.

In spite of the results that are the opposite of conscious purpose, the independent public service myth still prevails. It has now become a *raison d'etre;* it is used as a barb to ward off public participation in government. The tenure which was to eliminate graft now permits employees to ignore the public they were to serve. The reduction of patronage available to politicos has given more of it to senior bureaucrats. Where the public once could "throw the rascals out," now they cannot even influence the initial selection process which picks those who are to serve them.

Nevertheless, political abuses of the personnel system and the organization's policies happen anyway. The system creates career leaders who are unable or unwilling to blow the whistle or otherwise ward off individual politicos' intrusions into the personnel process. The system also protects those on the inside, except where its leaders are colluding in the rape of their own colleagues as in the McCarthy era. So in effect we have the worst of all worlds, a system that is generally self-protective, yet unable to withstand partisan political abuses.

The Myth of Scientific Management

Given the Western inclination to look upon "science" as the panacea for all problems, it is not surprising that we have turned to a pseudo-science, the modern witchcraft of quantitative systems analysts, for advice in coping with our disintegrating social institutions. We have mistakenly equated the ideal of "rational management" with "efficiency." We have made such a "rube goldberg" of our formal systems and continue to make them more complicated in frenetic efforts to shore them up that we are easily convinced that no layman can even understand, much less act upon them in a constructive way. Therefore we turn to people who speak in tongues, with flow charts and graphs, statistics, arcane theories, and x-fold exercises to bureaucratic nirvana. We want to believe that someone can make sense of it and when someone offers to do so in a "scientific" way we are eager to abdicate the field. Into this void has come the social scientist *qua* professional public administrators and personnelists described earlier.

The political or managerial generalist must believe the vested-interest based assurances of the so-called professionals in order to assume roles at the top of the pyramid where the real world is represented by decision trees and option papers in the currently used management technology. And a large number of tenets reinforce this myth. They relate to the efficacy of statistical predictions in the social sciences, including economics. Policy analysis is touted as a science and people believe that paper program evaluations can substitute for real world experience with the issues at hand. We have managed to substitute an abstract paper-based procedure for the decision making of people actually involved in the world of policy implementation.

In the field of internal management the reality is that a few highly questionable assumptions about human nature and its intrinsic malleability or lack thereof have been extrapolated to form a long series of interlocking techniques for testing, measurement, evaluation, control, developing of inferences about, and attempts at motivation and development of human personalities. Limited, experimental research instruments have been given wide currency as personnel management devices.

The existence of the myth has discouraged us from looking at basic assumptions and alternatives to the current school solutions calling for refined instruments, closer controls, and greater second guessing of individual decision making about one's own development.

Accompanying this "manageable" view of individuals is the view that a social organism is something which can be driven as one would an automobile, as long as you have the right person in the driver's seat. Since the formal structure of a public organism is generally prescribed in an explicit document, supported by a physical setting, it is understandable why people look on it as an apparatus and relate to it as one. Individuals in so-called leadership roles give orders, rearrange the walls and furniture, and play with pieces of the machinery such as travel quotas, telephone calls, and reporting formats in the expectation that the human organism will respond as directed.

The reality in complex social organisms is that more often than not an exact correspondence between outcome and command is fortuitous. Yet we persist in our belief that units of the federal bureaucracy should be expected to react in a martinet-like manner to orders from its leadership. Perhaps an image similar to that of a military review with units following intricate patterns of movement to shouted commands issued through a bureaucratic hierarchy underlies our expectations. We seem to forget that the individual movements which make up the beautiful parade ground display result not from the commands, but from an internalized set of decision points acted upon by each person in his or her own way. The individuals act; the commands are for the spectators.

Nevertheless the basic image of command-response pervades much of the thinking devoted to managerial approaches. Techniques for moving information and conveying commands are honed by experts on managers' staffs to reassure them that they are in control. It is assumed that the technology is real and the people are only feeding into it. Little recognition is given to the dichotomy between the actual thought and behavior of the members and what data they decide to include into the formal management system. The extent to which actual performance matches the manager's expectations is a function of conscious decisions of employees and not of the management's technology. Yet the myth is a virulent one and still influences much of writing on management despite Chester Barnard's *Functions of the Executive* mentioned earlier.

The Myth of Officialdom

Chapter 4 provides a description of the impact of the "official" self-image of public employees, both elected and appointed. Because we accept the traditional notion that governors, at whatever level, derive their authority from the nature of governments above and beyond the citizenry, we ascribe to them a special power. This special powers mentality assumes that certain privileges exist for the office-holder and that it is at his or her sufferance that citizens are permitted to have access to time, attention or information. It is a curious anachronism for a democracy whose Constitution starts out, "We the people of the United States, in order to . . . secure the blessings of liberty to ourselves and our posterity, do ordain and establish this Constitution . . . "

Our history has been one of struggle over how to implement that rhetoric and truly create a government of the people. When George Washington was first elected, Congress literally spent several weeks debating whether and what kind of title he should have in order to garner "true respect." Fortunately, Washington himself had his feet on the ground and the simple term "Mr. President" kept our chief representative somewhat closer to the rest of us.*

Acts of the Congress and the Executive and decisions of the Supreme Court, acquiesced in by "the people" have made us fall back a step and a half of the two taken in our Declaration of Independence as beings with an inalienable right to govern ourselves. Only the scandalous behavior of Richard Nixon finally stimulated Congressional action to prohibit Presidents from treating their "official" files as personal property. Citizens had to engage in a legal struggle for access to Henry Kissinger's State Department telephone conversations, meticulously transcribed and filed at taxpayers' expense.

Many of the legal arguments would be unnecessary and the officialisms unacceptable if enough people would come to agree in practice that it is really *our* government and not that of some higher authority to which we must petition. The response patterns to the concept of official and its many symbols that have been deeply ingrained in most of us make movement in that direction very difficult.

If you ask an American whether the citizens of our society have the ultimate responsibility to make democracy work the answer in all probability would be a decisive "yes." But the same person would agree that the democratically elected and appointed government then comprises an "official" entity, never pausing to question the contradiction in terms. By accepting the concept "government = official" the citizen then has little room for complaint if public employees take steps to distance their "officialdom" from public scrutiny and involvement. The sense of elitism, classification of information, defense of "perks," and lack of

---

*But the concept of an Imperial President is still very strong in American society.

responsiveness to the public characterize the "officials" of a democracy just as they do the "officials" ordained to their posts by gods, kings, and absolute dictators. By accepting the central myth all the tenets that are "logically" consistent with it follow in due course, and it is these implementing ideas and their impact that produce the contrast to what one intended. By agreeing to the concept of "official" one is automatically denying the fundamental principle of self-governance, because the obverse of officials is the existence of subjects. You cannot have one without the other. And it then follows that those who have been ordained have the right to give orders and set up procedures to secure the defense of *their* institution. So the outcome is not the preservation of democracy, but the setting up of a new kind of oligarchy. It is those implicit corollaries of implementation of the "officialdom" myth that must be taken into account if we are to understand how things go awry.

These simplistic yet powerful myths and their nets of supporting tenets constitute a significant portion of the concepts that make up the basic images and concepts of our bureaucratic organism. In this capacity they exert a powerful influence on all other elements that has the cumulative effect of creating ineffectiveness that not only renders counter-productive many current programs, but also debilitates the institution for the long haul.

In addition to the general bureaucratic myths and tenets, each department or agency has its own set of parochial myths that grow out of its unique roles or experiences; they shape distinctive subcultures in different parts of government. Some are shared by several units. One such recurring myth that is found in many groups or cores scattered throughout government is that of "elitism." The implications of this myth are so important that it was extensively treated in an earlier chapter. *Suffice it to say here that the myth of elitism is one of the principal variables that condition the intellectual and emotional approaches to policy and program products in the agencies where it exists.* It is one of the primary reasons for many of the non-democratic attributes of the present bureaucracy; its protectors are only doing what they consider normal for a "chosen group."

Bureaucratic institutions of government today protect themselves with calls for public obeisance to these allegedly valid principles. The fact they get away with it indicates the power of myths to blind even keen observers to the incongruities between theory and practice. Since everyone recognizes the inadequacies of the bureaucracy there is pressure for action, but unfortunately action must fall within the limits set by the myths to be permissible. For this reason, people support the use of the ineffectual tools described in Chapter 5; they do not threaten the myths directly. The myths are potent because so many elements in society have considerable investment in their continuation: the bureaucracy itself, the merchants of tests, the teachers of test-takers, the academics whose reputations are based on the study of the system, the outsiders who benefit from it, and all those who seek government employment.

Because many of the concepts I call myths and tenets are so strongly held by some, I sometimes feel as though I were attacking people's assumptions about God. There is no way to test directly religious myths; therefore we are left to judge their validity by the impact the implementing tenets have on human behavior and social interactions here on earth. If we accept that logic then we can assess the relative merits of various organizational myths by what effect their tenets have on lives and events in social organisms. If we are willing to submit our beliefs to the William James test of pragmatism we learn very quickly that the basic principles on which our permanent public service is organized have led us astray. Seemingly logical assumptions have had implications in practice unforeseen by the early proponents. The only way out of the quagmire appears to be a radical rethinking of such basic myths. They have fed into the lifestream of government in such a circular way that the Gordian knot cannot be undone without neutralizing their impact. Let's review how that works.

Person: Co-Creator of Self

Skilled observers like some mentioned earlier are beginning to perceive the interactive process of co-creation that characterizes our formal social groupings. They are beginning to write about the mutually shaping relationship between humans and their social creations.

Rosabeth Kanter, in a most perceptive study of the problems of "stuck" people in organizations has begun to unravel the interactive relationship between the behavior of individuals and organizational structures they and others have created. She writes:

> . . . organizational behavior is produced in the interaction of individuals, seeking to meet their own needs and manage their situations, with their positions, which constrain their option for the way they can act. The total interaction is a dynamic one: certain responses touch off others and provide the moving force behind cycles and chains of events.

Michael Maccoby poses the question, "Have you ever thought about how your work influences the kind of person you are becoming?" and his writing demonstrates an understanding of the reciprocal influence of work on character. In speaking of institutions Adam Yarmolinsky completes the circle by asserting, "What an institution does and what it is are alternatively cause and effect."[16] Among others there is a growing awareness of the manner in which the human structuring of work and environment reflects back on the developing psychological and behaviorial make-up of people themselves—of the way we interact with our reality and create it as it creates us. *As we conceptualize and order our lives, the actual doing makes of the dream a reality.*

For example, conceiving of people as lacking initiative we create structures that do not reward initiative and lo and behold the members are passive—the prophecy fulfills itself. Thinking of people as machines we create a mechanistic system that turns human beings into cogs. Those cogs, having lost the capacity to think globally, when in positions of organizational authority face the outside world with tunnel vision.

Given the existence of this circular principle, if we wish to change the social reality outside us the most direct and lasting way is to change our visions of what we are within. We can no longer think of the dichotomy "man versus system" when the reality is a reciprocal, interactive process. At its most simplistic level, the central reality is that "I am what I am because of what I think I am and what I do to others and organizations that influence the way they impact on me." Arthur Young[17] calls it a reflexive universe, where the involuntary reflex has evolved to what is now the human capacity for considered action. *The co-creating relationship has been there all along, but only now are we becoming conscious enough of it to begin intervening in a planned and advanced manner in our own creation.*

In an attempt to dissect the tangled skein of interactions among thought, behavior, and organizational elements, I have set forth in this chapter a holographic framework that identifies the major elements of social organisms and several of their internal dynamics. As "self-image" seems to be the key to human behavior, "composite-images" seem to be the key to organizational behavior; these images shape the organization's structure, climate and work outcomes which in turn affect attitudes and behavior and on and on. Although the process is circular, I believe efforts that deal directly with these cognitive patterns will be more effective in bringing about reform than dealing with formal systems or behavioral training.

The very core of these composite images are myths and tenets of the kind described earlier. If we are to have dramatic change substitutes must be found for them. We must also replace at the same time the formal structural elements which are inconsistent with the new ideas. Although the internalization of new concepts is necessary to start change, they will wither very quickly if supporting organizational elements are not in place to sustain and reinforce them. The situation would be analogous to a husband learning in group therapy that a new way of relating to his wife will solve their marriage problems, but finding that she is unwilling to change her life style to coincide with his new ideas. His new-found role and resolve to carry it out do not last long without support.

RENEWAL OF THE BUREAUCRACY IS POSSIBLE, but not through the people inside trying to invigorate the existing patterns of communication and work, nor through an excathedrally ordered reshuffling of organizational structures and hierarchical relationships. The training skills and techniques of outside experts are not sufficient. Of equally little import are spasmodic attempts at civil disobedience, external research studies, legal protections for whistle blowers, and greater snooping by Congressional staffers. Even though they may be intrinsically desirable, they will not remake institutions.

Renewal requires carving away the accumulated debris of ideas and practices that have become hindrances to progress, much as owners scrape the barnacles from the hulls of their ships to speed their passage through the sea. The influence of myths whose large number of operational tenets has led our institutional evolution astray must be recognized. Only those that can pass the scrutiny of reality testing should remain to help form the conceptual base, along with newly discovered insights, for the next phase of institutional development. After identification of the counter-productive myths, the next steps will be to conceive more humane and democratic replacements and to design new formal structures that overcome the stultification resulting from our current managerial paradigm. When similar conceptual transformations occur among enough people the principles that govern social organisms will ensure that both form and actual performance become congruent with the new primary images.

Institutional leaders, from the President on down, will be effective reformers only to the degree they succeed in reshaping American responses to some of the basic questions around which we have built myths like those described here.

Part III
Reintegrating Government and Society

7
Self-Correcting
Institutions

A prophet is not without honor, but in his own country, and among his own kin, and in his own house.

Jesus of Nazareth

Each person attempting to abstract a model of organizations usually develops some version of the ideal state, when all the parts of the organism mesh well and the right things happen at the right time to produce the right product and a euphoric membership. Some use the term organizational health; others call it effectiveness, fit, or some such positive term. "Health" has a value connotation to it, whereas "effectiveness" may be more neutral. The Mafia could be considered an effective organism, but not necessarily a healthy one. Self-renewing is another term that has been used to describe the ideal condition. This is not purely an academic issue; one's approach to government management is shaped by the theory one holds about the organization at or near perfection.

Some consider an effective organization as one (1) with a well-defined role agreed upon by the organization's members and its clients, (2) whose members perform in a manner congruent with that role, and (3) whose performance improves over time. Others say a healthy organization is:
- Open to new ideas, people and tasks.
- Adaptable to changing circumstances.
- Creative, producing new approaches/products.
- Productive; the necessary work gets done.

Chris Argyris has three criteria for an effective organization. It must:
(1) achieve its objectives;
(2) maintain its internal health; and
(3) adapt to and maintain control over the relevant environment in any given situation.[1]

Argyris maintains that an effective organization is inherently psychologically healthy for its members. To paraphrase him, there are three elements that are essential to psychological health. First, the nature of one's work calls forth that component of personality which is most central to the individual. Second, individuals must have some control over their own destiny. Third, individuals must be able to learn and grow as a result of their experiences in the work environment.

The concept I like to use for the ideal conscious social organism is "self-correcting." It takes into account the effectiveness criteria mentioned above and adds a purposeful aspect to them. It implies public organizations should move ever closer to fulfilling their public mandates. A self-correcting institution is one that is consistent with the aspirations of its constituency (members and outsiders), establishes concrete goals and accomplishes them, facilitates the personal growth of its members, and continually seeks to test its assumptions in light of new experience.

It is clear that most current government organizations fail to meet these standards. This chapter contains practical ideas for developing public organizations that will meet them.

New Element Criteria

How can we overcome the liabilities of the problematic bureaucracy? Taking the holographic model as a framework it is possible to postulate alternatives for each element that should move us toward self-correcting democratic institutions.

Government employees should see themselves as, and in fact be, citizens selected by their peers for service to the country. Both career and politically appointed employees must have the same sense of direct public accountability, with a passing-the-buck attitude totally unacceptable at all levels.

The bureaucracy's body of beliefs must be subjected to continual questioning by the members of the institution. There must be provisions for testing internally-held ideas against perceptions and data available externally. The objective should be organizational self-knowledge that is as up-to-date and as comprehensive and profound as possible.

The psychological set should include a sense of personal security, but it should differ from the current bureaucratic security which is bought at a great cost to personal initiative and autonomy. It should not be a security that is bought every day by obeisance to norms and procedures superfluous to the normal work requirements.

The behavioral norms would be what Chris Argyris has called Model II behavior:[2] open, fully communicating, and susceptible to confrontation and public testing. People should have a greater stake in above-the-board, publicly accountable behavior than in playing bureaucratic games. Norms should be primarily task-oriented and free of the burden of bureaucratic rules currently a part of the closed career system.

The roles of 3rd Century institutions should be based on issues or problems rather than functional or sectoral categories. Omnibus conglomerates would be out of place, as would smaller units that go on operating after the problem leading to their creation has been resolved.

The keynotes of 3rd Century structures should be simplicity and flexibility. We must overcome the current tendency to deal with the problems of a complicated system by adding additional complications, compounding the error as it were. Ironically, the more complex the issues the greater the degree of internal simplicity and flexibility that is required of the organization.

The interface between government organizations and the public should be significantly altered. The objective should be to reduce to the minimum possible barriers between the government and public sectors. We must go beyond even the idea of permeable membranes to an actual reintegration of government and society. The interface must be explicit, with a high volume of communication and complete reciprocity in the flow of information. It must not be susceptible to censorship and bureaucratic rulemaking without the consent of the voters.

That the workforce of the 3rd Century government should include the best talent our society can produce, in the requisite fields, goes without saying. That it should include the most appropriate modern technology for its various needs is another *sine qua non*. Also we must be able to relatively quickly change the mix of skills in the workforce to keep pace with changing problems and priorities.

In other words, the employees in government, at all levels, will have to reconceptualize their roles—going from that of policy maker and program controller toward that of worker, analyst, and facilitator of public-private cooperation. Conversely, citizens will have to perceive of government as the public tool or aid for social action instead of assigning it control and absolving themselves of personal responsibility.

The day must be over when the government thinks it has to "protect the public from itself." A more open, in-and-out public service is feasible now, with a whole new generation of sophistication (broader education) and activism (public interest groups) making it possible for in-depth public monitoring of government processes to occur. New mechanisms would have to be established to meet all these criteria, but they are feasible today.

Possible Alternatives

We must search for alternative organizational patterns, but there are no perfect ones waiting to be plucked from the air. There are no extant shining examples of comparable 3rd Century organizations. The most that can be found are small units that have managed to avoid the rigidities and individually demeaning aspects of the larger system, but even they cannot escape the pervasive shadow of bureaucratic overkill.

Our most practical recourse then is to examine the deficiencies in the current reality and hypothesize about the contrasts, experimenting and building a synthesis, to come up with alternative concepts worth testing. Some seeds for details of a new reform blueprint and intervention strategy can be found within the current organisms.

It is not surprising that some of the most effective individuals in the buraucracy seem to be those who disregard the myths and act according to contrary patterns. This does not mean simply turning 180 degrees, although some of that is required, but we must seek variations that are indicated by current negative experiences. Adding to them the experiential insights collected in social organisms which are founded on other images and assumptions can give a fairly complete alternative set of patterns and corollaries.

Using this two-pronged approach makes it possible to identify several congruent new components for each of the eight model elements. The total package provides the blueprint for a promising experimental change strategy. Taking the substantive concepts outlined in this chapter and the intervention process discussed in Chapter 8, a committed group of leaders should have a better than even chance of constructively reshaping the bureaucracy.

The first hurdle is to convince ourselves that we already possess the seminal ideas and skills. Our current organizational practices are far more primitive than they could be; they are based on outdated values perpetuated by traditional pattern-setting elites who view most people as objects to be manipulated. But that perspective does not represent the best thinking available in our society. With sufficient motivation we could eliminate the numerous, overly complex structural barriers we have constructed for ourselves. Although we cannot legislate a new meaning into the work lives of public employees we can "de-legislate" current obstacles to substantive accomplishment.

The key to social change is the modification of elemental perceptual patterns; the organism's self-images and basic assumptions. If an organization's members are willing to give up certain patterns and incorporate appropriate new ones then it becomes possible to put into operation reinforcing procedures, systems, and structures that can change attitudes and norms and eventually the organism's performance. On the other hand, if basic patterns are not modified and formal changes are introduced the latter will become distorted to conform to the pre-existing images and assumptions. It may be possible to mandate simple structural reforms in an organism with such force and persistence that eventually ideas, attitudes and norms become compatible with them—through the continuing patterns of reward and punishment—but I am aware of no case where this has occurred. To use such unilateral means to eventually elicit greater decentralized control, which is what is called for in the 3rd Century, appears to be a contradiction in terms. The medium being stronger than the message, it seems likely that such change-upon-command efforts would succeed in having the opposite effect.

The only viable option then is a rethinking of existing myths and the development of harmonious elements that encourage the growth of the attitudes and behaviors consistent with the new organizational vision. We can present an internally consistent set of alternative elements for a new kind of humanistic and democratic government. The following pages are a first step, one person's positing of a possible future.

Self-Images

A review of the primary self-image of citizens in government is the starting point in the creation of a self-correcting public service organism. Several facets of this image require reconfiguration to give us a new concept of public work.

The terms public service and public servant have developed a self-serving connotation that warrants their removal from our lexicon. Instead let's start thinking *"publicly paid employees," "public employees,"* or just *"government workers."* The reason for replacing such simple words with others is the implications they have for assumptions, attitudes, and behaviors. It makes a significant difference if employees perceive of themselves engaged to fulfill a specific contract instead of being anointed for life. Because such concepts are the base from which the character of government organizations evolves several substitutions are essential to profound reform of the federal bureaucratic mentality.

"Representative" replaces *"official."* The concept of representing the public and deriving one's status directly from the public should not be limited to the Legislative Branch. Elected and appointed people in the Executive Branch are no less representatives of the public than Senators and Congressmen, only their constituency is different. The term representative would cover all paid workers in the federal establishment.

The difference between *"representative"* and *"official"* is an anachronism, dating back to early groups whose function it was to represent the people before an official body that derived its existence from another source (God, the church, brute force, or wealth). In our form of government all public sector positions are established by the citizenry and do not fall in the old official category. It is time we made our practical concepts consistent with the principles of our constitution.

By placing the adjective *"democratic"* in front of the word *"government"* we almost totally change its meaning. The top-down connotation of power is replaced by a joint-participation one. The reason such a metamorphosis did not completely occur in our own society is because many of the traditional monarchical thought patterns shaped the new government and for two hundred years it has retained something of that tradition. This is only natural since new concepts of democratic institutions were not deeply ingrained throughout the new States. Most people transferred much of the old rhetoric to the new setting because they did not understand its implications. The subsequent would-be protestors who have been accepted into "officialdom" have lived up to the almost universal dictum of socialization processes; they became "more Catholic than the Pope."

"Program-developer" places *"policy-maker."* Rejection of the concept of "official" and full acceptance of the modifier "democratic" to denote our form of government leads logically to the next essential substitution: the superseding of the image of government employees as authorities having the right to make policy by a vision of them as qualified people chosen to work with other institutions and public groups in the development of publicly conceived and broadly supported programs.

For too long those employees empowered by the people to serve public needs have tended to arrogate unilateral decision-making authority. In recent years there has been more acceptance of the idea that government actors must take into account public opinion in their decision making. Note, however, that the emphasis has been on "taking into account," not on questioning the assumed right to decide. How slowly steps are made in the evolution of ideas!

Past	*Now*	*Needed*
"Listen to"	"Take into account"	"Involve"

We need now to progress to a collaborative decision-making process involving systematic public input, required advance disclosure of options, and joint Presidential-Congressional approval of the final choice before promulgation of government decisions.

"Implementor" replaces *"governor."* The concept of federal workers as the governing part of government should be supplanted with the image of implementers. The term government should be reserved for the total institution: formal organizations, elections, public groups, and the procedures that weave them all together in the process of self-governance. This means that people on the public payroll should see themselves as implementors of policies which they have helped develop, but over which they have no more of a proprietary interest than anyone else.

The real issues implicit in the changes proposed here are: "What should be the nature of power exercised by the public's employees? Where does control reside? Who participates in making decisions?" I recognize that I am suggesting a dramatic reallocation of perceived authority, but I do not believe the alteration is inconsistent with the ideals of most Americans. We do not need governors to tell us what to do; we need public employees to help us do what we have decided to do and cannot do without public organizations.

Assumptions

We will also need to revise our suppositions about the nature of organizations and how people ought to behave in them.

A New Visual Schema of Organizations

We must discard the triangular, two-dimensional picture of organizations. Some other schema should be placed into general usage. There is no magic version; mine should perhaps only be considered along with any number of sketches. The one which society's dominant communicators choose to disseminate and reinforce should, however, portray all the principles of social organisms described in the last chapter.

A number of variations from the triangle have been develoepd in attempts to depict other characteristics of organizations. One is the sociogram approach which illustrates the multiplicity and relative frequencies of interactions among individuals or offices. Another is the wheel/spokes design which places an individual in the center and arrays other people or functions around him/her. A third is the use of concentric circles which picture the relative importance of relationships in receding degrees of value.

Each of these has as its objective a more realistic portrayal of individual roles and relationships than the triangular framework. Any reduction of the complexities of social organisms to a simple line diagram is an absurdity, but since it seems to be a necessary symbol in the shorthand of human communications, it should be as fullblown as possible and still susceptible to easy retention.

A New Multilevel Definition of Social Organisms

Chapter 6 provided a review of the limitations of several textbook attempts to dissect the various elements that make up organizations. While I am not presumptuous enough to claim that my model is all-inclusive and that its taxonomy is completely unimpeachable, it does appear to me to cover the basic layers of reality or levels of abstraction that must come together for formal groups to create complex products from an idea. These basic layers are: Ideational, Psychological, Behavioral, Systems, Resources and Product.

A New View of the Individual in Public Organizations

First of all, differentiation between "employees" and "management," or between "supervisors" and "subordinates," should be eliminated. All individuals on the public payroll are employees of the public, managers of the public trust vested in them. The concept of employee-management relations would disappear and along with it the dividing of employees into union and non-union groups. (The proposed structural and personnel system arrangement should obviate the need for collective bargaining as a protective device.)

In my proposed contract between individuals and the "system," rights and privileges would be minimally described, in essence the same for everyone, and would devolve on the individual by virtue of his or her selection as a public representative.

Organizational Behavior

To develop a system in which all are in charge of self and at the same time directly accountable to the public which selected them will require the adoption of some powerful new assumptions about people and what motivates them to accept responsibility. It will require the rejection of the myth that centralized control is necessary, and possible. Instead we must assume that other individuals can be trusted as much as one can trust oneself and that individuals can and desire to take responsibility for their actions.

The corollary assumption is that overcontrol and *a priori* accountability in fact undermine the likelihood of a full measure of performance; the current authoritarian approach to management is counterproductive in terms of the morale and the internal motivation that leads to superior performance.

Another very important assumption to make is that monetary income can be largely neutralized as a factor in motivating job performance, along with the more superficial inducements of symbolic titles and prerogatives. It is possible to deemphasize extraneous incentives and allow more attention to be focused on the intrisic value of satisfaction for a job well done. People, if given the opportunity, would prefer to get rid of such superficial incentives, which only result in unfounded envy or squabbling.

Of central importance is the necessary new assumption that qualifications for providing government services for the commonwealth can be acquired in many sectors of society. There is no arcane art, nor specialized knowledge and skills that can only be secured through an inbred, college-to-grave career system. Since the bureaucracy's method of socialization of neophytes has so obviously not met our society's needs we should open the windows and continually bring in those who have been tested in the outside world.

Psychological Set

Psychological attitudes and interpersonal norms are the two elements of the organism which are somewhat more derivatives than generators in the circular and reciprocal interactions among elements. Therefore it is necessary to articulate these desirable elements and then attempt to develop images and design structures and procedures which will be conducive to their realization.

Openness to new ideas and a willingness to experiment and learn from mistakes are prerequisites in a self-correcting organization. A sense of being a self-starter, not always waiting for directions is another essential. A feeling of being accountable to the public in general, in contrast to single agency loyalties, is a central requirement. Confidence in one's qualifications and pride in one's contribution will reinforce the desire to be accessible and responsible. This carries with it an acute awareness of one's limitations as well as strengths. And finally a sense of personal security, based on an acceptance of one's status and the knowledge of being in control of one's destiny (to the extent that anyone can be), forms the bedrock for all the other necessary attitudes required to be employed to serve the larger society.

Interpersonal Norm

J.K. Glassman wrote in the *Washington Monthly* in October, 1976:

> It's ironic that as America gets more meritocratic, as economic advance is open to more people, it gets increasingly systematized in a way that discourages people from striking out on their own.

He and many others have recognized that we must turn around the pressures in public bureaucracies that result in *status quo* perpetuating behavior and develop norms which stimulate creativity. His allusion to the entrepreneurial type is an appropriate image. The term entrepreneur conjures up a vision of a person who strikes out on his own, takes risks, is innovative, accepts responsibility and is motivated to create a personal product.

Those characteristics are necessary for our 3rd Century public organizations, but they must be balanced by two other categories of principles: one governing interpersonal relations and the other related to organizational processes.

The key is a combination of individualistic, creative risk-taking that is non-manipulative of others, where one's intentions and strivings are "up front" for all to see and are open to challenges from colleagues. Chris Argyris is the only writer on the subject that I know who has successfully walked this tightrope and been able to formulate guidelines for interpersonal behavior that are practical and effective. His three interpersonal principles are simple to understand and as difficult as hell to put into practice. They are:

(1) Complete sharing of relevant information.
(2) Joint decision making on all trans-individual issues.
(3) No action taken without participants' internal commitment.

Argyris* says the antithesis of this is behavior characterized by hidden

*His underlying philosophy of the nature of man is also consistent with the proposed new images/assumptions outlined in these chapters.

motives, efforts to unilaterally control others, guarding of information, and fighting to always win over others (Model I behavior). No one has more accurately described the underlying principles which govern today's bureaucratic interpersonal norms.

The beauty of Argyris' principles is that they also establish a framework for organizational process norms: (1) Any member of the organization should have access to all the information that any other has access to. (2) Anyone who is directly affected by a decision should have an opportunity to participate in its making. (3) Individuals should only be involved in organizational activities to which they are internally committed. In this type organization all communication flows, decision processes, control relationships and roles and responsibilities should be explicit, susceptible to change by group action, and equally binding on all members.

Structure

It is difficult to determine the dividing line between personnel systems and organizational structures. They both are simply formal and relatively permanent mechanisms for ordering the human parts of the organism, to each other and to the task. Perhaps these two statements are adequate definitions: Structure primarily orders human relationships directly for the production of the organization's goods or services. Personnel systems determine the nature of individual ties to the overall entity.

If that is the basic purpose of personnel systems then acceptance of the perspective within this book would result in a complete revamping of both the philosophy and practices of the public personnel function. The structural changes proposed here would give individuals more control over themselves and their performance. They are based on the assumption that power is not a fixed sum and that more people can be given more power, with the total capacity of the organization to fulfill its objectives being strengthened.

Let's first look at some organizing principles that would help restructure bureaucracies into self-correcting organizations.

Internal Structures

In attempting to design 3rd Century internal arrangements we must keep in mind the overwhelming character of bureaucratic structures and procedures, their tendency "to keep everyone down," even for privileged tracks who are only kept down less. Kanter, in her excellent description of the *status quo* in large organizations, demonstrated how "being stuck" results in low morale, passivity, poor performance, cliques, grievances and pessimism about the future.

The dismantling of the pyramid represents an alternative for everyone, not just a privileged, or currently disenfranchised few. A flat and simplified hierarchy at the agency level would be replicated within smaller units. Managerial staff would be minimal and most subunits would be normally led by one of the group's professionals or technicians. At the functional unit level administrative and personnel staffs would be practically non-existent.

Information flows and decision channels would be established as appropriate, but very few even semi-permanent "chains of command" would be used. All but three of the layers of supervision, included in the present pyramids and listed on page 34 would be abolished. The three remaining would be agency head, functional unit executive, and task or program leader. Other leadership roles would be rotated among members of an office, committee, task force or whatever the most appropriate group formation happened to be for the task at hand.

Large numbers of employees would be assigned *ad hoc* self-directed tasks that might go on for long periods of time.

It would be an accepted routine that a part of each day would be devoted to individually-selected, non-structured program activities. Government would cost less yet each employee would have a more significant role. (The deflationary impact of eliminating so many non-productive functions would be much greater than all of the current efforts to control wages arbitrarily.)

The neat placing of everyone somewhere on the triangular grid would be relegated to the history books. No personalized and permanent claims could be laid to particular niches. There would be no financial and honorific title advantages to it. Everyone would be secure in the larger firmament and could be expected to give up easily out-dated tasks or positions to move on to higher priority or more currently useful activities.

Employees would be encouraged to work toward abolition of their current jobs—resolve the problem to get on to something else or find a better way to do it so that it does not require as many people. As part of the inducement to keep from perpetuating non-essential jobs, people should be offered the opportunity to create their own new ones to better carry out the purposes of the particular public function.

Each unit would establish its own administrative procedures for office hours, space and equipment allocations, etc. Travel would be authorized by unit chiefs and reimbursed on a pre-established package basis. Time and attendance records would be kept by the individuals and flexitime would be authorized in all agencies. This would eliminate the need for bloated support staffs and their pyramids of administrators.

There is plenty of evidence that elaborate structures are not necessary for human security and effectiveness. Japanese firms have the concept of permanent employment in a larger system and their employees' personal ranks are separate from position grades. (The latter principle has been a part of the concept of the U.S. Foreign Service for more than 30 years.) Worker-owned firms in the U.S. have not evolved complex hierarchies. They only become necessary when symbols assume more importance than the task. Such has been the unfortunate legacy of our historical good intentions about being fair and rewarding people for their performance, but there comes a time to reassess and refine our understanding of what it means to be human; the hair-splitting artificiality of our complex grade and title pyramid has proved to be more dehumanizing than constructive.

There are several work organizing principles that have proven to be useful in enhancing organization performance:

- Each employee and function must be well-grounded in the substance of the organization's work. There is no such thing as a "special" isolated role—whether managerial, staff or operational. Therefore look carefully at special assistant and service-only positions of all kinds, including layers of supervision that are perceived as just that.
- The positions of assistant or deputy are usually dysfunctionally oriented upward, existing to service the superior, and breaks the link between two levels of people who are doing things. This problem is doubled when the position is both assistant and deputy. Energy that should be focused downward is absorbed in fragmented and duplicative work.
- The opposite of the above is that the most solid performances are turned out by those with concrete assignments, responsible for managing their own tasks. This is another way of expressing the old saw that performance is best where authority and responsibility meet.

■ *Unit Size.* Instead of creating more and more omnibus units in pursuit of reducing the overall number of agencies we should aim for greater decentralization. Instead of trying to centralize and reduce the number of autonomous decision units, we ought to rationalize their relationships and clarify their respective roles.

The lesson to be learned from Barry Stein's work[3] is that there can be considerable decentralization within larger organizations, including government; in fact improvement in the quality of the product in the future will depend on it.

In order to make it possible for employees to manage effectively tasks/programs, seek improvements in their performance and be held accountable for it, departments and agencies will have to be broken down into appropriate units, given a mandate and resources and left to get the job done. Leaders responsible for discrete functions or programs (integral work units) would report directly to Presidentially appointed executives and not through a chain of intermediaries.

■ *Reduced Managers/Supervisors.* One of the clear directions to be taken is a reduction in the number of people who do nothing but allegedly "manage people." They may be needed at the start-up of new operations, but such roles should disappear as the new approach to assigning responsibilities becomes clear; no one should detract from the control of worker/producers who can take care of themselves. Experience in worker-owned firms in the U.S. has confirmed this; quality of performance and productivity is very high and employees have an ethic of conservation.

■ *Modern Technology for Communication.* Such decentralization of operations would be possible in the government sector only if there existed a widespread, shared policy perspective and philosophy, one which was kept current and continually reinforced through direct exchanges between elected officials and the Cabinet and the Presidential executives throughout government. Although currently unused for this purpose technology exists which could effectively replace hundreds, if not thousands of policy interpreter go-betweens.

A closed circuit TV network could include all the 1,000 political executives and other managers as deemed appropriate. Weekly sessions with the President could include all of them and daily group discussions could be held on special issues, involving only the necessary executives. Flexibility would range from one-on-one dialogues, question and answer sessions, to especially prepared general policy guidance programs. Given this sort of network there is no reason why any executive could not have a very clear understanding of the Administration's policy position in his or her area or be aware of the views of counterparts in other agencies.

The focus of the above network would be general policy, but each integral unit should be able to engage any other(s) on a teleconferencing arrangement that would include voice, video, or document exchange. Questions about interagency activities, unresolved issues and other coordination matters could be handled on a daily basis.

In addition all agency information systems and data banks would be accessible to all employees in each agency through computer terminals operated through the telephone system.

Now let's move to the second structural arena, that of the personnel system.

A Facilitative Personnel System

From the current emphasis on the personnel function as human resource management we must move to a minimal mode of facilitation and support. Personnelists should only involve themselves in workers' lives when asked. They should be ombudsmen, insuring that the limited formal, explicit system is implemented fairly. The appropriate style is a light-fingered one.

The basic themes of the 3rd Century self-correcting approach are to: (1) reduce complexity, (2) minimize rules and record keeping, (3) provide maximum employee choice and flexibility, and (4) transfer responsibility from the system to the individual. In other words, the current concepts of personnel management would be turned upside down; the focus would be on employees as actors instead of objects to be acted upon. Instead of would-be social engineers, employees in the personnel office should be lovers of individual freedom and initiative for others as well as themselves. Such principles are consistent with what we now understand to be the circumstances that are conducive to greater individual initiative, creativity and acceptance of responsibility. It is important to keep in mind that people can behave responsibly more easily when the system in which they live is responsible. The essence is the provision of a basic foundation of individual and family security with a great degree of latitude on most of the details.

Such a light-fingered personnel operation would be dependent on the existence of a few uncomplicated, but relatively permanent (25 years) frameworks that were kept uncluttered by refinements, exceptions, and ornaments that become objects to fight over, causing grievances and diverting attention from the basics of constructive work. The essential questions to be resolved are few. They are level of pay, professional category, career status, benefits and retirement. The criteria they must meet are simplicity and independence from complicated data or formulae; they must be sparse enough for everyone to see clearly all the angles, and they must be consistently applied. We should not try to tie down all the loose ends. In American society we try to make everything fit neatly together: age, education, job level, rank, salary, formal power, title, benefits, etc. Let's give up this hopeless tasks that mires us down. Below is a sketch of the basic components that could make it possible for such a system to work.

Permanents versus In-and-Outers. The workforce objective should be to balance satisfactorily the needs for continuity (institutional memory and experience) and fresh energy and ideas from the outside.

Some people, such as Charles Peters of the *Washington Monthly,* have advocated that 50% of the workforce be career and the other half be partisan appointees. That approach would give us schizophrenia instead of catatonic paralysis in government. Instead of such divided loyalties we need a common commitment by all employees to the general public. I would suggest that no more than 50% of the public workforce should be long-term and the others would be reservists with a five-year limit on tenure.* (Actually slightly less than 50% would be in each category because I would reserve 5% of the overall total to Presidential appointment.) I would also go so far as to say that the equal division should be maintained at each independent agency, and probably even to a smaller unit breakdown. Then there should obviously be some flexibility of mix, but no task or program office should be all one or the other.

Similarly, the 50-50 break should apply to all four occupational quadrants (described below). Pay and benefits, including contributions to eventual

*The Peace Corps was fairly successful in implementing this limited appointment concept.

retirement should be equal in career and reservist categories. The same public panel selection process would control entry into both categories. Applicants would have to opt for one status or the other. Those who work as reserves would have to leave government a year before reapplying for career status.

Presidential appointees. Presidents would have a number of appointments equivalent to 5% of the total civilian govenrment workforce to fill as they please (except for those few also subject to Senate confirmation) with terminations of appointments mandatory upon the President's departure from office. Twenty percent of that number could be in a political executive category (with a salary range of $61-70,000—using the sample formula given below). The balance would be divided equally into the four quadrants, thereby giving the President a slight edge in the ratio of higher paid jobs.

Occupational Quadrants. There would be four distinct occupational groupings: Support, Technical, Professional and Managerial. The Managerial could not exceed 10% of the total and each of the Technical and Professional groups could not exceed 25% of the total. Support jobs would be clerical and specifically defined repetitive operations. Technical jobs would be equipment-oriented including computers or involve more complicated operations such as accounting, routine writing, etc. The Professional jobs would be those calling for people like lawyers, physicians, architects, engineers, and those with graduate academic training. A more detailed sorting out of the current occupational groupings would have to be accomplished with some fairly tough negotiated decisions being made. As arbitrary as such a process might appear to be it would certainly be as valid as the current, daily hair-splitting exercises that occur in the name of "scientific job-analysis, position classification, and employee grade-level determinations."

A potential employee would apply to the job category most appropriate for his or her qualifications and, after appointment, would be eligible to compete for any job with the same designation. Each manager or team leader would have under his or her control a mix of positions in 3 or 4 quadrants and could only engage people in the same ratio.

The only "ranking" would be the four quadrants. It is very important when considering the need for further differentation of jobs or people to avoid any sort of relative ranking or grading, either in terms of titles or salaries. Ranking is *ipso facto* a win/lose situation, where a simple differentiation can be win/win. Organizations would be much more healthy if there were no artificial castes; distinctions among people would only be on the basis of current jobs.

Salary. A salary range would be established for each quadrant. As an illustration, a formula might be $10-20,000, $15-35,000, $25-50,000, and $40-60,000 for the four groups, respectively. The salary ranges would be divided into five levels. Everyone would enter at the bottom level and after two years of longevity would move to the next level. The whole set of ranges would be adjusted periodically to keep abreast of general inflationary cost increases.

Such a system appears to be reasonable enough to attract the necessary talent, yet simple enough to understand, and almost totally eliminates the whole arcane art of civil service position and pay management. In order to implement the principles of "comparability with private sector counterparts" these specialists use "indexation and weighting methodologies," of "intergrade deviations" and "uncorrected residuals" to "fit curves" to achieve results that satisfy no one. By reducing the level of complexity most of the grievances about alleged inequities would disappear.

The pay decision factors in this system would be reduced to two: what quadrant do you appropriately fit in and how long have you worked for the government? The salary level is in the person, not the specific position.

Benefits. The emoluments, in addition to salary, which would be equally available to all employees would be health care programs, sick leave and annual leave, and contributions to a retirement fund. Each employee, regardless of length of service, would receive an annual allotment of sick and annual leave to be accumulated, used or paid for as the employee desired. Record keeping on work and leave time would be left to the individual. The same per employer and family member rate of government contribution to a health care program, of the employee's choice, would be made for everyone.

Sabbaticals. In addition to bringing the public more directly into the process of government and the heavy use of in-and-outers, provisions must be made for larger percentages of the careerists to take time out periodically and look at what they have been doing from a different perspective. We have seen how exposure to the bureaucratic environment for too long shapes behavior. Experiences of people who have benefited from a year of external training, research, or work in another sector of society, such as that provided by the Intergovernmental Personnel Act, is convincing evidence of the efficacy of exchanging lenses every so often. Such sabbaticals should be encouraged and the new simplified compensation system set forth above would not penalize people who did.

Retirement. A fixed percent-of-salary government contribution to a common retirement program with a uniform annuity/contribution formula would be made on all employees regardless of length or category of service. The same would apply to both careerists and reservists, as well as Presidential appointees. As a result of the national review of the $3.3 trillion government funded or controlled pension plans now underway by at least four groups and some committees of Congress, the variety of civil service social security and private sector plans could be made more equitable. The government should encourage multi-source retirement systems that combine contributions from many different jobs, inside and outside government. Retirement systems should be made compatible in all publicly funded sectors, and more private pension plans would follow close behind, in order not to disadvantage the in-and-outers. The current system discourages many who would like to wean themselves from the bureaucracy because you are penalized in terms of retirement credit unless you stay 30 years or reach age 55, or some other "sit out your time" formula.

The above simplified approach to personnel systems would be conducive to facilitating a focus on the essentials of government service, getting the work done in the most creative and self-satisfying manner. In order to implement them most of the current personnel practices would have to be modified.

Selection. The whole farce of pretending to test for life-long suitability for a particular career would be junked.* The career applicant would only have to convince the selection panel that he or she had potential for growth and was a flexible, self-starter. The reservist would only have to demonstrate to the satisfaction of the selection panel that he or she was better qualified for the work in question than competing applicants. Being aware of the requirements of the job to be filled, the candidate would put together a personal dossier for presentation, in a face-to-face interview. The same process would be applicable to aspirants for career status and reserve status. The personnel office's role would be to advertise vacancies (not protect them for insiders as is now done), provide staff support for public selection panels, and process the contract, health, security (where required), and retirement forms. An online computer system with job openings would be accessible from all parts of the country.

The actual selections would be made by a public panel, composed of three people picked by lottery to serve for a year, on a when-needed basis, as in the juror system (except that no professions or other categories of citizens would be exempt). Panel members would be compensated for actual salaries lost. Each panel would handle the same employment category on a continuing basis in order to maintain standards. The members' terms would be staggered to provide continuity.

The initial selection process proposed here would place the primary responsibility for evaluation of qualifications on the candidate and the public panel. It would greatly simplify the bureaucratic entanglements, avoid the current bias to self-perpetuating cultures, and insure open competition for career or reserve appointments.

Entry contracts would establish the conditions of employment: occupational category, salary, and benefits, and would be the base document for the employee's subsequent negotiations for assignments within the system. Liberal use would be made of part-time and occasional employees.

■ *Promotion.* This double-blade sword that wounds more than it knights, tying the system and individual into procedural knots in order to carry on the merit charade, would simply be absent from the new system. Basic salary levels would be wholly adequate, with provisions for periodic longevity increases and cost-of-living adjustments as indicated by the general society's economic indicators. Moving from one of the four occupational quadrants to another

---

*For example, the PACE exam is being abolished. None should replace it.

would not be handled as a promotion function. The individual would simply decide when he or she wanted to make an attempt and would get in line, with personal dossier in hand, to compete before the panel with all other applicants for the desired quadrant.

Incremental salary boosts as enhancers of motivation and rewards for performance or personal ties would just no longer exist. Reinforcement for good work would be the recognition of peers and the public and the opportunity to take on more challenging and responsible duties.

■ *Performance Appraisal.* This tail would no longer wag the dog; the need for an elaborate system of make-believe evaluations to rationalize a personalized promotion process would have vanished along with the concept of grade ladders and climbing the rungs. A string of merit badges would no longer be a required part of the employee's baggage.

Employees, in the normal course of work, would receive feed-back on their performance from colleagues and users of their products. As they desire, individuals could collect for their personal dossiers the comments of others, to include with samples of their work.

The illusion of "equitable and valid" assessments would be relegated back to the world of academia and social science experiments and employees would be left in peace, with a sense that they exercised some control over their own destinies.

Permanent employees could be removed from the rolls after three such recommendations from supervisors and a review by the public panel. This new concept would require a legislative and judicial modification of the view that government employment, for the incumbent, is a "property right." This principle, unfortunately, has been upheld by the Supreme Court. The 3rd Century precepts must focus on due process and public procedures, but no one should have a right to a sinecure.

■ *Assignments.* There would no longer be pretensions of centrally controlled or top-down assignment function. Individuals in a market place manner would negotiate "contracts" with executives and/or task leaders with authority to obligate funds for people and programs. Offices with anticipated or actual vacancies would make them known, along with a statement of general qualifications, to all interested parties through the personnel system; this basic tenet of the current Civil Service merit promotion system would be made to work. Individuals seeking new contracts would apply to the leader in charge of the job, who would, after a specified period of advertisement, make a selection from among those applying. Since no monetary inducement would be involved both applications and selections would more likely be based on work-related factors. There would be no motivation to try for the job unless you wanted to do the work; the desire to provide financial assistance to a friend or colleague could not be satisfied through the job-filling process.

Support for the principle of equity would be access to information on job openings, the right to present oneself, and the public record maintained on job descriptions and incumbent qualifications. Experience has shown that a top-down effort to insure equity among radical, ethnic, and sexual groups succeeds no more than individual managers are willing for them to. The proposed system would recognize that and put the manager's record in the public domain. Access to information would be assured through a central computer data bank, which could be scanned by employees at will and programmed to notify people when their pending interests might be met by new vacancies. Leaders filling jobs would be obligated to react to all applicants and make a public record of their final decisions.

The central personnel system would monitor the information distribution process and decision records and call questionable circumstances to the attention of the job internal/public inspection and evaluation teams.

■ *Training.* Consistent with the philosophy pervading this whole personnel approach, the training function would be a laissez-faire, serve the needs of the client operation. In other words, individuals would decide whether and when certain training would help them do their jobs better or to get new jobs. Each career employee would be entitled to up to one year of training out of seven and reservists could obtain up to six months in the five year stint, but no one would be required to take training courses. Training needs would be met by private institutions who make their courses available to any government employees for a uniform, government-wide negotiated schedule of fees rather than by expensive in-house operations.

■ *Career Development.* Comparable to training, the career-development function would be a do-it-yourself one. The system's obligation would be limited to providing information about the various kinds of government opportunities and relevant statistical data. Each agency could have an occupational counselor to assist employees in obtaining career and training information and in self-assessment.

No agency-wide talent searches, assessment centers, special tracks, or other allegedly omniscient and omnipotent approaches would be used. Individual growth would have to be sought by the individual and the system's responsibility would be limited to facilitating it. Career development could just as well be improvement in the handling of one's current job, taking on a more difficult assignment, or changing quadrants, but the choice would be the individual's.

Parallel with this new do-it-yourself concept of career development would be a dimunition of emphasis on specialization. The result of that irrational urge to be rational and the pressure to squeeze people into the pyramid underlie a tendency of our schools to train people to do one thing. They learn to treat a symptom, when what we need are people who can understand the whole and work themselves out of a job. Over-specialization has led to fragmentation of work and its feeling of alienation. The result is disorder, not order. As Wendell Berry has shown us, over-specialization has caused people to lose contact with the organic whole of life, the ins and outs, the connections that bind us all together with each other and with the earth.

The purpose of this facilitative system is to permit individuals to take charge of themselves, keep in touch with the whole, and find the best way to use their talents in public service.

Responsibilities

The new structure described above can be facilitated, and in fact must be accompanied, by an improved approach to establishing government units. As demonstrated in Chapter 2, there is no rational and consistent way of allocating responsibilities for carrying out publicly required functions. We must move toward a problem/specific program basis for the establishment of discrete units; new ones would only be authorized for defined purposes, stated in terms of objectives for public services.* The idea of large sectoral departments would become a thing of the past.

■ *Roles.* Each unit within a larger agency would have a clearly defined charter, either in terms of statutes or executive branch contracts between Presidentially appointed executives and unit leaders. The key element is simplification. The role definition would include operationally definable objectives so that at the end of a one or two year period performance could be evaluated.

■ *Mandate.* Each unit should comprise a line item in an agency budget and its budget justification would in effect be a decision package for public, White House, and Capitol Hill review of the role, assessment of performance, and approval of continued funding. Each mandate would include limitations on personnel (specifying numbers for each quadrant) and financial resources. And a very important item, each mandate would contain an enforceable sunset clause indicating when the unit would be terminated. Renewal would require the same process as the initial establishment: agency preparation of justifications, public hearings, and Presidential and Congressional review and approval.

■ *Contracts for Production.* Most of the straightforward production of good and routine services should be handled by contractors selected through a truly competitive process (in contrast to current practice) that would be monitored by the public groups described below. Non-profit organizations could be more widely encouraged to take over needed social services.

■ *Beyond Permeable Membranes.* The absence of a super-structure of managers and administrators, the proliferation of instantaneous communication channels across organization lines, the freedom of personnel

---

*The High Altitude Pollution Program of the FAA is a unique example in government of several of the attributes called for here: a program based legislative and budgetary mandate, a public (international) monitoring group, and complete openness of information.

movement, and the more active involvement of public groups in the life of government in the 3rd Century would keep organizations in closer touch with the realities of the external environment. However, two other innovations would insure even more institutional responsiveness to the needs of the general public.

Joint Inspection-Evaluation Groups. Each program unit would be required to establish a joint agency-public inspection and evaluation group to do an annual review of operating efficiency and assessment of program effectiveness. The report would be published and would become a part of the annual budget request material reviewed by the White House (OMB) and the Congress. Public members would be chosen in the same manner as selection panels. The likely claim by some that neophytes could not understand the programs well enough to evaluate them should be ignored. The general public can understand the technicalities on which court trials turn and if a program can be designed that is not susceptible to citizen evaluation it should not exist. This procedure might very well incorporate aspects of the federal program report card idea proposed elsewhere. The Office of the Special Counsel, set up by the 1978 Civil Service Reform Act to support whistle blowers, filled through the selection process set forth here could be a precursor to these Inspection-Evaluation Groups.

Of course the personnel system changes described earlier should reduce most of the need for audits to uncover wrongdoing. The objective should be to create an open enough system so that "whistleblowers" are not needed; attempts to provide protections for them in the 1978 Civil Service Act is another treat the symptom, ignore the cause, approach.

Public Legislative Impact Reports. Each piece of legislation creating a new program or modifying an existing one would have a required impact statement prepared by a general membership public interest group, i.e., not one controlled, supported, or predominantly peopled by members of groups, firms, etc. that would either directly benefit or be negatively impacted by the act. The statements would be available at the time of Presidential and Congressional consideration of each proposal. The basic concept here has been used in the requirement for environmental impact statements established by the National Environmental Protection Act. The objective is to open up and influence the nature of the decision making process. Experience with environmental impact statements has shown they, like any report, can be tools for obfuscation, but the independent public creation of the proposed reports would help mitigate that problem.

Congress Needs to Step Back

Parallel with the dramatic changes in the Executive Branch, the work of the Congress must be reshaped to emphasize debate on principles and review and public approval of proposed legislation. The refocus should be accompanied by a withdrawal from the vastly overstressed "solve every policy and program issue through new legislation" approach of recent years. The answer to one bureaucracy having failed to come to grips with many basic issues is not the creation of another on Capitol Hill, the fact that it has a few advantages over the Executive bureaucracy notwithstanding. The checks and balances of a legislative review function are needed and Congress should devote itself exclusively to that role—it is large and complex enough without adding administrative, program review, and policy initiation activities. With its oversight hearings Congress should reinforce the public inspection function described above and represent the general public interest.

A National Representative Presidency

Implicit in these new concepts is recognition of the fact that the President and the White House staff cannot *manage* every part of government. They place the President in the position of giving policy guidance and setting priorities and leaving agencies the task of developing proposed programs and legislation. Public groups would get involved at an early stage and the President and Congress in the final passage and signing of legislation. Giving the power to veto specific items of legislation to the President would be consistent with this concept; a recent Gallup poll showed 70 percent of voters favor it.

This approach would have the President perceived less as an initiator of specific programs and policy innovations, and as more involved in shaping the broad trends of public policy, instead of being forced to be, and unsuccessfully so, the ultimate administrator of his/her own dominions. The President would be the public's chief representative in a formal review and approval process with the Congress. We have been naive to expect that detailed policy leadership and solutions to all problems can emanate from the White House. We must place the emphasis on agencies taking more initiative, in the glare of public scrutiny envisaged in the companion recommendations.

The Cabinet form of government should be emphasized over the current Chief Executive concept. Even the conservative report of the Murphy Commission discussed earlier expressed the view that this change in emphasis is necessary. The difference between the two is that the latter accepts and attempts to implement the myth that a single executive authority can effectively steer the ship of state and serve as supreme catalyst and final arbiter for the vast machinery of government in the most powerful and complex national government on earth. The former approach would accept the view that the administrative buck-stopping point has to be different for different issues and operational areas. In this concept the President appoints, with the advice and consent of the Senate the members of the Cabinet, meets with them regularly, attempts to integrate and coordinate their various efforts, and serves as the final reviewer of policies and legislative proposals that have been developed and publicly vetted by the various departments and agencies. This would include the power to review and reject the decisions of regulatory bodies, a power which has been undermined by the Administrative Procedures Act for many agencies within the Executive Branch.

The value of this modification to current thinking is that it recognizes the futility of the present struggles to centralize and raise an excessive number of program decisions to the highest level. It would leave time and space for the President to engage in the conceptual and value-oriented leadership required to mobilize our multi-faceted society to concerted national efforts. It would allow the President to play the role he or she can best play: an ombudsman of the people as the only elected official (with the Vice-President) with the whole nation as a constituency. Of course such a change would not be wise with our existing isolated bureaucratic career services. The only formal, non-judicial way the public now has of digging into and exerting influence on its behavior is through the channel of the Presidency and its politicized staff in the bureaucracy. As is already obvious this leverage is too weak and/or biased to be effective for most public issues. But, within the context of the other changes outlined here, the modified Presidential role would be appropriate.

This proposed change of emphasis in the role of the President would in fact be more consistent with the implications of Article II, Section 2 and Article I, Section 7 and 8 of the Constitution than the current practice. The myth of the pyramid has caused us to attribute to the President, at the apex of the triangle, powers impossible to actualize. It would also require us to ask of candidates what government theory and social principles they stand for instead of whether they have a managerial background. Now the public thinks it needs a manager or a strong executive, but we do not need a manager for an intrinsically unmanageable entity; we need someone with ideas.*

People

What kinds of people and human skills will be required to move toward the kind of governmental organism postulated in the preceding pages?

First of all we need more public employees who can deal with the problems of emotional human communications, including obtaining critical feedback from other units and the public, handle conflict resolution and consensus building, and understand basic human psychology. They must be able to work in an open system.

There are some who would argue that public employees would not be able to consider unpopular options in an open government without the protection of

---

*Some foreign analysts have said FDR was the last U.S. President of that genre.

confidentiality. I do not accept that argument; we have progressed beyond the stage where it was considered appropriate to kill the messenger who carried bad news.

With employees who are skilled in more effective ways of handling such issues, we will find efforts to reform our institutions easier than our past untutored experience would indicate. Thousands of such citizens exist, but up to now they have been outside the partisan machinery. They now need to join the challenge of institutional renewal.

The first task of self-education for those who wish to serve the public would be to develop an awareness of the impact of their behavior on others. It is a current blind spot for most managers and supervisors; they have never learned to obtain feedback from others about what they do and tend to behave in a manner that discourages people from being open and honest in their responses. The greatest obstacle to constructive change in organizational relationships is the lack of insight into interpersonal styles and a lack of a standard by which to judge performance and progressive movement. Subordinates tend to manifest the same constricted behaviors that they find so inhibiting when engaged in by seniors.

The personnel experts who deal with the "soft human underbelly" of organizations will be required to shape new visions of their role, develop different patterns of thinking, and learn more effective models of interpersonal relationships. At the same time, intensive research and experimentation must go on to provide the understanding and tools that a new breed of leaders will need to carry out their redefined roles. Teachers will have to restructure curricula, research and publishing habits, and attitudes and patterns of thought.

People in government service must develop a sound understanding of the state of the organization itself. Periodic thorough diagnoses must be made of the way things really work, or more accurately, of the way they do not work. The organizational climate, what people really think about themselves and their work, must be clearly in view. The condition of communication channels, the quality of decision making procedures, the kinds of processes for resolving internal conflict, and the appropriateness of them for the task at hand and must be explicitly evaluated and reviewed by employees.

Needless to say, greater emphasis should also be placed on demonstrated substantive competence in the hiring of new people into the government workforce. Public selection panels should require evidence of accomplishments relevant to the tasks for which a person is engaged. *People should be hired in government only after they have demonstrated competence elsewhere.*

Without regard for current roles, total organizations must engage in the process of learning how to pull themselves up by the bootstraps, into the position of a robust team looking for a problem to resolve. Only when its human relationships, intellectual perceptions, and emotional motivation are in tip-top form can a unit be asked to take on the task of continuing self-renewal. With the right leadership and public support some of our currently debilitating government organizations could carry out such a self-analytic and self-educational effort and uphold a mandate for reform of the current bureaucracy.

The preceding pages include some of the attributes that are essential in the elements of government organizations if they are to become the self-correcting institutions we need. In addition to these new criteria for the organizations themselves, we need new thinking among professionals interested in public work.

Misplaced Professionalism

For the 3rd Century we will not need a profession of government service, but we will require more substantive professionalism in government. Chapter 3 commented on the significant and often dysfunctional role played by differing images of professionalism in shaping the behavior of organizations. The tug of war between those who think government workers should be authoritarianly controlled bureaucrats and those who call for inner-directed public administration professionals, answerable to their own standards, continues. This is fortunate since a victory for either one would have foreclosed a more desirable option: a work-force of substantive professionals whose avocation is public service. *Posing a significant threat to our institutional future is the growing industry of educational and other interest groups pushing to legitimize an independent profession of public administration.* Their accomplishment of this objective and securing control of the entry process into government service would only further isolate the federal bureaucracy from the citizens it should serve. Altruistic and openness rhetoric notwithstanding, the end result, given the organizational dynamics described in this book, would be a more closed elite, arrogating for itself the role of deciding for the rest of us.

There is no question that we need a heightened sense of professionalism in government, that gives employees a greater awareness of their personal responsibility for their own behavior in public positions. We need a sense of self that would result in less willingness to serve as super staff aides all of one's career; reducing what Adam Yarmolinsky[3] called "heliotropism" in which everyone views him/herself in terms of taking final responsibility for anything. Assuming oneself responsible for something makes it less likely that one would always opt for not making waves. Acts of going public on government faults would come more often if employees perceived of themselves as abiding by a code of conduct more universal and enduring than the prevailing bureaucratic currents.

With this greater sense of personal responsibility would come increased motivation and better quality performance. Instead of waffling and muddling through one might get decisions and concerted action, better quality performance all around. Maybe a sense of responsibility for following through on policy, not just being present at the creation, would evolve.

Such a powerful role and potential independence could only be permitted to a group in whose selection and promotion the public maintained an effective method of participation. In the system suggested in this chapter employees would owe their government roles to the public that chose them and their professional standing to their peers who maintain an interest in monitoring their public performance. This combination of open selection and external review of prior professional qualifications would protect us from the current inbred tendency of some professions to put their own interests above the public's. Such an arrangement could give an entirely new perspective to those on the inside.

The making of public policy could then perhaps be seen in a whole new context—concern for the human needs of the larger society. The current internally competitive system, including the career assignment and promotion rewards, with its emphasis on rationality makes employees less feeilng, less caring, less sensitive to the needs of others, and even less alarmed about the injustices in our society and the world. There is now too much stress on the view that a fine mind can rationalize almost any policy or program, no matter how outrageous or inappropriate. Undervaluing the compassion in themselves, public employees become incapable of caring about the human needs of others.

If we could succeed in developing non-bureaucratic, publicly selected and mandated groups of professionals in areas such as environment, health, foreign affairs, economics, etc., who could work equally well in government and in the private sector we might succeed in breaking down the "iron triangles" that now deprive the public of the full and accountable use of its government. Such an open and publicly interactive system as that described in the preceding pages would make it less likely that the government would pursue special interests counter to the general public's expectation. Traditional secret deals domestically and with other nations would be hampered. No small benefit would be the need for fewer employees as professionals reintegrated fragmented tasks and assumed broader responsibilities; concurrently the role of administrative and people managers, in contrast to producers, would wither. The reduction in intervening layers and functions would increase productivity and effectiveness.

Such a change would not necessarily come about with more *trappings* of professions (look at lawyers in Watergate), but with a strong, independent code of ethics and a personnel system that encourages public accountability it is at least possible; with the current system it will never occur. *Our hope lies in a new concept of substantive professionalism in government instead of the professionalization of government.* The question remains, is it feasible to do anything about it?

The existing bureaucratic, authoritarian model of our public organizations is antithetical to a corps of inner-directed professionals. With their current operating assumptions the political leaders of the Executive Branch would not know how to relate to a truly professional group of subordinates. Conversely, employees who have a sense of professionalism would find it untenable to work where the right to practice one's profession depended solely on bureaucratic dispensation. A whole new set of assumptions about structure, procedures, decision making, hiring and promotions, and working relationships would have to be adopted in order to nourish this professional service ethos.

Although a revolutionary idea, the turning away from efforts to create public administration "professionals" toward more effective use of substantive professionals in a new world of non-bureaucracy would be possible in the overall application of suggested new elements described in this chapter. A clear ethical standard and an enforceable system of public control of tenure would be prerequisites to the consent of elected officials and their constituents to even experiment with such an idea.

What would the outcome be? How would the people in such a new system act? Would they take advantage of the decentralized structures and personal autonomy to run roughshod over the taxpayers?

One important thing psychologists have learned about human behavior is that the requirement that one behave in a submissive, controlled manner before one's supervisors seems to result in authoritarian behavior toward subordinates and outsiders. People pass on to others what they get in terms of treatment.

Most subservient and patronizing bureaucrats, in their demeanor toward senior officials, behave callously and capriciously in depriving other employees and private citizens of legal rights and human dignity simply because they were considered beneath or outside the bureaucrat's circle. The whole present authoritarian system reinforces this we-they dichotomy that deprives people of their dignity and makes them insecure. The behavior of manipulated and anxious bureaucrats can only improve. Ironically, the new system with its greater individual autonomy, responsibility, and power would result in more cooperative, sharing and genuinely helpful behavior. We have all observed many times the constructive and humane behavior of the few people in government who are already accustomed to considerable personal autonomy and feel they have the defined responsibility and the power to act decisively. The effect of the new system proposed here is to give those same modalities to everyone, including the public taxpayer-owner of the system. We have nothing to fear but the kind of behavior each of us manifests when we feel in control of ourselves and are relating as equals to others.

Some Positive Trends

Currently there are a number of positive, but isolated developments occurring within government and the society at large that are consistent with the overall strategy espoused here. They should be reinforced and incorporated into a generalized reform program. Their existence also indicates recognition of the need for the kinds of approaches advocated here. The problem has simply been that groups pushing for one specific change or another have usually done so in reaction to particular manifestations of the bureaucratic problem. To be fully effective they must be reinforced by complementary and supportive actions on all fronts.

The development of broad-based public interest groups (like Common Cause and Nader's various committees) which do not constitute any single economic or ideological interest has been a valuable asset in exposing the "iron triangles" described earlier.

3rd Century government will require many counters to these triads; they must be generalized, process-oriented groups with members who are concerned that the practices of government are not consistent with our publicly enunciated ideals. They must be different from the literally hundreds of single-issue groups that flowered in the 70s to pursue narrowly defined objectives. To make the bureaucracy more open and accountable will necessitate the continual scrutiny of public spirited citizens whose involvement is not motivated by the desire to grind a particular personal or policy axe, but by an interest in the long-range health of the organizations and their interaction with the public. The joint public/agency groups described earlier would provide mechanisms to facilitate such public monitoring and participation in the process of governance.

A related development has been the rise of privately produced research/news sheets about specific areas of government waste, activity, regulations, etc. These non-partisan efforts to provide a fuller flow of information to the public about the goings-on in government should be supported and encouraged to expand. The regular press does very little of this day-to-day education of citizens about the doings of their public employees. An equally important part of the problem is that even when people are aware of what is going on there are few effective and timely routes to take action. Without suitable recourse, people only get more frustrated by access to disturbing information. The 3rd Century institutions must both permit access to information and provide means for public response and influence.

The concept of "sunset" legislation which would require all government programs to be reauthorized—or liquidated—over a ten-year cycle makes sense in a world where the suicide of a bureaucratic unit never occurs. The principle is attractive, but other changes would have to occur to avoid the review becoming another rubber stamp approval process, like the fiscal year 1979 ZBB exercise where one small program in the whole federal government was abolished.

An idea advanced in 1978 by former Ambassador to Yugoslavia Laurence H. Silberman has merit. He suggested Presidents be required to submit to Congress periodic reports rating federal programs as "excellent," "adequate," or "satisfactory" and a ranking of programs within each department. Obviously such an internally generated report would be subject to all the bureaucratic gaming of other in-house decisions, but when coupled with a relatively independent audit mechanism it would offer some hope for explicit differentiations of quality or relevance. Bills embodying this concept have been introduced in the Congress.

The recent extreme examples of public dissatisfaction with the Executive bureaucracy (e.g., Watergate, Vietnam, the revelations about the offensive practices of the previously sacrosanct FBI, CIA and IRS) and the steps toward democratization of Congress (e.g., election of committee chairmen, more hearings open to the public, and a faster turn-over of members) have led to much greater involvement of Congress in the early steps of developing public policies. The Congressional demand to "be in on the take-offs as well as the landings" has led to more openness and interchange between the executive and legislative branches, with some helpful fallout for the public at large. This slight alteration in the routine is an improvement and should be encouraged, but more effective use of Congressional time must be made, perhaps with the movement toward the Presidential and Congressional policy review roles suggested earlier in this chapter.

An existing element of the bureaucracy which has come under much criticism, the advisory commission, is based on a sound concept, but has been faultily implemented. Legislation establishing new programs has frequently called for the formation of citizens groups to advise, monitor, or assist the bureaucracy's implementation of them. (Before the Carter Administration started reviewing, with a view to eliminating many of them, there were over 2,000 such groups on the government rolls.) The belief that public oversight and advice would keep the programs more relevant and better managed is a reasonable one. But as so often happens the intent is thwarted in the implementation. Through the current operation the commissions become coopted, and in effect become integral parts of the bureaucracy they are charged to keep an independent eye on. Such things as per diem, travel, office and staff support, access to material, rights to publish, etc. develop a vested interest in the particular unit of bureaucracy to which the commission is appended. This seems to occur even when the members come to their assignment with no prior biases, and it is even worse when the members are chosen, as they too frequently are, from the benefited special interest sector. Many people are appointed to their positions as political party payoffs and take them as a means to enhance their public image or actually land a full time job. Such groups generally evolve into the role of "a friend in court," i.e., before the President and Congress, for "their program." The baby should not be thrown out with the bath water and the concept of publicly supported public participation in government should not be lost for the 3rd Century; independence sustaining modalities should be devised to replace the current coopting ones.

An experiment tried during the last few years by President Carter and some departments has shown promise as a means of contributing to greater public influence on the bureaucracy and to making it more accountable to the citizenry. It is called a "town meeting" and involves senior officials in answering questions raised by citizens (in contrast to the traditional speech-making or preaching modes of public contact by officials)* in a series of large groups, smaller workshops, or radio/TV call-in programs. These experiences have exposed senior career people, frequently for the first time, to the thinking of private groups without special interests, and, in some instances, significantly influenced their views on both the substance and process of government policy making. The weakness of this practice is that there is no systematic way to maintain an ongoing dialogue nor to allow follow-up by citizens on the impact of their contributions. Short of a nationwide network of computer consoles which permits everyone to vote from one's home on the day-to-day policies of government,[10] it should be possible to dramatically expand the opportunities for unfettered exchanges between citizens and their public employees and elected representatives. The use of problem solving workshops involving government employees and private citizens to deal with policy questions should be widely instituted.

Many ideas have been considered by the bureaucracy to make itself more human-oriented and thereby more effective. One of these has been experimentation with the concept of "flexitime" discussed in Chapter 5. While commendable as a principle the testing that has been done with it has not produced dramatic changes because the larger bureaucratic context has been untouched. Current efforts to improve employee morale and performance, such as job enrichment, rotating assignments and project clustering, would be unnecessary in the 3rd Century organization. Their objective would be accomplished implicitly in the new arrangements called for in this chapter.

Efforts have been made in various agencies, particularly in the Department of Commerce, to improve the human climate of work relationships through the use of group dynamics and interpersonal process specialists. This willingness to deal with such personal and important issues is laudatory, but like other such isolated and single-element interventions its overall impact on institutional performance has been limited. Nevertheless, this emphasis on and education of people in group processes will be an essential component of the management and development of 3rd Century institutions.

This chapter has provided a vision of a possible replacement for the bureaucratic pyramid model of government, or any other sector, organizations. It leaves us with the question of how do we get from here to there.

---

*This process is also very different from formal public hearings which have a judicial tone to them and bring forth professional public statement makers.

8
New Committees
of Correspondence

> Lewis H. Lapham has called for the revival of an "articulate
> minority" of people "who live for others and not for the
> opinion of others, and believe that they can forge their energy
> and their intelligence into the shapes of their own destiny and
> their own future."
>
> *Harpers*[1]

The fulfillment in its 3rd Century of the domestic aspirations of its citizens
and the potential global role ascribed to the United States by Jean-Francois Revel
will depend on the American society's ability to make its national institutions
self-correcting in the face of new challenges and the internal trends of
stultification. The days are over when the country's route to national strength
and global influence could be unbounded expansion across the continent and
unfettered growth, with its objectives based on consumer production and its
wastes simply discharged in the wake. Faced with a changed and more restricted
resource base, threats to our quality of life from its by-products, and the
atrophying of internal social organisms, the post-industrial society must look
inward to develop new avenues of human growth, more appropriate technology
for constructive interaction with the environment, and a conscious process for
social renewal. The last is both the most formidable and most essential challenge
to be dealt with by the United States in the next few years.

At some point in recent decades our federal government establishment
became a drain on the life force of our society instead of a stimulus. The amount
of resources it consumes is now all out of proportion to its constructive
contribution. It inhibits rather than facilitates creativity and growth.
Bureaucratic favoritism and systemic incompetence have become the hallmarks
of our so-called modern merit system. More detrimental to our society than
blatantly personal abuses of the system is the faceless inefficiency and lack of
responsiveness that is now manifested by the bureaucratic leviathan as it eludes
being accountable to the public. Sustained by symbiotic relationships with sub-
groups of Congress and outside special interests, units of the bureaucracy live in a
world of their own, beyond the pale of influence of the general public which they
were designed to serve. *It is now time to ask whether we have gone too far in
creating a public service too insulated from the public and its direct involvement.*

Our federal bureaucracy is now an institution out of phase with the needs of
the larger society. It does serve certain powerful groups in our quasi-capitalist

society, but it is clear that the interests of most citizens are not well served. Our concept of representative democracy, with a few elected to look out for the needs of the rest, has been rendered almost impotent by the creation of a self-directed and thereby misguided bureaucracy. The increasing bureaucratization of Congress itself has abetted this trend.

Perhaps in some past eras it was possible for outmoded institutions to be recycled through the passing of generations, with the young bringing on change as it was needed, but now the required rate of institutional change is much more rapid than the generation cycle. The answer is not to return to the 19th century political process of filling government jobs. We still need both continuity and protection against the occasional abuses of politicians. With our avenues of representation neutralized by the larger system we must seek new mechanisms to ensure the voices of citizens in all sectors of society get a more equal chance for a hearing. We must now consciously create a new kind of government organization, one that is more conducive to the actualization of the principles of a democratic society.

After over two centuries since John Locke and Tom Paine, it is time to take up again the great debates about the ordering of relationships and influence among the members of the human race. That period of enlightenment led to the founding of a new era, giving Western civilization a new lease on life. Now we must attempt to do what neither the Greeks nor the Romans succeeded in doing: to leap from a stagnating epoch to a better one.[2] *We must find the balance between being two self-critical or too self-admiring and become a self-conscious society again.* The early nineteenth century saw Americans debating about the impact of their institution building acts on the achievement of the new republic's ideals. We need to revive that self-testing mode of public discourse about the shaping of our institutions.

But public debate alone will not reform the bureaucracy; its life support systems are too strong. Neither will violent protests overthrow it; its grasp on society is too pervasive. It cannot be ignored; it occupies too large a part of our lifeboat. Citizens must be actively engaged in the internal process of institutional renewal and continuing democratic government.

As we contemplate the difficulty of bringing about reform in the organism of government it might be instructive to analyze and draw inferences from recent social change phenomena. If the thesis of this book is correct and the federal bureaucracy has assumed the nature of a society within a society then the parallels should be obvious.

Reconstruction laws did not change the social institution of black versus white in the South, but intellectual and attitudinal change in the 1960s made it possible for some civil rights legislation to be passed and generally implemented in our society. According to no less an authority than Andrew Young, many Southern businessmen were moving to restructure black-white relationships before the law began to embody desegregation principles. Conversely, the existence of statutes and regulations has not affected the behavior of many sectors where prejudices and discrimination continue to prevail. Prohibition did not change the drinking habits of many Americans and its repeal reflected a recognition that law without widespread public support is a weak reed. An Equal Rights Amendment will not make women equal, but its ultimate passage will indicate that times have changed enough for the legal act to be largely redundant. Legal changes in the institution of divorce, child custody, and alimony are following modifications already occurring in practice. Women (and men) liberate themselves from arbitrary constraints when they recognize their impact and conceive of more satisfactory alternatives.

These examples make it evident that profound social change is not brought about by mandate. It requires the thinking of new thoughts by a lot of people after they have decided that things do not work and understand why their expectations do not pan out. The term organizational change is a misnomer; what is really involved is collective human change.

But it is easier to conquer and manipulate the physical environment than it is to channel human personalities. It is easier to change the course of a river or the profile of a landscape than to bring about a shift in the attitudes of a dozen people. The challenge then is to mobilize large numbers of people without resorting to demagoguery and authoritarianism; it is crucial that the process be consistent with the democratic ends.

This may seem to some to be a process that is overly solicitous of the individuals involved but political analysts tell us every other day that foreign and domestic policy, to be effective in the long run, must be based on a societal consensus; it must have the support of the American people if it is to outlive the reign of one administration or be satisfactorily implemented. For example, in the spring of 1976 Clayton Fritchey on the *Washington Post* editorial page contrasted the Marshall Plan and NATO, "covenants . . . openly adopted after the most open public and congressional debate," with the Bay of Pigs, Vietnam, Chile and Angola. The lesson is that, although having the appearance of ambiguity and indecisiveness, the mobilization of a popular consensus before government policy and program changes are put into effect is necessary for success.

For a revolution in the Washington bureaucracy to succeed, (a) a large group of employees on the inside, (b) a vocal and energetic public force, and (c) a significant group of academic and media pattern builders must begin to think new thoughts and act in new ways. Only through such a large movement will the small pockets of deeply vested interests be swayed or, if not swayed, have their specific benefits that derive from the current fragmentation and ambiguity in government exposed and nullified by public votes. Therefore the strategy that is required is not one of forcefully overcoming opposition to implementation of the new concepts of Chapter 7 and inscribing them in some so-called Reform Act but one of developing within enough people such a new vision of institutional potentialities.

To bring about reform in the bureaucracy is then without question a herculean task, one that must involve insiders and outsiders—bringing into face-to-face debate both those who push for reform and those who will vigorously strive to protect the *status quo.* The latter will be in active opposition, but the greatest obstacle is the large silent majority whose psychological and intellectual inertia must be converted into a force for reform. If that can be accomplished, then groups with special interests that are well served by the current circumstances and who will mount a formidable defensive campaign will be rendered ineffective. In other words a means must be found to link up the energies of willing bureaucrats and active citizens in a joint debunking of current myths and a forging of new institutional patterns. In addition to encouraging people to think new thoughts, we need a forum to hone them and a process to convert them to action. To suggest a possible way is the purpose of this chapter. We need a 3rd Century "Committee of Correspondence," modeled after Samuel Adams' design in 1772 for a way to circumvent the British restrictions on the Massachusetts legislature's effectiveness as representatives of the colony.*

In order to convince people of the need for an extra-institutional creation we must deal with the views of some of my historian colleagues who argue that the dramatic shift I am calling for is inconsistent with the historical experience of modern Western society. They argue that such institutional change, and large-scale societal change, is a result of the basic flows of aggregated behavioral patterns in which single events have only a transitory impact and are difficult to predict or track. They argue that even widespread experimentation gets only incremental change; a thousand 1960's flowers bloom, but only a few become permanently rooted. A great surge may be made, but most of it falls back on its source.

This view is not unlike that which is held by some who believe we are caught in the currents of an unconscious, but inexorable transformation. Much historical evidence can be adduced for these "go with the flow" views, but the human race and its biosphere simply no longer have time for arm-chair, Spenglerian social theories. The analysis in this book has shown that closed social organisms cannot keep pace with our rapidly changing world. It is a time for people to become pro-active vis-a-vis themselves and their own institutions as they did in a dramatic way three centuries ago with the material resources of the planet.

If one accepts these conclusions about the need for institutional renewal and the nature of effective social change, one must then confront several crucial questions: Is the mood in America conducive to significant conscious change in its central institution of government? Can disparate interests find an approach that constructively focuses their energy? Is there a process that would be broadly

---

*Within two years a "committee" had been established in practically every colony. They comprised the network that served as a basis for the first Continental Congress.

perceived as consistent with our democratic ideals? The answer to the first question is a matter of judgment; are citizens ready to take on the burden of self-government? The other two involve strategy.

The requirements for our 3rd Century reform strategy are twofold: how to remake an institution by stimulating or causing enough people inside to take the necessary steps to change themselves and the way they carry out their work, and how to build a public movement that will both stimulate and reinforce the efforts of those involved in the internal renewal. The key to both of these is a theory of conscious social change in which the analytic and problem solving process is the guiding force rather than a set of *a priori* specific structural objectives. But before moving into strategy, what about the readiness of key people inside and outside government?

Resistance to Change

Even if a few bureaucrats are ready to create a new world that would in effect put themselves out of a job and many small private groups have envisaged a possible new society, and are seeking to achieve it, what about the public at large? Is there a widespread sense that the "evils" of the *status quo* are no longer sufferable (comparable to the beginning of our 1st Century) and that dramatic change is preferable?

It is clear to most of us that dissatisfaction is high, but even a cursory analysis of its causes raises issues that many wish to avoid tackling. To call for a fresh interpretation of what is needed in a national government raises fundamental questions about popular conceptions of the nature of man and society, questions that are usually left to the philosophers by most people who only know how to live with the current mythology. The assumptions are so deeply imbedded in our neutral patterns and the bureaucratic tenets of social systems so pervasive that we are afraid to question too much—it is perceived that to do so would be extremely painful. Even to raise the question makes many defensive.

Most academics, from whom one should expect new ideas, stand by their methodology and statistical manipulations, concocted from a distance, and refuse to engage in "subjective" discussions which pit experiential and from-the-fray data against their abstractions. As in the case of the bureaucrat, format has become more important than substance. To engage in academic conferences and publishing one must submit to the superficial rules of data collection and presentation. If the result appears to hang together neatly then it is considered "substantive research." The relationship of the initial data abstractions to real life is seldom questioned. When one does the person is reacted to as an outcast, criticized for venting his or her spleen. The treatment from traditional colleagues is not too different from that received by the bureaucrat willing to break ranks.

The entrenched bureaucrat is equally dogmatic, hiding among the rule books or behind platitudes about ultimate reality. In a heated debate, an opponent of some managerial changes in an agency rested his case by strongly affirming "the way things are is the result of human nature and you must recognize the difference betwen ideals and human reality." Such a statement exemplifies a common opinion in our society: the behavior of man is beyond his own redemption. It is a widely accepted view that reflects a lack of understanding of the dynamics of human behavior.

Eric Hoffer has written: "We can never be really prepared for that which is wholly new. We have to adjust ourselves and every radical adjustment is a crisis in self-esteem; we undergo a test and we have to prove ourselves. *It needs inordinate self-confidence to face drastic change without inner trembling.*"[3] (My emphasis.) He goes on to say that "drastic change is one of the agencies which release man's energies, but certain conditions have to be present if the shock of change is to turn people into effective men of action: there must be a tradition of self-reliance . . . . When a population undergoing drastic change is without abundant opportunities for individual action and self-advancement, it develops a hunger for faith, pride, and unity." This leads to protection of the familiar and to less innovation—the opposite of what a self-adapting society must have. America is now caught in the dilemma of needing change yet having created people who are not resilient enough to effect it.

Yet to live long in its 3rd Century as a nation in reasonable control of its own destiny the American society must go through a phase of institutional renewal or revolution.

The process that is required is akin to the 16th Century Reformation movement—it will be that agonizing and profound. To be of value the outcome must be just such a restructuring of our basic assumptions about people and organizations. To meet William James' wise criteria for a useful approach, it must be *both* internally logical and provide the real world results that our society needs, which our prevailing organizational philosophy does not.

Most of us have had some insights, even if only fleeting ones, that produced visions of a better way to live and work together. Yet, we have been unable to actualize them and in fact are often afraid to try. For example, almost 100 senior government officials gathered at a conference in April of 1979 found to their surprise that most of them shared many of the ideals about a possible government for the future that I have outlined in Chapter 6, but they left the meeting unable to see their way to taking concrete steps toward their vision.

What is the basic nature of this reluctance on the part of established groups to make conscious change and how can people work to overcome it? How can they come to believe that the new vision they have is worth personal change? How do people move from looking for the solution "out there somewhere" and learn to look within themselves?

Would-be reformers must act on the basis of theories about resistance to change, so perhaps it would be useful to summarize one of them here.

Ronald Lippett, in 1958,[4] wrote that there are basically four factors which contribute to inertia in organized groups:

The first is a *reluctance to admit weaknesses*. People do not wish to admit to defects in themselves, which would be implied by changing the way one has been behaving. After all, the leaders of an organization believe they are where they are because of the validity of the system's various processes. A former Director General of the Foreign Service was heard to state, only quasi-facetiously, "The personnel system has to be accepted as effective by me (since it resulted in my becoming the DG)." For a senior career government employee to call into question the very basis on which he/she achieved success is extremely threatening. If one admits the fallibility of the system one may have to then question the validity of its choice of him or her for the current role. "What can be wrong with what made me the success that I am?" This factor is very important in understanding why elite groups or agencies have been little affected by all the so-called reforms of the system—the answer is the "successful" careerists have been in charge of the reforms.

There is also a socially ingrained *fear of failure* or awkwardness in trying to initiate a new practice or behavior pattern. Doing things the same way over time results in a sense of competence and security in the knowledge that one has mastered a given process. Recurring processes satisfy basic human needs and the contemplation of disrupting that pattern is threatening. One asks the question, "Why should I trade something I know I can do for an untested method?" This factor becomes particularly important in a bureaucracy which does not encourage and reward risk taking and more likely than not places a penalty on trying something new and thereby revealing a lack of tested competence. When the pressure is great to close all the chinks in one's armor, stumbling steps to learn to walk in a new way are infrequently tried. The natural fear of failure then becomes heightened by the bureaucratic intimation that nothing short of always being right is acceptable.

A series of unsuccessful attempts to change results in a sense of futility, *a fatalistic expectation of failure*. By the time many people reach adulthood they already consider themselves failures. Others learn in the workplace to lower their sights; the bureaucracy is particularly deflating. Among jaded bureaucrats one hears over and over again, "What's the use? This effort will turn out just like the last one. It will hardly get off the ground before somebody leaves or it's sabotaged." Career people in government have become very pessimistic about the ability of the system to follow through, with the interest of enough significant people who will devote the time and energy to making the change stick.

The final one is the fear of *losing some current satisfaction*. While the first three are more applicable to those on the inside, this last applies to outside groups as well. If a private citizen has a well established personal network in the current bureaucratic arrangement and hears talk of a revision of relationships that would break up those satisfying ties, the change is perceived as threatening.

Only infrequently would the kinds of change discussed in this book affect the safety or physical well-being of government employees. Some of the suggested changes might be perceived as reducing the likelihood of expected promotions and thereby impact on one's long-term material gains, but for those on the inside we are basically talking about psychological needs. They may be individual desires for status, power, influence, social ties, accomplishment, personal challenge or the absence thereof, or the personal regard of others. If the hierarchy gives some special access and one proposes to create a collegial structure that removes the secure contact the change is likely to be opposed. When an individual likes personalized bureaucratic channels and is asked to deal with a team he or she is likely to resist. And on and on, whatever is important to the individual that is threatened by change will be resisted.

Our would-be performers must keep in mind these very human obstacles, both within the bureaucracy and in groups outside, in the formulation of a change strategy. Stress should be placed on process as opposed to outcome to avoid the fear of failure that is aroused when ultimate goals are stated too specifically. The novelty of a radically new approach should reduce the sense of futility that arises with the *deja vu* phenomenon. And finally the concentration on the more profound satisfactions that come from self-reliance and pride of creation will reduce the individual concern for more ephemeral ones. One should keep in mind that the anticipated satisfaction of certain currently unfulfilled needs can serve as a powerful motive force for change. People only need a small ray of hope.

Bureaucratic Inertia

An important point to keep in mind is that natural resistance to change is not all bad. These same forces that resist and reject formal change efforts in the bureaucracy, whether activated by management or from the outside, or from within the organization's own professional staff, also reject *ad hoc*, random changes that, if allowed to take root, could continually knock the organization about in a willy-nilly fashion. In government they have prevented some of the more wild-eyed schemes from being implemented in a way that would have significantly lowered even more the current level of performance. In addition, when constructive reforms are introduced, these inertial tendencies provide enough time to allow the new ideas to take root and flourish. Also the continuation of required functions requires strong defenses to keep operations on track.

It should also be remembered that the complete absence of defenses can be just as indicative of poor health as ones that are too rigid. A phenomenon more distressing than bureaucratic resistance to change is the resignation that results in passive obsequiousness to each new authoritarian figure. Consequently, this book does not view all resistance to change as an ogre that must be slain or a cancer that must be cut away. It is a predisposition that springs from the human instinct to protect oneself and, especially in organizations, one's way of life. Instead of trying to bulldoze it out of the way, the reformer must challenge individuals to new heights.

Traditionally change agents have chosen either one or two ways to cope with resistance to their reform strategies: by focusing on the direct use of power or cunning for implementation or by trying to coopt people through giving a sop to placate or bribe the opponents.

As we have seen in earlier chapters—the former is the way bureaucratic managers have generally gone about it. Peter Vail[5] wrote, after a bibliographic search project, that:

> Running through the literature . . . was—and is—an 'assumption of unilaterality!' That is assumed that a manager can do just about anything he wants to, that sources of 'resistance to change' can be 'overcome,' that people can be influenced to do what the administrator wants them to do if only he can develop the requisite 'interpersonal skills,' that fundamentally the administrator can implement any program provided he gives enough thought to the strategy and tactics associated with doing it."

Many people now realize that this is another example of our misplaced faith in the robot-like view of man and society: the view that says that if some of us could only learn the details of the clock-like masterplan used by the deity who put us together we could then run people the right way. We now know that legislation or direct orders will not bring about profound change. Human beings resent manipulation and distrust their manipulators.

In recent decades a human relations task has been espoused by some theoreticians and managers. This approach would have the change strategist analyze the causes of resistance and, through systematic interviews or other data gathering techniques, devise measures that would undermine the resistance forces. These measures range from offsetting compensation (more money, better offices, or grander titles) to promises for the future. The trade-off approach was the principal tactic of the Carter Administration's effort to weaken resistance to its proposed Civil Service changes.

The effect of this so-called humanistic approach has not been much more successful than the proverbial caveman's club in reforming the bureaucracy. Both strategies have only succeeded in lowering the motivation, raising the level of hostility, reducing meaningful communications, and in general weakening the capacity of the institution of central government to carry out its assigned roles.

Bringing about change of the kind we now need in government is not a matter of running people the right way nor psyching out the reasons for resistance and assuaging them. It is more a question of providing opportunity and alternatives for people who are already inclined to progress.

This requires a third approach for dealing with resistance: the attempting of change which most of those concerned perceive is necessary and useful. In other words the changes should be widely perceived to serve the basic needs of the individuals involved and the society at large. They must be seen as overcoming barriers to personal growth and effective performance.

There is considerable malaise in the federal bureaucracy which is a predisposition to change. If people can only begin to discern some of the root causes of their institutional constraints and conceive of positive alternatives they wil gladly shed much of their resistance. The difficulty with the current situation is the lack of alternatives which are perceived to be both viable and more consistent with the members' aspirations for selfhood. Change will be sought when people feel enough stress as a result of a recognition that their basic assumptions are not working and they can see another reasonable option.

People inside government daily face institutions that do not work. They are well aware there must be a better way. As one member of the Navy Department said, "If the citizens knew how bad it really is in Washington there would actually be lynchings in the streets." Provided with a way to replace the parts of the current system that do not work, people on the inside would not hesitate to assist in the co-creation of a new day in government.

It is my thesis that elucidation of the myths that bind us into today's unhealthy institutions and the existence of a focused mechanism through which to consider new thoughts will revive the embers of hope that smolder in almost all burned-out bureaucrats. Hence the proposal for a new "committee of correspondence" that would serve as both catalyst and medium for recognizing our blinders and illustrating possible new vistas. Change of the depth and magnitude we require for our 3rd Century can only come from acts that are motivated by a compelling vision of the future we desire.

Personal Contributions

Hoffer's insights on resistance to change support the principles of this book, with its advocacy of greater self-control and individual responsibility. The conceptual and structural changes recommended would enhance the tradition and environment deemed prerequisites to dramatic change by Hoffer. In other words, a self-correcting mode would be entered. Ironically enough it would not be a new departure for our society, but would be a re-creation, within a modern context, of the open-ended, do-it-yourself circumstances of the first phases of our history. The lessons are before our eyes if we would but only look.

If people naturally resist the pushing of changes which they do not understand, which they perceive as threatening, and in which they have not concurred, is it not reasonable to ask if a radically different approach might give more positive results? When the imposition of change results in struggle against it, would not active participation, by those affected, in the development of the change proposal reduce that opposition? People resist things they do not understand, yet real involvement from the early stages would provide that understanding. If a person is involved in a project and has some real control over its impact on him or her is it not less likely to be threatening?

From this simple reasoning it would appear that there are certain criteria which, if applied to plans for change, would go a long way towards insuring support and implementation. They are simply stated as:

- Full communication is required from the beginning between designers and those to be affected.
- Active participation in the formulation of the actual plans by those concerned is required.
- Those who carry them out must concur in the proposed changes.

Experience and common sense demonstrate that only efforts to bring about change which meet these criteria are likely to have some chance of success. A completely above-board "committee of correspondence" taking on all comers, with an open testing procedure for developing action plans, would meet those criteria. Thought must be given to stimulating personal participation in a change that grows from within the current bureaucracy.

Promoting change among insiders requires the adoption of a different view of management-employee relations. "Getting at the truth of resistance" cannot be accomplished just by use of the traditional bureaucratic or political meetings set up to dispense the facts. People will perceive that approach as only one more effort at manipulation. Therefore, the "committee" must relate to but avoid being constrained by the current bureaucratic and political structures and hierarchies. It is essential that a mechanism exist at each stage for public employees to have access to the forum outside normal bureaucratic channels. People must perceive and in fact be free to contribute to the process without regard to existing roles and procedures.

Participation

Thirty years ago organizational psychologists began to understand that participation in planned change by the groups to be directly touched by it reduced the level of resistance.

"Group participation" became a by-word in organizations, but by the late 1960s people were questioning whether or not it really made a difference. What had happened was the occurrence of a typical social evolution phenomenon—that which started as "substance" became translated into "form." Whereas the earlier participants really participated, in later years they were only allowed to be tokens, who by their presence were expected to give legitimacy to decisions already taken by "the authorities." This latter practice was a charade and awareness of it served only to heighten employees' disillusionment with the bureaucratic system.

Paul Lawrence, in the *Harvard Business Review* in 1969 wrote:

> Subsequent research has not altered the general conclusion that participation, to be of value, must be based on a search for ideas that are seen as *truly* relevant to the change under consideration. The shallow notion of participation, therefore, still needs to be debunked.

If the idea of participation is included in the change strategy, but is not honestly and fully carried through, the situation will result in a backlash.

Communication

Communication attempts may also be real or a sham; obviously the former is required if change efforts are to be effective. One of the problems reformers of a bureaucracy have to overcome is the convictions held by most of its members that the formal communications channels are selectively used. The gatekeepers frequently present only certain aspects of a subject while pretending they are giving a complete and valid picture. Given the general employee's awareness of Bureaucratic Games and most individuals' appreciation of the distrustful psychological climate in which he/she lives, very few are willing to accept "official" communications at face value. Our 3rd Century activists must recognize the existence of this practically insurmountable barrier to communication that is in place even before they come on the scene. Consequently, it is absolutely necessary to establish a new and credible communication medium for the reform effort.

In addition to the psychological and social isolation within current bureaucratic organisms, the rigidity of their hierarchical structures presents blocks to both vertical and horizontal flows of communication. Ideas going upward get part of them screened out at each level and those going down get reinterpreted at each stage and similar phenomena of distortion occur throughout the organization as each turf keeper interjects his special view. Due to these built-in hazards, all personnel involved must get uncensored presentations about diagnoses of problems and the proposed solutions and their ramifications. Where possible, face-to-face encounters should be used and when that is impossible complete circulation of the primary source material should be made to all participants. Everyone should hear or read both the critics and the defendants' view.

Consensus Building

The reform process must have several specific products, the first of which is the tentatively agreed upon action plan; people should be able to see the entire process sketched out in advance. While all might like to engage directly in analysis, with full discussion and involvement, a point in time must be reached where decisions have to be made. In our current system that includes the legislative process, executive action, group consensus, and individual commitment. The specific decision points depend on many factors, some of which are based in the Constitution and statutes. The essential preconditions are that all participants understand the decision making rules of the game, see them as being fair to all, and accept them as binding on their own behavior. No set formula is required if the above standards are met. Various options can be a majority vote rule, a total consensus requirement, or decisions taken by a certain leader or leaders after participants are satisfied the full case has been made and presented fairly to those decision makers. The keys are fullness, fairness and openness. When these requirements are met then the problem of most of the resistance has already been resolved. Stacking the deck with backroom deals, closed sessions, classified information, and less than fully open public hearings must be avoided. The best guard against suspicion is a requirement for full publication of proposed decisions, with public analyses of their impacts, in the "letters of correspondence" medium before votes or decisions are taken.

Testing

As any hypothesis should be tested before being embraced and fully acted upon, so must the early assumptions about resistance to bureaucratic change be looked at in light of actual experience and evaluated as the change effort progresses. By having the involvement of those from whom resistance was predicted engaged in the diagnostic and solution generating phases, perhaps one will find that some of the expected resistance does not occur. Given the kind of process suggested here, in the glare of public scrutiny, one may find restraint in the special-cause pleading that normally can only occur in private. It pays to publicly validate hypotheses about people and their likely reactions to reform; one may be pleasantly surprised.

Public Involvement

Some of the same concerns, and ideas for coping with them, must be taken into account as we turn to the public's necessary role in bureaucratic reform.

Insights developed by observers of previous change attempts have not been incorporated into recent executive and legislative approaches to reform; our contemporaries in government still depend on closed decision-making, traditional bureaucratic channels, and authoritarian procedures. Although outside opinion is frequently solicited, there is no way for those who provide it to see a direct impact on the final product. They frequently do not even know what happened to their input nor what other people have said. All goes into the "black box" of the President and his advisors with only public speculation on why the outcome is what it is. This was as true of the Carter Administration's Reorganization Project as it was of past administrations.

In our need for bureaucratic reform, we are left with a paradox: change must come from within, but those on the inside cannot be expected to start and follow through on such a process without public involvement and support. The current institutional realities pose difficulties for the reform-minded politician or appointed manager; they must work with a short, fixed time frame and are expected to leave their marks by making a dramatic shift in a specific policy or practice. (President Carter and his team spent two years learning the ropes and then had to start running for re-election before they could apply the lessons they had learned.) Strategic thinking is pushed aside by tactical considerations. Consequently, there is little chance that sustaining power for reform will come from the leadership of the existing institution.

Even when a new President or appointed executive starts with good intentions they are not likely to last the duration. Progress on profound change is slow and as the end of a term or re-election time approaches the greater becomes the pressure for a quick-fix. One's ability to withstand the demands for dramatic results is in inverse order to the magnitude of the promised changes—the greater the heralded objectives, the less likely the chance that realistic restraints will be appreciated. For these reasons we cannot expect the Executive Branch leadership to lead to reform change.

These principles also characterize Congress and private groups whose existence depends on the perpetuation of the *status quo*. The political process of pressure groups and votes, which is always in reaction to events, is not suited for creating new social departures. Neither will reform come from something vaguely called the public; there is insufficient knowledge of the internal reality and, by the complex nature of the bureaucratic problem, inadequate concentrated expertise in the hands of any single group. So what will be the nature of public involvement?

The new re-founding parents, the members of the "committees of correspondence," will come forth on the basis of their personal qualities, not as a result of their formal institutional roles. They will include some people with inside experiences and others with outside perspectives; they will all be people with a sense of considerable autonomy and an intense interest in building for the future.

Are there enough of them to provide more energy than those who defend the inertia of the current bureaucracy for various economic and political reasons? Some of the more obvious defenders are: (1) Political party leaders, particularly those who would resist the demise of much of their patronage. (2) For the same reason, many in Congress would oppose the proposals. (3) The "almost there" level of careerists who see themselves on the verge of gaining new and important positions in the current system would resist changes that might deter achievement of those aspirations. (4) Special interest groups who have sweetheart relationships with various benefactors in the existing bureaucracy would be loath to give them up. (5) Union leaders whose role would be diminished by the 3rd Century system would attempt to undermine its implementation. These groups have already demonstrated their prowess in derailing past reform efforts.

Since the opposition of such groups is largely a given, at least initially, the question of heretofore underattended public inertia must be addressed by a determined reform movement. How does one involve the concerned but skeptical public? It is only in this large "silent and suffering"majority that there is enough potential energy to overcome the vested interests. It is crucial because so many of our citizens will have to do much rethinking if we are to make any progress, and that group will have to include a large number of teachers and other idea developers outside government.

Serious reformers who desire to involve the public must possess two intellectual prerequisites. They must believe enough people possess sufficient social understanding and intellectual skills to really make a difference. The idea that the course of events is largely beyond a people's conscious control must have been banished. Secondly, they must eschew both the conventional wisdom that "strong management" will turn the trick and the current piecemeal social engineering theories of organizational change. If their strategies are to have any chance of success they must be holistic, taking into account all elements of social organisms and their interactive relationships. The problem must be treated as it really is, cultural and organic, not organizational. The activists must understand enough human nature to stimulate the critical self-awareness that will build motivation for self-change within the society and the bureaucracy. For this reason a significant part of this chapter has been devoted to the phenomenon of human resistance to change.

■ *Public Will.* It is a matter of judgment whether or not the American society is intellectually and socially mature enough to successfully engage in such a process of internal, conscious self-renewal of its public institutions. Many factors would indicate we are not ready: the parochialism of much of Congress, the national leadershlp selection mechanism which rewards politicking skills more than knowledge and leadership, the very process of bureaucratization described in this book, the sway a few financial and industrial interests have on thought in America, the superficiality of most of the media, the self-interest of many citizens and the unwillingness of most to get involved in the larger issues, and the limited supply of activist intellectuals in the society. But all of these things, real though they are, are counterbalanced by many assets: a growing awareness in America that something has to be done internally to avert what many see as a demise in important facets of our national life; a large number of self-help groups who have undertaken meeting needs with their own hands; networks of thinking activists who are questioning the validity of current conventional wisdom for maintenance of a democratic society; a technology of communication that makes possible in a very short time period the kind of public analytic and education process called for, one that would have taken centuries in ages past or at least decades up until the 1980s; the potential availability of the relatively small amount of human and financial resources needed for the catalytic group; and the pressures of increasing numbers of unresolved issues that will energize normally apathetic citizens to respond favorably to such an explicit and publicized "project hope."

A Possible Strategy

If the public, its employees and their managers all find themselves at odds with and frustrated by their governmental institutions, why are we not able to mobilize enough energy and direct it in the appropriate path to bring about innovation and reform? How do we escape the paradox of people being unable to initiate change at the same time they express such dissatisfaction with the present? How can we organize effective action?

The simple answer is you start with a look at the whole institution, and you start with the basic concepts which were the source of the institution and have evolved with it over time. In order for the different elements of an actual change program to make sense, as they are introduced into the arena of ideas and people begin to react to them, there must already be an established conceptual framework or theory that gives a reasonable explanation of the current state of affairs. The basic conceptual approach and historical analysis must make it possible for people to see the relationship of the proposed changes to the existing situation and its inadequacies, and to relate them to the problems of their own experience. The rationale for the proposed changes must clearly arise from such a larger set of understandings and must indicate how they will resolve the generally agreed upon deficiencies. For example, the lack of such a context made it impossible for people to adequately assess the specifics of President Carter's "civil service reform package" and their likely implications.

The most important step in the development of this intellectual context is the explication of the current basic images and institution-shaping assumptions. This phase must include a profound discussion of their relationships to current bureaucratic attitudes and practices. Such an act of elucidation should lead to a general metamorphosis of the way people think about a few key concepts. A widespread consensus would evolve about their incompatibility with the anticipated demands of our 3rd Century.

In order to avoid going off half-cocked on another quick-fix scheme it is necessary to develop this kind of an intellectual understanding of the root of the problem. The alternatives are there, laid out before us in our everyday experience; we fail to recognize them until we look with a new definition of the problem.

It is not appropriate here to design a detailed blueprint for action by a self-conscious reform group, but the conclusions of the preceeding chapters have implications for the nature of a strategy. Some of these are sketched out in the following paragraphs.

At each step in the process there should be adequate ventilation of differing opinions about current myths and their impacts. The process must insure public testing of various analysts' views. People should have an opportunity to present personal experiences, research findings, and individual theories to those responsible for fueling the public debate. It is only through such an open, challengeable procedure that enough widespread profound thought will be given to the basic principles which need to be changed. This analysis is essential if we are to garner broad agreement for new patterns of thought. Public concept development had reached a point in the late 19th Century in America where it would support a structural revolution in public institutions. Today we need a similar level of conceptual consensus, within the buraucracy and in significant public sectors, before we launch proposals for specific formal changes. There is an adequate level of general desire to reform the current bureaucracy, but ideas about what the real problems are and what viable alternative solutions exist are still very inchoate. A few individuals and groups have pet ideas, but nowhere has there been a comprehensive and in-depth analysis of the type required before sweeping reforms are launched.

The requirement for public discussion and consensus building calls for a new approach to communication with both employees and the public. A new medium, clearly labeled as such, should be established with a newspaper-like distribution system to insure that anyone who desires can have timely and full access to the same information as anyone else. It should be the organ for substantive debate, procedural announcements and descriptions of tentative proposals, inviting comment before formal executive/legislative action is taken. The current bureaucratic and public media channels of information dissemination, as described earlier, are clearly not credible instruments for the magnitude and importance of the task. What is called for is a series of letters (literally communications in all media) among the new "committees of correspondence."

The process by which decisions are to be reached should be well-publicized, in this extra-official instrument, and open to challenge. People and groups must know when and where to make an input and how to raise challenges if they desire. As results come forth everyone must feel that it was as open and fair as could be expected. Consequently, the work of this group cannot be funded by government grants or other money with strings. We must keep in mind the point Gene McCarthy has made, "The American Revolution was not funded by matching grants from the Crown."

Public discussion and decision-making processes are indispensable in effectively dealing with opposing views. They must be dealt with directly and openly, with citizens able to see where the lines are drawn and to have adequate information to decide which positions to support.

An open, public process of developing support for specific problem definitions and solutions does not guarantee the former are the most valid and the latter the most appropriate. Theoretical assumptions and extrapolations need testing in practice. This fact should caution us against implementing partial solutions throughout the government before trying them out in pilot experiments. Since partial remedies are clearly more often counterproductive than not, they cannot be effective if the other elements of the organism are not congruent or moving toward consistency, it is necessary to try out a comprehensive plan in one or more suitable agencies before introducing the principles government-wide.

If this quality of debate and testing is to be possible, new analytic tools are required; different lenses are needed to get a different perspective on the problem. The test of the suggested analytical approach developed in Chapter 5 is whether it leads to useful insights into the "quagmire" of government bureaucracy today and helps in the development of a constructive reform strategy. The ultimate proof will come only from others trying it out on a large scale, but its perspective can be immediately useful in thinking about and designing strategies to cope with the organizational difficulties we face.

Its concept of interacting levels helps explain some of the misguided organizational behaviors we have today; the influential role of myths and other primary images is central to the behavior of social organisms. The holistic approach is helpful in illuminating reasons for the failures of previous fragmentary change efforts. Conversely, it suggests some new approaches that take into account the linkages among all elements of an entity, for future reform attempts.

It also points to some general organizing principles that could lead to more effective public institutions. But to bring some of those principles to life out of the current fudge factory of government is the task of live people.

What is required is a strategy that offers individuals in government the opportunity both to serve the needs of the larger society and to have a role, within a citizens effort, in the shaping of how their service will be defined and carried out. Public employees need to have a clear understanding of how their activities fit into the bigger picture and how to engage in redefinitions of their public roles. Straggling bureaucrats would be on the forefront of reform if they saw real opportunity being offered, but they would resist manipulation for the purposes of others.

Given this or some similar analytic approach, what must would-be social and political leaders, interested public groups, and private citizens do to accomplish the dismantling of the pyramid and to create a self-correcting alternative?

First, many people representing various sectors of society, including at least the executive and legislative branches, academia, the press, foundations, and broad-based public interest groups must collectively decide that the time has come for a profound and comprehensive institutional revolution.

There must be a volunteer coalescing of such people into an identifiable task force, with unfettered financial commitments, and with an agreed upon procedure for serving as a catalyst for formal government action (when the time is appropriate). No sector of society, government or otherwise, should have a dominant position in the task force. I have suggested it become a new "committee of correspondence," patterned on the group that played such a key role in the building of consensus and support for the first governmental revolution in America two centuries ago. Its formation should include an invitation to all interested comers to join in the exercise as they desire.

What are the necessary elements for a plan of action, contrasted with a change plan? When the "committee" gets organized it should establish an action plan that involves at least the following phases:

- A public and publicized analysis of the organismic elements of our federal bureaucracy and their impact on the quality of public policy and programs. The steps in this phase are: (a) publication of tentative hypotheses from a number of sources, (b) testing of them through the assessments of practitioners at all levels, (c) revising and republication, (d) solicitation of comments of criticism or confirmation, and (e) publication of and elucidation of the new concepts. This step is the identification and dethroning of myths: the beginning of the upending of bureaucracy.

- Development of proposed formal changes deemed necessary to actualized: the newly agreed upon governing and organizing concepts and to reinforce the desired attitudes and performance. The design of the proposed changes should be based on an interdisciplinary assessment of the assumptions involved. They should be supported by interdisciplinary research.

- When a conceptual change dealing with all organismic elements is agreed upon, the passage of implementing legislation to authorize pilot testing will be required. The act should be clearly seen as experimental, with a proviso for periodic evaluation.

- The monitoring and publicizing of progress in the test agency should involve the extra-official "committee"; it should not be done by the bureaucracy. The evaluation process should meet the same criteria for openness and multi-source input that was required of the design phase.

- Evaluation and revision of the experimental structure for its contribution to the desired public products and service is essential before more generalized applications are mandated. Lessons learned in the pilot efforts should be built into implementation plans for other agencies of government.

- Encouragement and facilitation of other agency adoption of the new principles should be a part of the "committee's" role. As the results of the experiment become known, they should be widely disseminated. Others wishing to get on the bandwagon should be encouraged.

At some point in the above process the regular institutions of government, press, and education would pick up momentum and involvement in the reform, but the "committee" should remain alert and active until it is quite clear that the internal revolution is on an irreversible track.

The key aspects of the above action plan are: multi-based, open, self-generated involvement, and a testing-as-you-go philosophy. The "committee's" funding should have no strings attached; it should not relate to control of the process. The action plan should at least embody the principles outlined in this book as prerequisites for self-correcting, effective 3rd Century institutions. It should set the example by the very manner in which it acts as a catalyst or change agent. It should demonstrate the feasibility of a new kind of bureaucrat-citizen-politician collaboration. It should test the merits of the argument that public work is best when it is inner-directed and self-controlled. One should count on 5 to 10 years from formation of the group to government-wide implementation. A willingness to give the seeds time to grow is essential; dynamic patience is necessary to sustain the energy level long enough for enough people to start thinking and acting new ways.

Who could start such a chain of events? No special status is required. It could be a public personality: a foundation executive, a Member of Congress, a respected politician, or any well known individual. But it is more likely to be a few private citizens with a willingness to break new ground and a few resources to commit to the larger good. Are there enough such people?

It is my judgment that the necessary critical mass lives in America today. If only a few people will step forward and say they are ready to join others, we will see what has to be one of the most crucial, cooperative social and intellectual efforts in history: the assertion of conscious, self-control over what heretofore have been institutions whose natures were determined by what C. Wright Mills called social fate. Although trends tend to leave many pessimistic, I for one am optimistic about the potential of a freedom loving group of citizens to bring about the removal of obstacles we have set in the way of fulfilling our humane and democratic ideals. We only need a few to heed the advice of Lewis Lapham quoted at the opening of this chapter.

Bibliographic References

1. Organizations and Societal Decline

1. Jean-Francois Revel. *Without Marx or Jesus*. Paladin. London. 1972.

2. C. Wright Mills. *The Causes of World War Three*. Ballantine Books, Inc. New York. 1961.

3. C. Northcote Parkinson. *Parkinson's Law*. Ballantine Books, Inc. New York. 1979.

4. Ivan Illich. *Tools for Conviviality*. Harper and Row. New York. 1973.

5. Alexis de Tocqueville. *Democracy in America*. Alfred A. Knopf, Inc. New York. 1945.

6. Roger A. Freeman. *The Growth of American Government*. Hovver Institution Press. Stanford University. Stanford, California. 1975.

7. Gail Sheehy. *Passages*. Bantam. New York. 1977.

8. Robert Ornstein. *The Psychology of Consciousness*. Viking Press. New York. 1972.

2. Costly, Poor Quality Chaos

1. White House Media Liaison Office. "Government Reorganization - Progress." Memo to the Press. July 13, 1977.

2. Hugh Helco. *The Executive Wasteland*. Brookings Institution. 1977.

3. Max Weber. *The Theory of Social and Economic Organization*. Oxford University Press. New York. 1947.

4. Rosabeth Moss Kanter. *Men and Women of the Corporation*. Basic Books. New York. 1977.

5. Lewis H. Lapham. *Harpers*. December, 1978.

6. Lawrence Kohlberg. *The Development of Modes of Moral Thinking and Choice*. University of Chicago Library. Chicago. 1958.

7. Nathaniel Davis. "The Ethics of Discretion." *Department of State Newsletter*. October, 1974.

8. U.S. Department of Health, Education and Welfare. *Work in America*. MIT Press. Cambridge. 1973.

3. Diverting and Demotivating Complexity

1. R.D. Laing. *Knots*. Random House. 1972.

2. Dan Miller. *Manchester Guardian* article. October, 1976.

3. Eric Berne. *Games People Play*. Ballantine. 1978.

4. Morton Halperin. "Games Bureaucrats Play." *Foreign Policy*. 1971.

4. A Hollow Officialdom

1. David McClelland. "Two Faces of Power." *Journal of International Affairs*. 1970. Vol. 24. No. 1.

2. Elliot Jacques. *The Health Services.* Brunel Institute of Organization and Social Studies. 1978.

3. E.F. Schumacher. *Small is Beautiful: Economics As If People Mattered.* Harper and Row. New York. 1973.

4. Theodore Roszak. *Person/Planet: The Creative Disintegration of Industrial Society.* Anchor Press. New York. 1978.

5. Wendell Berry. *The Unsettling of America: Culture and Agriculture.* Sierra Club Books. 1977.

6. Barry D. Karl. "Public Administration and American History." *Public Administration Review.* September/October 1976. No. 5, pp. 489-503.

5. Abortive Reforms

1. John Gardner. *Self-Renewal.* Harper and Row Publishers, Inc. New York. 1963.

2. Alfred J. Marrow. 1973 draft review of government reform efforts.

3. I.M. Destler. *Presidents, Bureaucrats, and Foreign Policy. The Politics of Organizational Reform.* Princeton University Press. 1974.

4. Jay Shafritz. *Personnel Management in Government: Politic and Process.* Political Science and Public Administration Series. Dekker. 1978.

5. Paul Von Ward. "Henry Kissinger as Department Manager." *Life in Organizations* (edited by Kanter and Stein). Basic Books. New York. 1979.

6. Henry A. Kissinger. "Domestic Structures and Foreign Policy." *Daedalus.* Spring. 1966.

7. Graham Allison and Peter Szanton. *Remaking Foreign Policy.* Basic Books. New York. 1976.

6. Theory for Analysis and Action

1. Philip Selznick. *Leadership in Administration: A Sociological Interpretation.* Row, Peterson & Co. Evanston, Illinois. 1957.

2. Paul R. Lawrence and Jay W. Lorsch. *Developing Organizations: Diagnosis and Action.* Organization Development Series. Addison-Wesley. Reading, Massachusetts. 1969.

3. Harold J. Leavitt. *Managerial Psychology.* The University of Chicago Press. 1972.

4. Charles Perrow. *Organizational Analysis: A Sociological View.* Brooks/Cole Publishing Company. Belmont, California. 1970.

5. Anthony Downs. *Inside Bureaucracy.* Little, Brown, and Company. Boston. 1967.

6. Michael Maccoby. *IEEE Spectrum.* July, 1973.

7. Rosabeth Kanter. "The Job Makes the Person." *Psychology Today.* May, 1976. *Men and Women of the Corporation.* Basic Books. New York. 1977.

8. Michel Crozier. *The Bureaucratic Phenomenon.* University of Chicago. 1964.

9. David Garnham. "Foreign Service Elitism and U.S. Foreign Affairs." *Public Administration Review.* Vol. 35, No. 1. January/February, 1975.

10. Maxwell Maltz. *Psycho-Cybernetics.* Prentice-Hall. New York. 1969.

11. Kenneth Boulding. *The Impact of the Social Sciences.* Rutgers University Press. New Brunswick, N.J. 1966.

12. Patrick Linehan. *The Foreign Service Personnel System: An Organizational Analysis.* Westview. Boulder, Colorado. 1976.

13. Gregory Bateson. *Steps to an Ecology of Mind.* Chandler Publishing Company. 1972.

14. Paul Von Ward. "Performance Evaluation: The Annual Inventory." *Foreign Service Journal.* October, 1974.

15. Woodrow Wilson. "The Study of Administration." *Political Science Quarterly.* June, 1887.

16. Adam Yarmolinsky. "Bureaucratic Structures and Political Outcomes." *Journal of International Affairs.* Vol. XXIII. No. 2.

17. Arthur M. Young. *The Reflexive Universe: Evolution of Consciousness.* Delaconti. 1976.

7. Self-Correcting Institutions

1. Chris Argyris. *Intervention Theory and Method.* Addison-Wesley Publishing Co. Reading, Massachusetts. 1970.

2. Chris Argyris and Donald Schon. *Theory and Practice: Increasing Professional Effectiveness.* Higher Education Series. Jossey-Bass. 1974.

3. Barry Stein. A series of unpublished papers.

8. New Committees of Correspondence

1. Lewis H. Lapham. *Harpers.* December, 1978.

2. Deena Stryker. *Open Forum Quarterly.* U.S. Department of State. Fall, 1978.

3. Eric Hoffer. *The Ordeal of Change.* Harper and Row. New York. 1963.

4. Ronald Lippitt. *The Dynamics of Planned Change.* Harcourt, Brace. New York. 1958.

5. Peter B. Vail. "Public Administration is Administration in Public." *New Directions in Public Administration: the Federal View.* The Bureaucrat Inc., Reston, Virginia. 1975.